ASTROS LEGENDS

ASTROS LEGENDS

Pivotal Moments, Players & Personalities in Houston Astros Baseball

Greg Lucas

INDIANAPOLIS, INDIANA

Published by Blue River Press
Indianapolis, Indiana
www.brpressbooks.com

Distributed by Cardinal Publishers Group
A Tom Doherty Company, Inc.
www.cardinalpub.com

ISBN: 978-168157-223-9
LCCN: 2022940697

Cover: Tessa Schmitt
Book Design: Tessa Schmitt
Editor: Tessa Schmitt

Printed in the United States of America

10 9 8 7 6 5 4 3 2 1   23 24 25 26 27 28 29 30

TABLE OF CONTENTS

After a radio-television sports announcing career that lasted more than 45 years including play-by-play announcing stints with the NBA San Antonio Spurs, Houston Rockets, and Indiana Pacers and 25 seasons with the MLB Texas Rangers and Houston Astros, the Butler University graduate and native of Kokomo, Indiana started writing books.

His last three, including this one, have dealt with the Houston Astros baseball team for whom he spent 17 years in all broadcasting roles. *Houston to Cooperstown: The Houston Astros' Biggio & Bagwell Years* was published by Blue River Press in 2017. Earlier he had written *Baseball – Its More than Just a Game.*

During his on-air career Greg also did play-by-play for college football, basketball, and baseball plus dozens of other sports over the years totaling about 4,000 combined events and games. While he didn't write any books during that time, he read a lot of them. He still does.

In addition to this heavily revised and updated content to reflect more of the glory years of the Astros, his earlier volume *The Houston Astro's Biggio and Bagwell Years* needs no updating. Available directly through Blue River Press, the stories of the Astros first Hall of Famers live on in Houston baseball history.

Living in Houston, Texas with his wife of more than 50 years, Yong, a retired blood bank specialist medical technologist, and graduate registered nurse and proud of his son, Dr. Alexander Lucas, PharmD, Greg dotes on both and his adopted former neighborhood black cat, Mr. Midnight.

More books? Only the future holds that answer.

INTRODUCTION

Starting in 2015 when the Houston Astros rebounded from the worst seasons in franchise history, prior to the transfer of the club from Drayton McLane and into early years of a rebound under Jim Crane the club, has been the strongest team in MLB. World Series champions in 2017 and 2022, plus two other American League Championships between 2017 and 2023, made them at least a mini dynasty.

In 2023 when they won the American League West in a tiebreaker and advanced to the ALCS, it was for a league record 7th straight season. That included two World Series championships. Only the Braves in the National League had been to more championship rounds with eight. But they were able to capture the World Series only once during that run.

Players like José Altuve, who started his career before the change, were joined by Carlos Correa, George Springer, Alex Bregman, and Yuli Gurriel to make up the nucleus of the everyday lineup. They were later joined by Yordan Alvarez, Michael Brantley, and, in 2022, Jeremy Peña. The cast was never exactly the same and even those in the early nucleus like Springer and Correa moved on. But the Astros kept on winning.

The pitching staff included future Hall of Famer Justin Verlander who won two Cy Young Awards and also missed a full season after Tommy John surgery in just all or parts of six seasons. But it was more than Verlander. The Astro staff, while it was changeable, was built about young arms with just a bit of veteran presence both in the rotation and out of the bullpen. By 2022 it was the best full staff in all of major league baseball. But then injuries hit in 2023 and after the club lost Verlander to free agency for 2023 things were much weaker.

As a result of Penalties levied against the club for using

electronic methods to steal signs, they lost the manager that won the first Series and two American League pennants, A.J. Hinch, but won again with a future Hall of Fame skipper, Dusty Baker who also took them to two World Series and winning one in 2022.

After winning it all in 2017 they won a then franchise record 103 games in 2018, but lost to the Boston Red Sox in the American League Championship Series.

In 2019, the Astros won the league title and won a new record 107 games, but lost a strange World Series to the Washington Nationals when neither team won a home game. The Astros were cursed with having what is usually called "the home field advantage." They lost all four games at Minute Maid Park. The same mysterious problem would re-occur in 2023 when they lost four home games to the Texas Rangers in the ALCS.

The Covid pandemic caused the 2020 season to be limited to sixty games. The Astros were sub .500 at 29-31 but still squeezed into the post season as a wild card. They lasted long enough to battle for the American League Championship but were held off by Tampa Bay, barely. The Rays won the first three games, but the Astros won the next three. The Rays won game seven.

In 2021, the Astros were back. They won the American League title again, but were beaten by the Atlanta Braves in the World Series. In 2022 it was 106 more regular season wins and back to a championship in the Series for the Astros.

When the Houston Astros won the 2017 World Series, it is no surprise that it was the greatest single achievement ever since it was the first full championship in the franchise's fifty-six-year history. Since then, thanks to the Astros' success continuing, there are new moments to never forget.

The purpose of this book is to go beyond what may be obvious and make some calls on other Houston baseball legendary moments, players, and personalities. It is hoped you will have fun recalling the past and people involved in Houston baseball history; all are legends of Houston baseball. My system combines the event itself with the timing of and importance to the overall big Houston baseball picture. All items are interesting, informative, and worthy of memory.

Why 117 entries? That equals the greatest total number of wins compiled (regular and post season combined) in a single season by any Houston Astro team. It happened in 2022.

From the mid-1950s, Houston was always destined to eventually be a Major League Baseball city. The first game was special, but also something that was inevitable. The creation and opening of the Astrodome was important, too, but other stadiums were built so the game could be played indoors. The Astrodome's overall history and that it was the first of its kind ever built in the world makes it special, but it is not among the very top Houston legends—only one of them.

In the "what have you done for me lately?" category, it is impossible not to see many of the top Houston baseball legendary moments coming from the 2017 Series into the 2020s. You may think some others are worthy of pushing some of these off the list, but you won't get many fans of the dynasty that began in 2017 to agree with you. Over time, even the memories from 2017 are being downgraded by newer fans. The more the Astros keep winning, the longer this list will become.

1

Astros Golden Age: Four AL Champs, Two Series Champs

If not a dynasty, the Houston Astros were as close as any major league baseball team from 2017 through 2023. During the first seven years of that period they were American League champions four times and World Series champs twice. They were AL West Division champions six seasons in seven years. And they played for the AL title all seven seasons. That established an American League record for consecutive ALCS appearances.

How did they do it? After all they ran through two managers, three general managers, and only had the same players regularly in the lineup at two spots. And both of those players, José Altuve and Alex Bregman, lost some time to injury.

The answer: solid pitching and some players that never took

anything for granted. Just using the two World Series winners as an example, the 2017 team and the 2022 teams only had Bregman and Altuve in common. Pitcher Lance McCullers is also on that list, but with an asterisk. He missed quite a bit of time with arm miseries, including Tommy John elbow surgery.

Team management had a lot to do with the dynasty years. While the Astros farm system was never ranked among baseball's best and fielded a number of teams with losing records, it always seemed to be able produce some big-time major leaguers. Excluding some first round draftees like George Springer, Carlos Correa, and Bregman who were expected to be good. Yordan Alvarez, Jeremy Peña, Kyle Tucker, Framber Valdez, Hunter Brown, and Christian Javier were all system productions who were around by 2022 but were not on the club in 2017. This was after Springer and Correa both left for free agency to Toronto and Minnesota respectively.

Few teams can fill holes from the system with quality as the Astros have. And yes, there WAS one very significant reason why the Astros won their first two titles. Justin Verlander came to Houston in a late season deal from Detroit in 2017. While he did miss two seasons after Tommy John surgery, he was able to throw his third no hitter in an Astro uniform and take two American League Cy Young Awards while anchoring two World Series winners. He would not have a shot at a third after he left for the New York Mets as a free agent…until August 1, 2023 when the Astros sent two top minor league outfielders to the Mets and brought JV back! With the development of Hunter Brown and the unexpected success of 28 year old rookie J.P. France, there was no problem with the rotation depth for the last 50 games of the 2023 season. That kept the Astros in contention even if their fortunes would leave them one game short of returning to the World Series in 2023.

Two days after the final game, 74 year old manager Dusty Baker announced his retirement. During his four years in Houston he took all four teams to the ALCS…winning two and one World Series. For his 16 year managerial career as won of the winningest managers in baseball history he is expected to join the Hall of Fame in the future.

2

Alvarez 454' Bomb Makes Astros 2022 Series Champs

The Astros were on fire when the 2022 post season began. They were hot all year, winning 106 games after a slow first few weeks. In the post season they won their first seven games, sweeping Seattle and New York to gain entry to their fourth World Series since 2017.

In the series a somewhat surprise foe, the Philadelphia Phillies, represented the National League. They had gotten hot in the post season and eliminated both the Padres and Braves to make the Series. During the regular season ,Philadelphia had finished third behind the Braves and Mets in the East with just an 87-75 record. They made the post season as the final wild card besting the Milwaukee Brewers by one game.

However, if the Astros thought they could sweep Philadelphia, the Phillies had other ideas. The Astros had the home field advantage—if that mattered. They had the same thing in the 2019 World Series against the Washington Nationals and neither team won a home game. Having four of them resulted in the Nationals surprising victory.

This time the Astros only split the first two games at home—suffering their first post season loss in 2022 when the Phils took the opener 6-5 in ten innings. Houston had jumped out to a 5-0 lead with Justin Verlander not allowing any hits through the first three. But the Phils roared back with three runs in the fourth and tied the game the next inning.

No more scoring till the top of the 10th when Justin Realmuto homered. The Phils held on in the bottom of the inning and won 6-5.

Houston salvaged a win in game two. Again Houston compiled a 5-0 lead, but this time held on to win 5-2. Alex Bregman hit a two-run homer. And, in a footnote no game behind home plate had ever been or can be better than that recorded by umpire Pat Hoberg. According to analytic sources he never missed a ball/strike call going 129 for 129 on all pitches taken by the hitters.

As the series shifted to Philadelphia, the games were strange. In game three the Phillies hit five home runs and scored seven, holding the Astros scoreless to take a two game to one lead. But game four was another day…and one to remember.

The game was scoreless through four innings. Houston had not scored at all in 16 innings. But they broke through for five runs. Bregman's two run double was the biggest hit.

In the meantime, the Phillies who had tied a World Series record with their five home run game the day before were being befuddled by Houston starter Christian Javier. When he left the game after six innings and 97 pitches, he had not allowed a hit. And that dominance of Phillie hitters continued. Bryan Abreu struck out the side in the seventh. Rafael Montoya pitched a hitless eight. Then Astro closer Ryan Pressly finished it up. The no-hitter was only the second ever thrown in a World Series game and the first combined effort. Don Larsen's complete game perfect game for the Yankees against the Dodgers in 1956 was the only other time a World Series team had been held hitless.

The victory evened the best of seven at two games each.

In game five, the Astros relied on their pitching again. Justin Verlander struggled a bit, but only gave up one run in five innings and left with a 2-1 lead. The run he surrendered was a home run in the first inning to Kyle Schwarber. It was the 10th given up by Verlander in World Series history passing the old record of nine surrendered by Catfish Hunter.

Houston came back to tie it in the bottom of the first and took a 3-1 lead into the last of the 8th. Ryan Pressly had to get a five out save and was aided greatly by a leaping catch off the scoreboard by center fielder Chaz McCormick. When the Astros won 3-2 and things moved back to Houston no one was thinking home field jinx. And Yordan Alvarez made sure of that...and that no 7th game would have to be played.

Needing a win to stay alive, the Phillies finally took a 1-0 lead on another home run by Schwarber, his third of the series in the top of the sixth inning. But the bottom of the frame will live in Astros history.

Philadelphia starting pitcher Zach Wheeler had been keeping the Astros in check through the first five. After both José Altuve and Bregman reached base in the bottom of the sixth and the lefty hitting Alvarez due to bat, the Phillies elected to "play the percentages" and bring in left-handed reliever José Alvarado to face Alvarez.

The percentages didn't work. Within minutes the Astros had a 3-1 lead as Alvarez hit a ball to dead center field and high enough to fly over the batters eye above the field. The blast was measured at 454 feet and essentially took the Astros to their second World Series victory since 2017. The roar from the home crowd flat-lined sound decibel meters.

Houston was not through. Catcher Christian Vazquez singled home a fourth run and the Astros vaunted bullpen closed things out pitching scoreless 7th, 8th, and 9th innings.

In fact, the Houston pen set a major league record for lowest earned run average in a World Series throwing at least 40 innings.

The Astros pen threw 54 1/3 innings and allowed only five runs. That 0.83 earned run average was the lowest ever. It helped give Houston its second World Series victory and manager Dusty Baker the first in his long career guiding teams.

3

Houston Wins First World Series in Seventh Game 2017

Someday, the Astros winning their first World Series may serve as only one of the team's greatest legendary moments. It did, until 2022! Hopefully, they will win several, and the first will have to be ranked among them. But there is only one "first" and 2017 will always be special.

But timing is everything. There is no question that it was the first greatest legendary moment in Houston baseball history.

The actual clinching game was no classic, but what it meant was. Some of the individual feats in the seven games—and whole postseason—will receive their own mention, but winning the game that clinched the championship had to take the first top spot.

For the record, when José Altuve took a groundball deep in

the hole from his second-base position in short right field and made the throw to first baseman Yuli Gurriel for the Series-clinching final out, that was the greatest moment in Houston baseball. From that moment, the Astros were World Series Champions for the first time ever.

The final score of the clinching game was 5 – 1 as the Astros bested the Los Angeles Dodgers in the seventh game. The Series had been a great one with heavy offense at times held in check by clutch pitching. Each team had scoring chances in games they lost, but the Astros took advantage of a few more. The Series was really that simple—and close.

With the Series even at three games each, everyone knew what was as stake and just how good the Series had been to this point. As Houston manager A. J. Hinch told the media beforehand, "We're playing in one of the most epic World Series in history, and I think our players have appreciation for that." It didn't take long for his team to put in a claim for the title.

In Game Seven, George Springer clinched the MVP honors by the third inning. In the first, he led off with a double, then scored on a throwing error on a ball hit by Alex Bregman. José Altuve brought him home with a groundout and Houston led, 2 – 0, in the first.

Astro starter Lance McCullers got himself in trouble by loading the bases, giving up a double and hitting two batters. But he got out of it with no runs scoring.

In the top of the second, the game was essentially clinched by the Astros. Brian McCann walked and Marwin Gonzalez—who might have had the biggest hit in the Series in Game Two with his ninth inning homer off Dodger closer Kenley Jansen—doubled. Josh Reddick grounded out, but then McCullers hit a soft grounder good enough to bring McCann home. When Springer worked the full count off Dodger starter Yu Darvish and drove the next pitch over the wall, it was 5 – 0, and the game was essentially over. The homer was the 25th hit by the two teams in the World Series, which extended a new record.

Astro strong relief work from Brad Peacock and Charlie Morton closed things down. The Dodgers got some baserunners and mounted some threats early but could never get the clutch hits to get back into the game.

Starter Lance McCullers Jr. had little command of his pitches. Even spotted with the first inning lead, he struggled. In the bottom of the first, he threw 25 pitches and left the bases loaded. In the second, he survived thanks to a double play started on a line drive to shortstop Carlos Correa. In his 49-pitch outing that ended with one out in the third, he also set a record by hitting four batters. Manager Hinch got him out of the game before any of those baserunners could be driven in by the Dodgers, who continued to trail, 5 – 0.

Brad Peacock entered in the third and pitched the fourth. He got one out in the fifth before Francisco Liriano and Chris Devenski finished the inning, leaving two runners stranded. Los Angeles had left eight runners on base through the first five innings, including five in scoring position. The Astros had left only one on, but they had the 5-0 lead.

Charlie Morton entered the game for Houston in the sixth and was touched for a Dodger run on an RBI single by pinch-hitter Andre Ethier. The hit made it 5 – 1, with runners on first and second, and only one out. No one else scored. Starting in the seventh, Morton got hot and ended any Los Angeles hopes in the seventh, eighth, and ninth. He retired the side 1-2-3 in each inning. On that final groundout by Corey Seager to Altuve, the Astros were World Series Champs. There has been no legendary moment greater than that!

Although a very young player with hopefully a long career ahead of him, Alex Bregman said when he saw the Altuve to Gurriel play, "I just dropped to my knees and realized a childhood dream had come true. This team worked so hard for this. It's special to be part of this team. The coaching staff is unbelievable, ownership, our general manager, the city of Houston. We won this for them!"

In the next two seasons some people put a tarnish on

the Astros win due to their use of electronics to steal signs in home games. However, the record proved not all Astros took advantage of the activity. The sign stealing and can banging tip offs were only used at home. In the Series, the Dodgers lost two games in LA including the clincher. More on the saga of illegal stolen signs later in this book.

4

Marwin Gonzalez' Home Run in 2017 Series Game Two

Without Marwin Gonzalez's homer off Dodger closer Kenley Jansen in the ninth inning of Game Two, the Dodgers would have taken a two-game-to-none lead in the 2017 World Series. Judging from the fact the Series went seven games as it was, it is not hard to believe that, had not Marwin come through, the whole Series would have had a different winner. The Astros would have had to win four of five games for the championship, which would have been a very tall task. The World Series featured 25 home runs, and Gonzalez's was the single most important. And it was predicted by none other than Justin Verlander that Marwin was going to do something special.

"I told Marwin the inning before [that] he was going to win the game for us. I didn't think it would be a game-tying home run. I thought it would be a game-winning homer. That's what

I told him."

Gonzalez's homer may not have actually won the game, but without it, the Astros likely would not have won. Perhaps Verlander was closer to being correct than it seemed at the time.

Consider the circumstances. The Dodgers, with the temperature in Los Angeles registering as high as 103 degrees Fahrenheit, had won the opening game of the Series, 3 – 1. Clayton Kershaw struck out eleven Astros and the Dodger bullpen had bested the Astros. To even the Series before going back to Houston, the Astros really needed to take the second game.

However, the offense was being kept in check again. Entering the ninth inning, Los Angeles led Houston, 3 – 2. Star

Marwin Gonzalez hit a huge HR in the World Series.

Dodger closer Kenley Jansen had never blown a postseason save. He was on the mound.

Furthermore, Jansen had only given up home runs while ahead in the count with no balls and two strikes twice in his entire career. Gonzalez became number three. While hitting such a key home run off Jansen was not expected on any form chart, the fact that Marwin Gonzalez came through should not have been a total shock.

In 2017, Gonzalez had grown from a super utility player who could play anywhere and hit adequately into a real star player. Playing expertly at every spot on the infield and outfield, Marwin sparkled defensively and led the team in runs batted in (RBIs). Most of the season, he had been a solid .300 hitter. He finished at .303 with 23 home runs and 90 RBIs while playing in 134 games. His on-base percentage (OBP) of .377 and slugging percentage (SLG) of .530 were each third best on the team.

Game Two of the Series had many other heroes later, but without Gonzalez coming through in the ninth off Jansen, they likely would never have gotten the chance and the Astros would have had longer odds to pull off a World Series win.

Marwin Gonzalez's acquisition by the Astros was at the request of incoming general manager Jeff Luhnow. Jim Crane had purchased the team but was not officially approved as owner until a short time before the meetings. He would not make full staff changes until the 2012 season was over, but he had his GM in place. Gonzalez, a Chicago Cub, was unprotected in the minor league draft and selected by the Boston Red Sox at Houston's request. Luhnow, who really liked Gonzalez, had worked out a trade with the Red Sox for Marco Duarte. Gonzalez went to 2012 spring training with the job of either making the team or returning to the Cubs. Luckily, he never returned. Marwin served as the team's number one backup at three infield positions in 2012 and added more throughout his Houston career.

5

Yuli Gurriel Hits 3-Run Home Run to Tie 2017 Series Game Five

T he 2017 World Series featured two of the greatest games played in World Series history, Game Two in Los Angeles and Game Five in Houston. In Game Five, one huge hit by Cuban native Yuli Gurriel made it possible for the Astros to complete a comeback off the Dodger's best starting pitcher.

The Dodgers looked to be on their way to another win in a Clayton Kershaw start over Dallas Keuchel. They scored the first four runs in the game and led, 4 – 0. A victory would have given the Dodgers a three game to two lead with the last two games back in Los Angeles.

Keuchel was uncharacteristically ineffective. He went only 3 2/3 innings. Afterward, Dallas almost felt that he had not played at all. Keuchel noted, "Honestly, it felt like I didn't

Photo courtesy of Keith Allison

Yuli Gurriel's big swing was timely in the 2017 Series.

even pitch. I mean, I didn't pitch that long. I've never been so nervous in my life. The bubble gut feeling, the highs, the lows. I'm glad that us pitchers are with the number one offense and they provided a good show."

While Keuchel had been subpar up to then, Kershaw had been putting them down in order. He had faced only nine hitters through three innings. The Dodgers led, 4 – 0.

In the bottom of the fourth, the sluggish Houston bats came alive. After a leadoff walk to George Springer, José Altuve singled with one out for the first Houston hit. That was followed by an RBI double by Carlos Correa on a 0 – 1 pitch. Yuli Gurriel didn't even wait that long. He drove Kershaw's first pitch to deep left field and into the seats for a game-tying home run.

Although there would be many heroes before the five-hour, seventeen-minute game ended, without Gurriel's three-run blast, the Astros might not have had the chance to win it at all. Wiping out a 4 – 0 Dodger lead with Clayton Kershaw on the mound was crucial to the Astros ultimately winning the World Series.

People were getting to know more about the former Cuban player who had been signed by Houston during the previous season. Everyone following the Series knew he had made a racially insensitive gesture toward Dodger pitcher Yu Darvish during Game Three, but how much did they know of his years as a Cuban star?

Gurriel had been a star in Cuba for twelve seasons, hitting as many as 30 home runs and as high as .399 during season schedules of fewer than 90 games. He played one season in Japan for Yokohama and hit .305 with eleven homers and 30 RBIs over 62 games.

Gurriel played 36 games for the Astros in 2016 as he learned to play first base. He had been a third-baseman for most of his career. In 2017, the 33-year-old Gurriel, showed he was settled in as he hit .299 with 18 homers and 75 RBIs during the regular season. He was a key member of the batting order and tough in the clutch.

Kershaw found that out firsthand in Game Five.

6

Altuve Won Three Batting Titles. In 2021, Gurriel Got One.

t the conclusion of the 2021 season José Altuve had a team mate join him on the list of American League Batting Champions. Yuli Gurriel won the honor giving the Astros four hitting champs in the American League.

Jeff Bagwell once hit .368. Moisés Alou hit .355 in the National League. Those are the two highest single seasons for any Houston players. But neither won a batting title. José Altuve has won three! And the list of winners also includes Yuli Gurriel's name. Timing may not be everything, but it does mean a lot. When Bagwell hit .368 in 1994, Tony Gwynn hit an astounding .394! In Alou's big season with a .355 in 2000, Todd Helton hit .372 for Colorado. Both Bagwell and Alou finished second in the batting races.

Altuve has the next three highest seasons for an Astro

player, and each one of them won the AL batting championship. He won his first one in 2014. The Astros were still woeful as a team, but kept from losing 100 or more games for a fourth year, finishing at 70 – 92. Perhaps Altuve's individual success was a sign of things to come.

Altuve winning the hitting title was something no one could have predicted at that point. In one partial and two full seasons in the majors with Houston, he had yet to hit higher than .290. In 2013, his average had slipped seven points to .283, and his strikeouts climbed to 85. His OBP was a weak .316.

In 2014 Altuve was convinced to be a little less aggressive at the plate and to look for better pitches to hit. There were few pitches thrown anywhere around the strike zone that Altuve could not hit, so he was a free-swinger. However, while there were times he could hit a ball anywhere, there were also times in a pitch sequence when he would be fooled and flail away wildly with no success.

Coaches, most notably John Mallee, and José's own intuitiveness taught him to take more pitches and hone in on specific ones. The result was more hard-hit balls and deeper counts to work with. His walk totals didn't change much, but his strikeouts dropped from 85 to 53, and he had 48 more hits than in 2013. His OBP rose to a very commendable .377. Altuve claimed a slight leg kick added to help with timing was also a key.

The result was his first 200-hit season with 225 and a league-leading .341 batting average to become Houston's first league batting champion. He had to hold off Victor Martinez in the closing days, but won the crown by six points.

Although Altuve had a slight decline in 2015 hitting "only" .313, he started to show power with his first double-figure home run season with 15. He also collected exactly 200 hits.

In 2016, Altuve at 26-years-old became a super star. He won his second batting title with a .338 mark to go with 24 home runs and 96 RBIs. Altuve was no longer a leadoff or number two hitter. Though only five-feet, five-inches tall (as he will tell

Astros Career Top Hitters:
Moisés Alou .331 in 3 years
José Altuve .307 in 13 years
Michael Brantley .305 in 5 years
Jeff Bagwell .297 in 15 years
Bob Watson .297 in 14 years
Lance Berkman .296 in 12 years

you) and perhaps 165 pounds, he was one of the "big boys". José had 216 more hits, set a personal high with 60 walks, only 70 strikeouts, and a superb .396 OBP.

In 2017, he won his third AL batting title with another 204 hits and a .346 average while hitting 24 home runs again. His OBP reached Bagwell/Berkman levels at .410 while he stole 32 bases in 38 tries. After the season, he became Houston's second ever MVP by winning the honor for the AL. Jeff Bagwell in 1994 had won the same honor in the NL

The story on José Altuve is far from complete, but through his first 13 years in the major leagues, his Hall of Fame train is on schedule. Plus, in March 2018, he signed a contract extension that will carry him through 2024 in a Houston uniform.

In 2021 Yuli Gurriel, who had been producing clutch hits for the club since he joined it in 2016 won the league batting championship in a close battle with teammate Michael Brantley to join Altuve in owning a silver bat.

Gurriel hit .319. He also had a strong .383 on base percentage to lead the Astros and a .462 slugging percentage which was very good for a low home run hitter. He hit 15 long balls but had 31 doubles. He also only struck out 68 times in 605 plate appearances.

When his career in Houston ended, he had been on two World Series Champions. In seven seasons he hit .284 with 206 doubles, 94 home runs, and 435 RBIs in 801 regular season games.

In 85 post season games, Yuli hit .267 with eight home runs, finishing his Astros post-season career in 2022 with a .347 average, two home runs, and four RBIs in 12 post season games. A very strong way to close things out in Houston.

7

Jeremy Peña Wins 18 Inning 2022 LDS with HR vs Seattle

he Astros swept the Seattle Mariners in the 2022 Division Series but the three games were not without great moments. First, they won the opener when Yordan Alvarez cracked a walk off homer in the last of the ninth. And in the clinching final game, it took superb relief pitching from Luis Garcia in extra innings and one long ball for the win and clincher.

Lance McCullers arguably pitched the best post-season game of his career. He went the first six innings allowing only two hits and no runs. Seattle's George Kirby was just as good with one more inning on the mound.

Then, the bullpens took over. The Astros went to the bullpen six times allowing only three more hits. Hector Neris, Rafael Montero, Ryan Pressly, Bryan Abreu, Ryan Stanek, and rookie Hunter Brown did not allow a run. The Mariners also went through the whole staff.

Although at this point the game could have gone either way, Astro manager Dusty Baker knew his team. "These guys, they know not to panic. They don't get too excited. They don't get too down."

They could have. Both teams were not hitting many balls hard...or hitting the ball at all. They combined for a new post-season record with 42 strikeouts! Three-time AL Batting champ, José Altuve, was 0-8 at the plate.

By the 14th inning, the Astros went to the starting rotation to borrow Luis Garcia. As it turned out, he would throw the most pressurized five innings of his career. With the game still scoreless and being played in Seattle, allowing one run during those innings would end the game.

Understating his own effort, Garcia said afterwards, "Watching the whole thing, the guys (on the pitching staff) were doing a really good job and I'm really proud of them."

The whole Astro staff would be very proud of Garcia when things were finally done.

Then, in the top of the 18th, Jeremy Peña came to the plate. He was 0-8 at the time. But that was forgiven when he took a three-ball-two-strike pitch from Penn Murphy, the Mariner's ninth pitcher, to deep left center field at T-Mobile Park over the wall to put the Astros finally on top 1-0.

"That was a long game, but you've still got to lock it in, try to get good at bats," Peña said later. "I was just trying to stay inside the baseball and drive it into the gap." That he did. The ball went to the left-center gap and kept going over the wall.

But that is all they would get...or need...as Garcia, now in a spot to essentially save his own game, threw another zero in the last of the 18th and the Astros clinched the series.

The home run by Peña apparently really charged him up. The ALCS vs the Yankees, which resulted in another sweep and World Series win over Philadelphia, saw Peña named MVP in both. He hit .353 with two homers, two doubles, and four RBIs in the sweep of the Yankees. Then he hit .400 with a .432 OBP with a homer, two doubles, and three RBIs in the Series.

And it all started when he ended the game with an 18-inning home run in Seattle!

8

Chris Burke's 18th Inning Home Run to Win 2005 NLDS

It may be hard to believe, but there have been some legendary Houston baseball moments well before 2017. In fact, prior to the 2017 World Series, Chris Burke's 18th-inning home run in 2005—that led the Astros over the Braves and into the National League Championship Series (NLCS) against St. Louis—would have been on top of this listing.

Burke's home run off Joey Devine at Minute Maid Park ended a game that will never be forgotten. Like the big moments from the 2017 World Series, it capped an improbable Astro comeback in a very important game.

With a win, the Astros would eliminate the Braves without needing to go back to Atlanta to finish the Series. They would also have a more-rested pitching staff for the next Series against the St. Louis Cardinals.

For most of the scheduled part of the game at Minute Maid Park, it seemed a certainty the Series would have to shift back to Atlanta. The Braves led 6 – 1 to the last of the eighth inning. But then Lance Berkman hit a grand slam off Kyle Farnsworth in that inning. The Astros were within one run.

However, hopes were slim when, with two out and no one on base in the last of the ninth, light-hitting catcher Brad Ausmus faced Farnsworth. Then, Kyle made a mistake. He fell behind in the count to Ausmus, and when Brad guessed and got a fastball, he was able to drive it toward the wall in deep left-center field. Banging off the wall just above the yellow line that denoted home run territory, the game was tied at 6 – 6. The game moved into extra innings with that score.

It stayed that way until the last of the 18th. In the meantime, pitching staffs and benches were being depleted. The Astros even brought in starter Roger Clemens to pitch for three scoreless innings. Andy Pettitte, who had not even been in the park, rushed back in case he would be needed. Fortunately, Burke came through just in time.

Leading off the inning, Chris said later he thought about trying to drop down a bunt and beat it out for a hit. But the first pitch from Braves pitcher Joey Devine wasn't close and Burke took it for a ball. The next pitch was also off the plate, too far inside.

Pitch number three was magic—for Burke. Chris hit the inside fastball on a line toward left field. The question on spectator's minds was, "Would it be high enough to clear the twenty-one foot wall, or slam off the top of it?"

It was high enough. As Chris put it later, "I was looking for that pitch. I put the right swing on it and got it up and over the wall.

"I didn't hit it great," Burke recounted. "But I figured it was going out. I threw my fist up, and I remember giving Cheo [Astro first-base coach José Cruz] a five. When I got to third, the look on Doug's eyes [Mansolino, third-base coach] were as big as his whole face. Then, seeing the guys waiting for me at home plate. It's almost an out-of-body experience."

The Astros had won the longest post-season game ever. They had ousted the Braves and were set to take on the Cardinals for a berth in the World Series for the first time.

Chris Burke never had another moment even approaching that one again. The former first-round draftee from the University of Tennessee was blocked from getting much playing time by the presence of future Hall of Famer Craig Biggio at second base. His major-league career lasted only six seasons, and he was just a .239 hitter with 23 homers in 477 games. However, he hit two post-season homers, drove in four runs, and batted .286 in 13 post-season chances. And he had a moment few in baseball history ever have.

Before he became a hero, he thought of the fans. "The game was a grind. That's a long time to stay sharp mentally. I was almost feeling bad for the fans. They'd been going through it for nearly six hours."

After Burke hit the home run, the length of the game was forgotten, but the game itself and Chris Burke's heroics will never be forgotten by Astro fans.

9

Framber Valdez Runs Off Record with 25 Consecutive Quality Starts

In 2022, Justin Verlander won the Cy Young Award in the American League. But teammate Framber Valdez was not that far behind in the voting. And he deserved to be a finalist. His record was 17-6 with a 2.82 earned run average over 31 games started. He also pitched a team high 201.1 innings. Verlander had only one more win, but his ERA of a skimpy 1.75 pushed him to the top.

However, no pitcher on the team or in the history of baseball did one thing Valdez did in 2022. He set a new single season record with 25 consecutive quality starts. That was out of 31 total starts and had a huge effect on the Astros winning

106 games.

A quality start does two things: it eats innings allowing the bullpen to have some rest and it keeps a team in the game to give the offense some time to get going. Pitching six innings and allowing three earned runs or less is a quality start. Projected to nine innings that is a mediocre 4.50 ERA, but allowing three runs or less in six IS very good.

When Valdez set the new record, he broke the old one of 24 set by Jacob DeGrom of the Mets.

His success is a result of pitches that move...two seam sinking fast ball and his outstanding curve. Very hard to square up. When he failed it was usually a pitch without movement that found the middle of the strike zone. Or not having enough control to have the ball-strike count in his favor. During his streak and the 2022 season that rarely happened.

And his catcher, Martin Maldonado said a number of things have made Valdez, "It is a lot of calm, a lot of confidence, and a lot of maturity from him. He knows what he can do good. Listening more and taking great pride in his work and less emotional on the mound."

Maldonado saw that up close. Opposing hitters did too.

Manager Dusty Baker was impressed, "That is a remarkable streak. There have been some great pitchers that he surpassed and I am glad he accomplished it and we won the game."

The Astros beat the A's on September 18, 2022, 11-2, and Valdez picked up his 15th win during the run.

10

Astros Win First Pennant in 2005 But Are Swept by Chisox

Until the 2013 season, the Houston Colt .45s/Astros baseball teams had been members of the National League (NL). They had made nine post-season appearances between 1980 and 2005, but until 2005 had never been league champions. Either the Phillies, Mets, Braves, Padres, or Cardinals had always knocked them out early.

In 2005, that would finally change. The Astros were able to secure a wild-card post-season bid after only a 89 – 73 regular season record. They were eleven games behind the Central Division champion St. Louis Cardinals, who had won 100 games. The Astros record was one game better than the Philadelphia Phillies and just good enough for the single wild-card spot in the NL.

The Astros got past their longtime rival in Atlanta three

games to one, with Chris Burke's heroics in the 18-inning finale leading the way. They had won the opener with an offensive show to support Andy Pettitte in beating Atlanta, 10 – 5. Morgan Ensberg had three hits that drove in five runs. A five-run eighth inning clinched it with Jeff Bagwell, Ensberg, Jason Lane, and Orlando Palmeiro all having RBIs.

In the second game of the series, the Braves evened things as John Smoltz bested Roger Clemens, 7 – 1. Brian McCann's three-run homer with two outs in the second inning was the biggest hit.

With the series shifting to Houston, the next two games the Astros reclaimed the lead in the series with a 7 – 3 victory behind Roy Oswalt. The Braves negated an Astro two-run bottom of the first inning produced by an Ensberg RBI double and a Jason Lane sacrifice fly with two of their own in the top of the second thanks to a McCann RBI single and another by pitcher Jorge Sosa. A home run by Mike Lamb in the third gave Houston the lead they would not relinquish. Then came the classic 18-inning thriller that Chris Burke ended with his home run.

Next, the Astros had to face the team in St. Louis that had won the division by an eleven-game margin. Not only did the Astros battle to beat the Cards in six games, they closed down Busch Stadium II which would be replaced by the new Busch Stadium III the next spring.

Astro fans had hoped their team would not have to play a sixth game in St. Louis. Houston had raced to a 3 – 1 game lead in the best of seven. After losing the opener 6 – 3, they won the next three and were leading 4 – 2 with two out and two on in the top of the ninth at Minute Maid Park.

Closer Brad Lidge was on the mound. He struck out the first two hitters John Rodriguez and John Mabry. Houston was one out away from its first World Series.

Unfortunately, on a 1 – 2 pitch, the player Astro fans respectfully called "The Pest," shortstop David Eckstein, did what he did best. He got a piece of the pitch and flicked it into left field for a single. Whether that unnerved Lidge or not, he walked the next hitter, Jim Edmonds, on five pitches. According to manager Phil Garner, that was one of two major mistakes by Lidge. "The mistake is walking Edmonds. You have to make Edmonds hit the ball. You can't walk him." That gave the Cardinals' best hitter, Albert Pujols, a chance. Garner let Lidge know he didn't mind if he walked Pujols in this spot, even pushing the tying run into scoring position at second base. That had been the mantra all year with Pujols. Force someone else to beat the Astros, not Pujols.

That desire was not fulfilled on this night. Lidge threw a first pitch slider that was a strike. Then he tried another. Instead of sliding, the pitch hung over the middle of the plate. Pujols did not miss it.

The drive went high and deep into the night in left field, crashing hard against the plexiglass window above the train tracks below the roof. The Cardinals scored three runs with two out and led 4 – 3.

The Astros were retired in the last of the ninth, thus setting up a required trip back to St. Louis. They needed at least one more win. While the fans in the stands were crushed by the loss, as they had been only one strike away from clinching the NL pennant at home, the players were more conciliatory toward their ace closer.

Lidge himself said after the game, "He hit it a mile. It's tough, but I told everybody in this clubhouse, I'm looking forward to going to St. Louis and winning it there."

Though disappointed, the Astros took the loss as pros and looked ahead. Oh, there was one look back during the plane ride that took them to St. Louis. Jeff Bagwell and Brad Ausmus asked GM Tim Purpura if they could get the pilot to say something over the loud speaker. After Purpura heard the plan, he agreed, and soon the pilot informed those on board that if they looked out of the left side of the plane, they could see Pujols's homer flying past.

Some teammates and pitching coach Jim Hickey, who

were not in on the joke, were furious, but they all laughed when they found out who was behind the prank.

Fortunately for the Astros, they were able to nail down the pennant in their first try at Busch Stadium. Roy Oswalt, who would have started the World Series on full rest, was the starting pitcher in St. Louis. He was superb. Oswalt threw seven innings of three-hit ball, allowing only one run on a John Rodriguez sacrifice fly in the fifth after the Astros had already scored three times. Brad Ausmus had three hits and Craig Biggio had two while driving in a run. Morgan Ensberg, Adam Everett, and Jason Lane each drove in a run, Lane's on a solo home run.

With Dan Wheeler on the mound for the Astros in the last of the ninth, the Astros clinched the team's first pennant after Lane gloved a soft fly ball in right field. The team celebrated, and fans back in Houston did the same. In St. Louis, the bulldozers could be fired up the next day to start dismantling Busch Stadium II. The players and staff made a quick stop back in Houston before heading to Chicago to meet the AL-Champion White Sox in their first World Series.

The White Sox swept the Astros in four straight games, despite the run differential being the least in a sweep ever. Only six runs separated the White Sox and Astros. Houston had leads in two of the games and lost one of them in 14 innings, taking five hours and 41 minutes—the longest post-season game by time in MLB history at that time.

The 2005 Astro team had lost Carlos Beltrán and Jeff Kent to free agency after 2004. Jeff Bagwell was sidelined after shoulder surgery. The offense was far less potent than the previous season. When Bagwell returned from the disabled list (DL), he could not throw and could only pinch-hit. In the Series, he was used as the designated hitter. While he had hoped to try for a comeback the next spring, he could not and retired.

11

Best Trades Ever Brought in Bagwell and Alvarez

or years no trade in Houston baseball history had as long lasting or positive of an effect than the deal for a little-known AA level third baseman from the Boston Red Sox farm system in return for an experienced and talented major-league relief pitcher. That was the trade that brought Jeff Bagwell to Houston for pitcher Larry Andersen at the end of the 1990 season.

But in 2016 the Astros seemingly fleeced the Dodgers out of one of the greatest hitters in baseball, bringing Cuban-born Yordan Alvarez to Houston. That may turn out as big.

As for the Bagwell acquisition, the Red Sox were in a pennant race, which they would eventually win by two games over the Toronto Blue Jays in the AL East. But to get there, they wanted to shore up their bullpen. Andersen was a good pick up, as he appeared in 15 games the last month of the season while recording a stingy 1.35 earned-run average (ERA).

Bagwell had just finished his season with New Britain of the Eastern League when the trade was made on August 30, 1990. His first full minor-league year was a great one. He had hit .333 with a .422 OBP in 136 games. His trade may have had a lot to do with what was missing. Bagwell hit only four home runs!

However, to be fair and to put even that into perspective, it must be pointed out that home runs were rare in the Eastern League in 1990. The league leader, Rico Brogna, hit just 21, and only ten players in the whole league reached double figures. Still, lack of power for a corner infielder is not usually helpful in obtaining a first-class ticket to the major leagues.

Of course, Boston already had future Hall of Famer Wade Boggs playing third base and two others in the system ahead of Bagwell, Scott Cooper, and Tim Naehring. Jeff was expendable.

As for the Astros, the scouts knew Bagwell played hard and could hit for average. He was above average defensively. If he started the 1991 season at AAA Tucson, perhaps the organization might know more about what they had. They had a third baseman in Houston in Ken Caminiti so the position was not open.

A New England native, Bagwell wasn't so happy about the trade to say the least. "I was devastated," Jeff remembered. As he told writer Leigh Montville in 1993, "I was one of the saddest guys you'll ever see. All my life everything had been Boston. I was born in Boston. My father was from Watertown. My mother was from Newton, just outside Boston. Our house was one of those places where you couldn't mention the word Yankees. My grandmother was a huge Red Sox fan. I called to tell her the news and she started crying."

When Jeff had been drafted by Boston out of the University of Hartford two years earlier, joy reigned. The joy had turned to dismay. Off to Houston? Where exactly is that anyway? Somewhere in Texas?

As history has noted, Jeff Bagwell's skills were discovered quickly in spring training. Manager Art Howe determined he could be shifted to first base to get his bat into the lineup. Bagwell and the Astros never looked back. With maturity and hard work in the weight room, Jeff developed enough power to crush 449 home runs in a 15-year career. His 1994 season remains the best single season of any Houston hitter. He hit .368 with 39 home runs and 116 RBIs in just 110 games of that strike-shortened season. He led the NL with 104 runs scored, 116 RBIs, and a .750 SLG. For his career, he hit just under .300 and arguably was the best overall player in franchise history before chronic shoulder problems forced him to retire prior to 2006. The Hall of Fame beckoned in 2017, clinching the Astros trade for Jeff Bagwell as the best deal they may ever make.

But then came Yordan!

The big six-foot-five, 225 pound, Cuban-born Yordan Alvarez was traded to the Astros on August 1, 2016, before his professional career even began. In 2016, the Dodgers had signed him as an international free agent. The Astros had wanted to compete, but had already been fined by major league baseball for spending too much in signing veteran Cuban star Yuli Gurriel.

The Dodgers signed Alvarez but didn't have him long enough to learn what they had. He was raw with great power, but not a lot of experience in either Cuba or Haiti where he had moved. Could he handle professional pitching? What position could the big guy play? These were legitimate questions but didn't bother the Astros. Yordan had met the Gurriel brothers while in Haiti before Yuli signed with the Astros. He was even befriended by Astro scout Charlie Gonzalez. Gonzalez wanted the Astros to sign Alvarez. But they couldn't due to their punishment for signing the older Gurriell.

In June of 2016, Alvarez signed for two million dollars with the Dodgers. However, he was not a high priority and LA's staff may have not known him from pitcher Yadier Alvarez. When the contending Dodgers needed relief help with the big club, Houston was ready to help them out. They sent major league pitcher Josh Fields for Alvarez. Later, Los Angeles' President of Baseball Operations Andrew Friedman admitted trading Yordan was a mistake. Possibly for two reasons. There is reason to think the Dodgers thought they were trading pitcher Yadier Alvarez instead of Yordan Alvarez. The Astros knew the potential of what they were getting.

Friedman later said, "I obviously wish I would have said yes to other names the Astros asked for before him." Did he agree to the other Alvarez and not notice it was the other Alvarez the Astros wanted...or at that point was Yordan Alvare just another guy in the system? As with the Jeff Bagwell trade years before, the Astros were the big winners.

The general manager of the Astros when Bagwell was acquired from Boston was Bill Wood. As he recalled to Bill Brown in the book *Deep in the Heart*, "When we got Bagwel that trade and he went to the Instructional League, I got a phone call from Jimmy Johnson [the coordinator of instruction]. He said, 'You can't believe this kid Bagwell and his hitting ability. He looks even better than the praise he got from our scouts.'" Manager Art Howe saw in the spring that he had to find a spot for Bagwell right away.

12

Alvarez Gives Astros 2022 1-0 ALDS Lead Over Seattle with GWHR

rom his debut with the Astros, Yordan Alvarez opened eyes with his power and overall hitting ability. His first major heroic effort came in the opening game of the 2022 ALDS against the Seattle Mariners.

During the regular season, Alvarez hit 37 home runs and the Astros won 12 of 19 games against Seattle. Houston also had a whopping 118 – 72 edge in the all-time series. But this was the post-season and upsets happen all the time. There was one in the making in game one of the best of five set.

Astro starter and future Hall of Famer Justin Verlander was very hittable. In fact, when he left the game after just four innings he had allowed ten hits, six earned runs. The Astros trailed by four runs when the future Cy Young Award winner left the game.

Houston was able to climb within two runs to the last

of the ninth thanks to home runs by Yuli Gurriell and Alex Bregman. And when the game went to the last of the ninth, history was not on the Astros side. They were 0 – 48 in their post-season history when trailing by more than one run after eight innings.

But then came Yordan Alvarez in the last of the ninth. But he needed runners on base. David Hensley was hit by a pitch with one out. After José Altuve made the second out by striking out, Jeremy Peña kept the inning alive by singling to center.

Strategy took over. The Mariners brought in lefty starter Robbie Ray to face the lefty hitting Alvarez. It didn't work. On the second pitch Alvrez, who had hit ten homers and carried a batting average of .321 vs lefties, crushed a long drive over the wall. His three-run homer gave the Astros an 8 – 7 victory.

Afterwards, Mariner manager Scott Servais was questioned about his pitching move. "Bringing in a lefty to face Alvarez...we had been talking about it before the game and when the moment arose we went with it. That was the game plan going in."

As for the hero who was playing before his parents from Cuba, "I think its one of the most special moments that I have had in my career," the translater for Alvarez reported.

The walk-off home run was the first ever for a team trailing by multiple runs in postseason and just the second with a team down to its final out. Kirk Gibson did it for Detroit in the 1988 World Series.

The homer by Alvarez got the Astros off to a one-game-to-none start. They would not lose a postseason game in the first two rounds and later win the 2022 World Series over Philadelphia four games to two.

13

Niekro and Howe Led Astros into First Postseason

t was only fitting that the pitcher who remains as the winningest of all time while wearing a Houston uniform was the man responsible for putting the team in the postseason for the first time. The pitcher was Joe Niekro, although he did have a lot of help from another Houston icon, Art Howe.

It was in 1980. When one looks back at the standings, it appears rather simple. The Astros record was 93 – 70 and the second-place Dodgers were 92 – 71. But add those totals. There was one more game played than the standard 162. That's right, the Astros had to beat the Dodgers on October 6 in a one game playoff for the NL West title.

It was Joe Niekro on the mound and Art Howe driving in four runs with a homer and a single that did it. Houston won 7 – 1. For Niekro, it was his 20th victory. The second time he had reached that level as an Astro. During the 11 seasons Niekro wore Astro colors, he won 144 games, which remains the franchise record. (Overall, Niekro was 221 – 204 in a career that featured seven different teams over a 22-year period.)

Photo courtesy of B&M Photography.

The Astrodome filled up after a big win.

After the game, Niekro admitted the victory was a long time coming, "I've been waiting for this for fourteen years!" Howe was telling the press that he had hit a hanging curve for his homer and a fastball for his single. The homer was off Dave Goltz, and the single off Rick Sutcliffe.

Winning that game for the division seemed easy, but getting to it was anything but. The Astros had come into the final series in the season against the Dodgers leading by three games with three to play. They lost all of them, forcing the playoff.

The Dodgers won all three by one run each. Joe Ferguson hit a walk-off homer in the last of the 10th in the first game. Steve Garvey had three hits, including a solo home run off Nolan Ryan and scored both runs in Los Angeles's 2 – 1 victory in the second game.

The pennant race was tied after Ron Cey's two-run home run in the last of the eighth off Frank LaCorte, giving the Dodgers their final 4 – 3 margin. Cey would miss the playoff game due to injuring his foot by fouling a ball off it just before he hit the game-winning homer to make the playoff game necessary.

All this set the stage for the playoff heroics of Niekro and Howe.

14

José Altuve Discovered in Venezuela

Still a lot of career to be played, but the discovery of José Altuve by Astro scouts has to rank high among legendary Astro stories. Credit may go to Omar Lopez, or Al Pedrique, Pablo Torrealba, or Wolfgang Ramos. All have been linked to finding, recommending, or signing the superstar.

Despite the fact that Altuve is a major-league hitting machine with three batting titles to his credit, thinking he would be this good was no cinch. He was so small! When scouts first put him on their watch list, he was only sixteen years old. In addition to his 5-feet, 5-inches height, he weighed perhaps 145 to 150 pounds.

But Altuve could hit, field, and run. Still, after the first day of an Astro tryout camp in 2006, he was not invited back the next day. Altuve's father, Carlos, convinced José not to take that as the final word. He knew Al Pedrique had been intrigued at least earlier that summer, and Al had not been at the first day of tryouts. José agree to show up the next day whether invited or not. Pedrique was there and liked what he saw, although he didn't project José as major leaguer. A roster filler at A or AA might be his role. That size thing was too hard to ignore.

When Altuve was offered a $15,000 contract, he and his father were quick to accept. They were both confident that given a chance, José Altuve would make good.

After Altuve started his professional career, Astro farm director Ricky Bennett watched José play for a number of games in a row and said, "I couldn't take my eyes off him. He played with such flash and passion, always the right place at the right time."

Altuve started to show everyone at age 17 in his pro debut in rookie ball when he hit .343 in 64 games in the Venezuelan rookie league. The next two seasons, he started in the US Appalachian Rookie League with Greenville and was boosted to low-A ball at Tri Cities by the end of 2009 when he was only 19. He was hitting everywhere and stealing bases. By 2010, he started to appear on the Astro's radar after hitting .301 with 15 home runs, 67 RBIs, and 42 stolen bases in 125 games. He split time between Lexington and Lancaster that season. Astros scouting director Bobby Heck said, "Once he hit well at Lexington, we realized he would be a major leaguer."

Maybe so, but as good as he has become? Hard work and natural talent did that. José was good, but not great, his first two full years in the major leagues. He hit .290 and .283 respectively and stole 33 and 35 bases.

Then in 2014, Altuve blossomed into a superstar. He collected 225 hits, stole 56 bases, and led the American League (AL) with a .341 batting average. The next season, he dropped off a bit to .313, but still recorded 200 hits. That was the season his power started to show with 15 home runs. In both 2016 and 2017, Altuve won batting titles. He also hit 24 home runs both seasons. And he was named the AL Most Valuable Player (MVP) after the 2017 season.

Can there be any doubt José Altuve was the greatest find in Houston baseball history? The Astros showed their feelings when they signed him to a five-year contract extension to take effect in 2020 that would pay him a reported $151 million dollars over five seasons. When it expired after the 2024 season, Altuve would be nearing 35 years old. The team had wrapped him up through the peak—if not all—years of his career. With the contract and his credentials already, a spot to join Craig Biggio and Jeff Bagwell as Astros in the Hall of Fame someday would be no surprise.

Al Pedrique, the scout who first saw something in José Altuve, has had a long and outstanding baseball career. A native of Venezuala, Pedrique played 174 games in the major leagues with the Mets, Pirates, and Tigers from 1987 through 1989. He then became a minor league coach, manager, and scout. In the major leagues, he reached the manager's job with Arizona for the second half of 2004. He also served as bench coach for the Astros after serving as minor league field coordinator. He was an Astros special assistant when he saw something in small sixteen year old José Altuve that others failed to see. Pedrique later coached for the A's where he and Altuve renewed acquaintances in every Astros vs. A's series.

15
Carlos Correa Drafted First in First Round 2012

The pressure was on the Houston Astros when the June 2012 amateur free agent draft came around. With the new ownership and management in place, Jeff Luhnow and his crew would have to make the right pick with the first choice. Many in the past had failed. The Astros could not afford to. If the franchise was going to be rebuilt from within, it would have to obtain some future stars from the amateur ranks.

The consensus right choice in most baseball circles was outfielder Brian Buxton, a talented high school outfielder from Georgia. He had all the tools and was considered a sure-bet future star. Another name heard, but not rated highly by as many was 17-year-old shortstop Carlos Correa from Puerto Rico. Scouts liked what they saw, but would he become as good as Buxton? And, he was so young!

To the Astros scouts, it was almost a no-brainer. Correa had to be the choice. In addition to being talented as a ballplayer, he was a leader on the field and far more mature than his 17 years. He was a straight-A student and had registered a 1560 on the SAT in case college was a goal. His future looked bright no matter which way it turned. And he wanted to be a baseball player first. Correa would become the first player from Puerto Rico ever selected with the first pick in the baseball amateur free agent draft. This from an island that produced such major leaguers as Roberto Clemente, Ivan Rodriguez, Orlando Cepeda, Bernie Williams, and Carlos Delgado.

The Astros were also able to get Correa for less than the maximum price for the first pick ($4.8 million) and still had enough money available to select pitcher Lance McCullers Jr. in the supplemental first round. That first round combo may someday be remembered as one of the best two first round picks by a team in baseball history!

Already, with their careers young, both have been AL All-Stars. Both have been stars on a World Series Championship team.

Correa projects to be even more—maybe even a Hall of Fame player. For Astro fans that may be bittersweet if it happens since Correa opted for free agency after the 2021 season and left the team for the Minnesota Twins. With the Twins his star dimmed a bit as his hitting declined. Perhaps the Astros lost him at the right time.

But Jeff Luhnow and his crew, with what knowledge he brought from his days in St. Louis and the input from the outgoing Astro scouting department, made two choices that, no matter if he gets back into baseball somewhere, he may never be able to duplicate. After the Correa selection, Houston GM Luhnow said, "Correa has a chance to be a star who could hit twenty to thirty home runs, whether it's as a shortstop or, ultimately, maybe third base." Based on his major-league start, that projection may be low, and there is no indication that Correa won't remain a shortstop for some time. Injuries, which have cut two of his seasons short, are the main concern.

The loss of Carlos was quickly made up with Jeremy Peña's arrival in 2022 to take over. As outlined earlier in this book, all he did was become MVP in both the American League Championship Series and the World Series in his rookie season of 2022. The shortstop position in Houston remains manned as well as nearly anywhere in the game.

Correa was AL Rookie of the Year in 2015. Corey Seager of the Dodgers, the 18th pick in the 2012 draft, won the Rookie of Year Award in the NL in 2016. Addison Russell of the Cubs beat Correa to becoming a World Series Champion in 2016. Although not the hitter on the Correa-Seager level, Russell's steady glove anchored the Cub defense for a short time.

Correa won his first pick overall from his workouts with his team while winning the Victor Pellot (Vic Power, from his MLB career) Excellence Tournament in the early spring of 2012. Carlos was the MVP of the tournament, which included a two home run game. At the PG World Showcase that spring, he was clocked with a 97 mph throw from shortstop to first base. He also played for Team Mizuno and the Puerto Rico National Team that played in a youth Pan American tournament.

Astro scouts were won over. Carlos was coming from a low-income family that had moved several times due to homes damaged by floods and hurricanes. His father did as much as he could in working with Carlos and getting him on the best teams to develop his skills. By the time he was ten years old, he was one of the best, if not the best, players in his age group on the island.

By time he was 20, he was a major leaguer. By the time he was 22, he was a world champion. What does his full career hold in the future? His future great moments won't be wearing a Houston uniform. But while he was an Astro, he was great.

16

Craig Biggio's 3,000th Hit

n baseball, a player can reach a milestone that guarantees immortality. Until the so-called "Steroid" or "PED" era, most of those milestones were well-known and would guarantee entrance into the Baseball Hall of Fame in Cooperstown, New York. Lifetime Astro Craig Biggio achieved one of those milestones the honest way when he collected his 3,000th hit on June 28, 2007 at Minute Maid Park. His single off Aaron Cook was his third hit of what would become a five-hit night—only the second of his long career.

Biggio had tried to stretch the hit into a double to get into scoring position, but was thrown out by former teammate Willie Taveras for the third out. With the mid-inning break came the celebration. Both of Craig's sons raced onto the field. Wife Patti joined the group near first base, and then, at Biggio's urging, longtime teammate Jeff Bagwell, then retired, was summoned to the field as well. In the meantime, the sell-out crowd continued to roar in excitement and appreciation. The Astros went on to win that game, with Carlos Lee's walk-off grand slam being nearly forgotten. The night was all Craig Biggio's. After the game, Biggio put Lee's hit and his

Craig Biggio's 3,000th hit was his ticket to the Hall of Fame.

achievement in perspective. "I couldn't have scripted it any better. As a baseball player, the way the fans treated me ... I've said that for a long time. I love these guys. I love this city. I worked hard here, and they appreciated that."

Craig went on to collect more hits as the 2007 season wound down, finishing with 3,060 and a future ticket to become Houston's first Hall of Famer, which he achieved in 2015. Jeff Bagwell would also be enshrined in Cooperstown in 2017. They would be the first two former Astros to wear a Houston cap on their plaques. Neither ever played anywhere else.

Getting the historic 3,000th hit at home took some real scheduling by manager Phil Garner during a nine-game road trip that preceded Biggio's big night. Biggio was only 11 hits from 3,000 at the beginning of the trip. Garner had Biggio in the lineup for six of the nine games and used him as pinch hitter in two more. Biggio collected eight hits and had 2,997 hits when the team returned home. In his prime, he would have certainly started all nine games and had his 3,000th hit on a foreign field. In 2007, Craig was only hitting .238 and his replacement Mark Loretta was actually having a better year with a .300 mark. Keeping Biggio out of a few games so he would surely reach 3,000 in the upcoming eleven-game home stand was not a real hardship.

17

Springer is 2017 World Series Most Valuable Player; Peña Win Same Honor in 2022

o achievement is any greater than being named the MVP in the World Series and leading one's team to the big prize. George Springer did both for the 2017 Houston Astros. Jeremy Peña duplicated the feat in 2022.

What George did was tie a World Series record with five home runs in the seven games. Only Chase Utley in 2009 and Reggie Jackson in 1977 had hit as many. The best of both Babe Ruth and Barry Bonds was four. Springer also hit .379, with eight of his eleven hits for extra bases. He drove in seven runs. All of this from the leadoff spot in the Astros batting order. But what may have been even more important than the numbers was when he came through. Clutch was his middle name.

In the classic second game, he hit the final go-ahead home run in the top of the 11th. In Game Five, he atoned for failing on a diving attempt to catch a sinking liner hit by Cody Bellinger in the top of the seventh, which resulted in a run. Springer homered in the bottom of the inning to tie the game. The Astro won both Game Two and Five.

Then, in the clinching Game Seven, he doubled off Yu Darvish to open the game and later scored. In the next inning, he crushed a two-run homer, and the Astros never looked back, rolling to a 5 – 1 victory and World Series title.

Strangely, it didn't start out so well. In the Series opener, after a lackluster ALCS, he was hitless in four at-bats. But veteran Carlos Beltrán calmed him down. As Springer put it, "He told me to just go out and try to enjoy the moment because he'd been playing for twenty years and this is only his second time here. He told me to go out and kind of be who I am and enjoy it."

After the first game, George Springer obviously enjoyed it.

George Springer has had to overcome a lot more than just learning to hit major league pitchers. Springer has had to fight speaking with a stutter since childhood. He has been taking on the problem head on. While he will still occasionally have to pause, he has conquered the fear part of the affliction so well that he challenges it. He welcomes doing interviews. He welcomes being "wired" with a microphone during games. He tries to help others. He is a spokesperson for the Stuttering Association for the Young (SAY). He has raised money for the nonprofit organization by sponsoring bowling tournaments and other events that allow camps for youth with stutters to meet, work, and play together. As George says, "I'm extremely happy for all kids to go out and truly see they're not the only ones. I know from experience that that can be a very isolating feeling."

While Springer's exploits as an Astro will be remembered, free agency tempted him to Toronto and the Astros had a big hole to fill in centerfield.

The Astros in 2022 had a player who filled a big hole win the same honor Springer had won in 2017.

Jeremy Peña who took over at shortstop after Carlos Correa had moved on as a free agent to the Minnesota Twins.

During the regular season Peña hit only .253 and led the team with 135 strikeouts. But he hit 22 home runs, had 20 doubles, and drove in 63 runs. His defensive skill was recognized with the American League Gold Glove. A very fine rookie season.

Then came the postseason.

In addition to winning the third and final game of the LDS with an 18th inning home run in Seattle he heated up even more in the next two rounds. Against the Yankees in the Astros four game sweep Peña hit .353 with two homers and four runs batted in. He was named ALCS MVP for that effort.

Then in the six game World Series against the Phillies he hit .400 with another home run and three RBIs. That was good enough for Jeremy to be voted World Series MVP as well.

Peña for the full postseason hit .345 with four homers and eight runs batted in for 13 games.

18

World Series Game Five in 2017 Upstaged Game Two

**W**hile some of the heroics in the 2017 Game Five have been listed as legendary moments of their own, the game itself deserves full recognition. The final score was Houston 13, Los Angeles 12 in a long ten innings. There were 14 pitchers used and 417 pitches thrown. The official game time of five hours and 17 minutes was the second-longest World Series game ever. Only the 14 inning game between the Astros and Chicago White Sox in 2005 was longer. Both would be eclipsed by the seven-hour, twenty-minute, 18-inning Game Four of the 2018 World Series.

Still, the Astros have a "thing" for long postseason games. Their NLDS 18-inning win over Atlanta in 2005 went five hours and 50 minutes. In 2022, they played another 18-inning game in Seattle that took even longer, six hours and 22 minutes.

The Astros won that game as well. Game Five in 2017 with the winner taking a three game to two lead in the Series as it headed back to Los Angeles, had a lot at stake. And both teams had multiple chances to win or lose.

Things looked very rosy for the Dodgers when they jumped on Astro starter Dallas Keuchel with three runs in the first then added another in the top of the fourth. In the meantime, Dodger ace Clayton Kershaw had not allowed a baserunner the first time though the batting order—nine up and nine down.

Things—and the whole game—changed in the bottom of the fourth. George Springer led off the inning with a single. Alex Bregman was retired, but he hit a ball deep to the outfield for the out. Then José Altuve singled for the first Houston hit. Next, Carlo Correa ripped a double, scoring Springer. Altuve and Correa were on base, 4 – 1, when Yuli Gurriel hit the first pitch from Kershaw for a three-run home run to tie the game.

In keeping with what this game would become, the tie was gone in the next half inning. The Dodgers' Corey Seager and Justin Turner each drew walks from Astro reliever Collin McHugh to open the inning. With one out, Cody Bellinger hit a three-run homer to right-center field. Dodgers led 7 – 4 to the bottom of the fifth.

The Astros came right back. After two outs, Kershaw walked both George Springer and Alex Bregman. Kershaw left the game and was replaced by Kenta Maeda. José Altuve got the count to 3 – 2 and re-tied the game with a three-run homer 7 – 7.

The game remained tied at seven until the Dodger seventh, when Cody Bellinger tripled with one out after Springer made a diving attempt on the ball but missed. Los Angeles had an 8 – 7 lead to the bottom of the frame.

George Springer led off the last of the seventh but stayed in the box for only one pitch. He liked what he saw from Dodger reliever Brandon Morrow and re-tied the game at 8 – 8 with a homer. The Astros would add more. Bregman singled and Altuve doubled him home. The inning ended after Carlos Correa hit a two-run homer with Altuve on. The Astros led, 11 – 8, after the seventh.

But the game still had a long way to go. The Dodgers closed the gap to 11 – 9 on an RBI double by Corey Seager off Will Harris in the eighth. The Astros lead was 12 – 9 after Brian McCann's home run, which most felt was insurance, in the last of the eighth.

It wasn't insurance, it was necessary as it turned out. Los Angeles re-tied the score in the top of the ninth with three runs off Chris Devenski. A leadoff walk to Bellinger and a Yasiel Puig one-armed homer into the first row of the Crawford boxes in left field made it 12 – 11. Then, after an Austin Barnes double and a single up the middle by Chris Taylor, the game was even 12 – 12.

The Astros had a chance to win in nine, but after a two out double by Yuli Gurriel, Josh Reddick flied out to left field and the game went to the 10th.

In the top of the inning, Joe Musgrove gave up a one out single, but no other baserunners. The Astros came to hit in the bottom of the tenth.

Kenley Jansen, who had not been dominant out of the pen for the Dodgers, started well. He got Evan Gattis and Marwin Gonzalez out—the latter on a swinging strike. No doubt Jenson took joy from it since it was Gonzalez who had tied Game Two with a two out home run off him.

Then the Astros got a break when, for some reason, Jansen lost command and hit catcher Brian McCann with a pitch. Then he walked George Springer on a three-one pitch. Speedy Derek Fisher entered the game to run for McCann since he was in scoring position.

The hitter was Alex Bregman. On the first pitch, he singled to left-center. Fisher raced around third and slid home. The Astros had won 13 – 12 in perhaps the most thrilling back and forth, offensive-heavy game in World Series history. Bregman, as expected, was flying high when he spoke with the media after the game. "When you feel like you came through for your team and you see the joy on their faces, there's nothing like it. It's an unbelievable moment. You dream about it as a little kid. To be living a dream and one win away from the World Series is really special."

Manager A. J. Hinch described the whole game as many felt, "Just when I thought I could describe Game Two as my favorite game of all time, I think Game Five exceeded that and more."

19
World Series Game Two 2017

Until Game Five, many fans thought Game Two of the Series had the honor of being considered as the most thrilling game in World Series history. The importance for the Astros to win it and even the Series made it crucial. The Dodgers had won the opener. Houston needed the win to get a split in Los Angeles before the Series shifted to their home park.

ALCS MVP, Justin Verlander, would be on the mound for Houston. Rich Hill would be the starter for the Dodgers. A pitchers' duel could be expected. The Astros led, 1 – 0, into the bottom of the fifth. Houston had scored in the third on an RBI single by Alex Bregman that drove in Josh Reddick, who had led off the inning with a single and was bunted into scoring position by Verlander.

In the last of the fifth, Joc Pederson hit a two-out solo home run to tie the game. The long ball put the Dodgers on top the next inning when another two-out home run—this time by Corey Seager with a runner aboard—gave Los Angeles a 3 – 1 lead.

The score remained that way until a leadoff double by Alex Bregman in the top of the eighth resulted in the Dodgers relieving Brandon Morrow with closer Kenley Jansen. He got Altuve on a groundout to second, but couldn't retire Carlos Correa. His RBI single closed the gap to one run. The score stayed that way until the next inning.

Joe Musgrove, who would be a key reliever in the Astros Game Five win, had a perfect bottom of the eighth before the Astros came up in the ninth still one run behind.

That was when Marwin Gonzalez, after falling behind in the count—no balls and two strikes—hit a cutting fastball from Jansen on a line to deep center field that made it over the wall to tie the game.

Springer doubled with two outs, but Bregman grounded out to end the inning.

The Dodgers batted in the last of the ninth against Astro closer Ken Giles. He had a perfect inning, throwing only ten pitches.

In the 10th inning, with Josh Fields, the seventh pitcher that manager Dave Roberts had used, pitching for Los Angeles, José Altuve and Carlos Correa hit back-to-back home runs. Those would be the only Astro runs in the inning, but going to the last of the 10th, Houston led, 5 – 3. (Fields was the pitcher the Astros gave up for Yordan Alvarez the year before.)

That lead was not safe. Giles, after a low-pitch perfect ninth, was not so perfect in the 10th. He surrendered a leadoff home run to Yasiel Puig, but he regrouped. He struck out both Yasmani Grandal and Austin Barnes. Needing just one more out to close out the game, he lost his command. He walked Logan Forsythe, then threw a wild pitch with Enrique Hernandez batting. Hernandez singled to score Forsythe and tie the game at 5 – 5.

The Astros reclaimed the lead in the 11th after Cameron Maybin singled and came home on George Springer's home run. Houston took a 7 – 5 lead to the last of the 11th.

No breathing easy, though. With Chris Devenski on the mound and two outs, Charlie Culberson took a 2 – 1 pitch over the wall in left-center field, 7 – 6.

For Astro fans and slugging Yasiel Puig at the plate with two out, Devenski was able to pull it together. He struck out Puig on a full count to end the game. The Astros won, 7 – 6, in eleven innings and went home to Houston tied at one game each in the World Series.

"That's one of the best games ever. Both teams battling it out and the 'Stros finished on top," was a post-game comment from third baseman Alex Bregman.

For George Springer, the game was key. After a poor ALCS and four strikeouts in Game One of the World Series, he needed a boost. He got it in Game Two. George had three hits in five at-bats. He was relaxed at the plate after savvy veteran Carlos Beltrán had just told him to relax and have fun.

"I just think that when the lights turn on even brighter, you tend to subconsciously press and you want to succeed so bad that you start to do things you wouldn't do, or you start to come out of an approach that has worked the whole year," Springer reflected following the game. "So for me be able to tell yourself to slow yourself down I now understand why some guys struggle in the postseason and some don't."

Said manager Hinch, "If you like October baseball, if you like any kind of baseball, that's one of the most incredible games you'll ever be a part of."

He was right—then came Game Five a few days later.

20

Astros 2017 Series Tainted by Electronic Sign Stealing

ll was not good for the 2017 World Champs when a former pitcher on the team, Mike Fiers, went public with the news that the team has used electronic means to steal opposing pitcher's signs to give Astro hitters an edge during the year.

While stealing pitches had been very common in Major League Baseball for years, it came at a time when MLB was trying to stop it. All clubs had been issued memos that Baseball was going to crack down. The memo was not just for the Astros, but originally directed at other clubs as well including the Red Sox and Yankees. But it applied to all.

When Fiers made his social media comment directed at the team that had won the most recent World Series the Astros became a target.

The Baseball Commissioner's office then directed a full investigation against the Astros and their methods.

The Astros were found guilty of using the television monitors that MLB had allowed be installed near the dugouts to help expedite whether umpire calls could be challenged with the new replay rule more quickly.

For years, no TV monitors were allowed to be used by managers, players or coaches. In fact, the author of this book who spent time as a field level commentator with Astros TV had one incident when the home plate umpire, Ed Montegue, came over to the telecast position which was right next to where the manager normally stood and specifically said no one from the bench should be allowed to see my personal monitor. Removal of the monitor and expulsion from the game (of the author) would be the Penalty if a violation was seen.

When MLB went to replays all bets were off. The Astros took advantage. Those cited for coming up with the Astro system included player, Carlos Beltrán, who had been with the Yankees the year before. He told the team others had ways to steal signs that the Astros didn't. Coach Alex Cora helped create the system the Astros would use. ManagerA.J. Hinch turned a blind eye and how much Ge neral Manager Jeff Luhnow knew was questionable. That quartet would be the only victims of MLB punishment. The other players were given amnesty if they complied with the investigation.

Their system was actually crude and only worked when the club was playing at home. Video from a center field camera was directed to a monitor located just down the steps from the dugout in real time. When a certain pitch was called for an Astro employee would pound on a large, rubberized trash container. The hitter could hear it at the plate. All the "thumper" would differentiate would be off speed or not. It was not sophisticated enough to relay anything else. The edge to the hitter would be being ready for curve or change and being prepared for a fast ball if he heard nothing.

Because banging and making sound was used, large loud crowds at home were needed. Even if the Astros tried to use the system on the road—which they did not—an empty stadium in Oakland, for example, would have given them away quickly. Plus, they wouldn't have access to anything but what the game telecast was showing.

The Astros who used the system liked it. Others wanted no part of it. Not necessarily because of the "cheating" aspect, but in some cases for safety.

If an off-speed pitch is expected and the pitcher throws a fastball for some reason, a hitter leaning over the plate looking for a curve or slider might wind up being hit by a fast ball.

Other hitters don't want to alter their personal method of hitting and relying on their eyes and quick reflexes to hit. José Altuve, for instance, wanted the trash can beating to be kept quiet in his at bats. There were others on the team. Some admitted or did not deny they used the information. Carlos Correa did not deny. Neither did Marwin Gonzalez or George Springer.

An interesting sidelight to this was the Astros as a team actually hit better on the road than at home in 2017. They scored over 500 runs on the road to only 395 at home. Their batting average at home was .279 compared to .284 on the road. They even hit more home runs: 123-115 on the road. Further, in the World Series they won two games on the road where the system could not be used, including game seven. Any sign stealing value was negligible. And while there were some unfounded accusations the Astros were using "buzzers" inside their uniforms to receive information that was investigated and found to have no evidence of truth. It was essentially a social media invented accusation.

The Astros, as the fall guy for sign stealing electronically and using the trash can banging at home were fined $5-million and lost their first and second round picks in the 2020 and 2021 draft. The Penalty was imposed after the 2019 season which saw the team win the American League championship but lose to the Washington Nationals in the World Series. Neither team won a home game. The manager, Hinch, and general manager, Luhnow, were suspended and subsequently fired by team owner Jim Crane.

In a televised documentary aired on the PBS program, Frontline, on Oct 3, 2023, a fan of the Astros, computer programmer Tony Adams who had access to recordings of every Astro home game in 2017. He came up with a program to track sounds of the game including the can banging. He found that it stopped in September after a Chicago White Sox pitcher, Danny Farquhar suspected something was up and had his catcher change signs.

He also noted that not all players used the "banging" help. José Altuve was the most prominent. Computer analysis of all home games that year recorded over 8200 pitches and 1443 trash can "bangs" Nothing was heard during Altuve's at bats. But nothing was heard for anyone after the White Sox incident. This ended the Astros use of the system even before the regular season was over. No "bangs" were heard in any post season games by Adams. But Fiers went public and because what the Astros had done after memos had been sent to the teams, they had to be in the spotlight.

Cora and Beltrán who were implicated for instigating the operation were both suspended and removed from managerial jobs they accepted after they left the Astros. Cora was eventually re-hired by the Red Sox. Beltrán had been named Mets manager but was removed before ever taking over.

The Astros hired veteran manager Dusty Baker to take over in the pandemic shortened 2020 season and James Click came over from Tampa Bay to serve as General Manager.

Baseball followers who had little or no deep knowledge of history cursed the Astros whenever they came to town. Some wanted them to have to default on their 2017 World Series win. Others wanted players Penalized even without knowledge of who and how many of them used the system. Some players admitted but were protected by the terms set by MLB.

Historically, sign stealing had been a part of baseball for decades...some of it even using electronic methods.

In 1876 the Hartford club in the National League's first season had a shack set up on a telephone pole to see signs and relay them. In 1898 the first use of electronics was used by the Philadelphia Phillies. They ran a wire from beyond the center field fence to the third base coach's box. The coach for the Phils could feel a vibration that he could use to signal the hitter.

It was also in Philadelphia where signs were stolen and relayed using a mirror from outside the park.

Greatest quote from a Hall of Famer Rogers Hornsby: "Every team with a scoreboard in center field has had a spy in residence one time or more."

The 1951 New York Giants had a coach in their center field clubhouse with binoculars. He would relay the signs to a fellow coach in the Giants bullpen in left field who would signal what was coming. The 1951 National League playoffs featured Bobby Thomson's game winning home run. He declined to admit he had help. Team-mate Willie Mays said he was aware of the system, but never wanted to know what was coming.

Texas Ranger manager Billy Martin used a television feed to steal pitches. He had coach Jim Fregosi in the clubhouse watching a live feed. Fregosi had a walkie talkie and told Martin what signs the opposing catcher was using. The Ranger hitter was relayed the info.

If used stolen signs are so helpful why would players like Altuve, Mays and others not want them?

One story tells what could go wrong. In 1948 Joe Medwick was finishing his career back in St. Louis when he was told a curve was coming. He leaned in ready and a fastball came instead, sailing toward his head. The resulting fractured skull ended his career.

For baseball, the TV monitors are still close to the dugouts, for replay decisions, but are supposed to be delayed a few seconds. And an electronic pitch calling system is in use by most catchers and pitchers so no signs are given.

Problem solved....until some team figures how to steal those electronic signals!

21

In ALCS Rangers Got Revenge - 39 runs, 16HR at Texas in 2023!

he Texas Rangers ousted the Astros from the 2023 post season one win short of another World Series appearance. But neither team won a home game...shades of the 2019 World Series for the Astros.

In fact Houston set a record by winning a division title despite playing sub 500 at home all year. Oh but their road games! Like the three they played against their eventual conquerors in Arlington September 4th through September 6th.

While the defending champs struggled for much of the season as a result of injuries, subpar performances and a resurgence by American League West foes in Seattle and Texas in one three game series they began their quest to dominate again. They may have "won" the AL West by doing it.

The Astros totally annihilated Ranger pitchers in a three

game sweep. Houston's offense exploded for 39 runs including 16 home runs winning three games by 13-6, 14-1 and 12-3.

José Altuve hit five home runs. José Abreu hit two and did Martin Maldonado, Mauricio Dubon and Yordan Alvarez. Solo homers were hit by Michael Brantley, Chas McCormick and Yanier Diaz. The wipe out put the Astros in first place for the first time during the season and dropped the Rangers to third now suddenly in danger of missing even a wild card spot.

Altuve was superman. He hit five home runs in six at bats over two games including four on consecutive trips to the plate. That was accomplished in four straight innings, too. He hit one in the 9th inning of the first game. Then he his three more in the 1st, 2nd and 3rd innings of the next game. That had never been done before in major league history.

If Altuve was Superman, José Abreu was at least Batman. In the three games he drove in eleven runs including a seven RBI game in the final when he hit a grand slam and a three run homer.

After the opening win the Astros were tied with Seattle for first place. After the second they had taken the lead which they held after the series ended.

They would lose the lead later after losing series to two teams with the worst records in the AL, Kansas City and Oakland. Those losses assured them a losing record at home.

But back on the road to end the season they won five of their last six by taking two of three in Seattle and sweeping the NLCS playoff bound Arizona D-Backs in Phoenix while Texas dropped three of four in Seattle. Both the Astros and Rangers finished with identical 90-72 records, but the AL West went to Houston for beating the Rangers in nine of thirteen games.

22

Altuve Slams HR to Comeback win in Arlington

For awhile the Astros looked like they might pull it off and get themselves into another World Series when they swept the Rangers in Arlington thanks to a comeback win in the ninth courtesy of José Altuve.

The 2023 ALCS series had begun in Houston where the Astros, in keeping with their full season woes at home, dropped both games to the Texas Rangers. However, proving the defending champs weren't dead yet they won the next two in Arlington. In the third game things were going the Rangers way as they held on to a 4-2 lead into the ninth inning. Taking a 3 games to two lead to Houston where the Astros had not played well would give Texas a major advantage. It looked as though that would be the case.

But in the bottom of the 8th inning Astro reliever Bryan Abreu cut loose a fastball shoulder high and tight to Ranger slugger Aroldis Garcia. He was hit by the pitch and quickly turned around jawing at Astro catcher Martin Maldonado. Benches emptied and when things calmed down the umpires tossed the Astro pitcher and Garcia along with Abreu's manager Dusty Baker for what they deemed an intentional and successful attempt to hit Garcia.

Baker protested vigorously because it was just a two run game and that would put two runners on base. Baker said no one had told Abreu to hit Garcia and it would have been stupid anyway. His team could still win the game.

The umpires tried to mind read a bit since Garcia had hit a three run home run off Justin Verlander earlier to give the Rangers a 4-1 lead in the 6th. Then he showboated a bit running it out.

In the days of Ryan or Gibson or Drysdale, Garcia would have been decked for sure and maybe hit by a pitch. But even in those days it would likely have come at a later time and not during a close late inning playoff game.

No doubt Abreu wanted to back him off the plate in a attempt to drop his confidence level a bit. But to actually want to hit him? Not likely. Even so MLB suspended and fined Abreu for two games. Calmer heads at least postponed a possible suspension to the first two games of 2024 to not effect the post season.

Ryan Pressly entered the game for Abreu and despite the two base runners he inheirited no more runs scored. The Astros would hit in the top of the 9th still trailing 4-2.

The Rangers kept the same pitcher, José Leclerc, who had worked the previous inning some 25 minutes earlier in the game since he was their regular closer.

The Astros needed two to tie and three to take the lead. Who ever made the decision, Baker before he left the dugout or bench manager Joe Espada, Yainer Diaz was sent up to pinch hit for Jeremy Peña. Diaz singled to left. Now with the tying run at the plate little used lefty power hitter Jon Singleton hit for catcher Maldonado. He got ahead of the count...two two strikes and on 3-2 drew a walk.

The Astros had two on and no outs with Altuve coming up. He lofted a high fly ball to deep left field. And over the wall it went! The Astros had rallied from two down to one up in the top of the 9th!

Afterward Altuve; "That was the craziest game I ever played in." Manager Baker was more effusive, "That was a huge victory that will go down in history."

Indeed it might have had the Astros been able to carry through. The Rangers saw to it that they didn't. Still for one game, Baker: Altuve has a slow heart beat and he lives big moments. Number one he wants to be up there. Number two he's got a high concentration level. I mean this dude is one of the baddst dudes I've ever seen and I've seen some greats." The words of the man who was a team mate of Hank Aaron and managed Barry Bonds. Very high praise for José Altuve.

23

1986 Astros Win NLW Title as Mike Scott Throws a No-Hitter

 **W**hile the 1986 Houston Astros would win the National League West by ten games and clinch the division in the season's 153rd game, the way they did it was classic.

Mike Scott, the eventual Cy Young Award winner in the NL, threw a no-hitter against the San Francisco Giants in the clincher. The game was at the Astrodome on late Thursday afternoon, September 25, in front of a crowd of 32,808. Most of them were on hand to see a possible clinching game. The crowd was dressed as those from 1930s World Series films. Lots of business attire from people who had knocked off work early to witness what they hoped was the Astros winning a division title. The no-hitter was a bonus.

Seeing outstanding pitching was a given. In the two previous games, Jim Deshaies had struck out a then- record first eight hitters in the game against the Dodgers on the way to a two-hit, 4 – 0, shutout. Then, in the opener of the Giants series, Nolan Ryan blanked the San Franciscans, 6 – 0. He threw the first eight innings allowing only one hit. That set the stage for Scott the next day. He faced only 30 hitters, walking two and striking out 13 in collecting his 18th win.

In the ninth, with the Astrodome crowd mostly on its feet and screaming, Scott finished with a flourish. He struck out Dan Gladden. Then he struck out Robby Thompson. The last hitter would be Will Clark. He hit an easy hopper to Glenn Davis at first base, who raced to the bag to retire Clark and put the Astros into the postseason while ending Mike Scott's no-hitter with the same play!

Although the Astros would ultimately fall to the New York Mets in the National League Championship Series four games to two, Scott would be named series MVP for winning both of his starts, allowing only one run. However, his no-hitter to clinch the division has been remembered much longer by most Astro fans.

Astros Cy Young Awards:
Mike Scott 1986 NL
Roger Clemens 2004 NL
Dallas Keuchel 2015 AL
Justin Verlander 2018 AL
Justin Verlander 2022 AL

24

Four Pitchers No-Hit the Phillies in 2022 World Series

n 1956 Don Larsen of the New York Yankees threw a perfect game no hitter vs the Brooklyn Dodgers in the World Series. It was the only no hitter ever pitched in the fall classic. Until the Houston Astros did it in 2022. Only the Astros didn't have one pitcher do it. They used four!

It was in game four played in Philadelphia with the Phillies holding a two game to one lead. And it was one game after the Phillies had taken that lead with a one-sided, five home run game to beat the Astros 7-0 the day before in game three.

Phillie fans were at full octave fully expecting to keep rolling and jump into a three game to one lead.

It would not happen thanks to the Astro quartet of Javier, Abreu, Montero and Pressly. They would win 5-0 and not allow a single hit to the Phils.

It was the second no hitter ever in the World Series and obviously the first multi pitcher no-no.

Cristian Javier had started for Houston and went six

innings. Had started and won a three-pitcher no-hitter against the Yankees earlier in the season. Pressly also closed that one out.

This time Javier essentially blew the Phillies away. He threw 63 fastballs in his 97 pitches. Then he would throw a slider the Phillies could not handle. Javier struck out nine and walked two.

Bryan Abreu pitched the seventh and struck out the side. In the 8th a great catch by Astro right fielder Kyle Tucker saved a base hit off Rafael Montero, but he got three up and three down. Closer Ryan Pressly walked one, but got through the ninth to preserve the no hitter.

Philadelphia hitters in addition to no hits struck out 14 times.

The final score was 5-0 for Houston. Offensively, Alex Bregman had a two-run double. Yordan Alvarez, Tucker and Yuli Gurriel drove in the other runs.

25

Astros No-Hit the Yankees with Three on June 5th, 2022

 quartet of pitchers threw a no hitter in the 2022 World Series against the Phillies. And earlier in the regular season two of that number were part of a three pitcher no hitter in New York against the Yankees. The starter and finisher were the same. Christian Javier made the start on June 25th. Ryan Pressly closed it out.

The Astros won the game 3-0 so Javier got the win and Pressly the save. Hector Neris pitched the 8th and got part of the glory as well.

For the Astros it was their second multi pitcher no hitter against the Yankees in New York since 2003. In the first six pitcher game it was the last ever in old Yankee Stadium. This one was the first in the new Yankee Stadium.

This was a game the Yankees were supposed to win. Gerrit Cole was on the mound, their ace, and Cristian Javier was going for Houston. He was a good young prospect but not expected to outlast Cole and shut down the vaunted Yankee sluggers. But he did.

Javier went seven hitless innings with 13 strikeouts and only one walk. Meanwhile, Cole was good, but left after seven allowing the Astros only four hits and one run. He struck out eight. J.J. Matijevic's home run in the seventh off Cole was all the Astros would need. However, José Altuve would homer in the 8th and the third run was driven home by Yuli Gurriel hitting for Matijevic in the 9th.

After Javier left the game with seven innings and 115 pitches under his belt, Hector Neris, who walked two in his 8th inning making Astro fans nervous got through it. "I have to get it for my team. I have to get it for Javy," said Neris after it was over. Pressly had a two strike out three up three down ninth. The setting was huge said the closer, "To do it in New York It's the best feeling in the world."

It was the teams 14th no hitter since the team founding in 1962. That number would reach 16 during the 2023 season.

26

Astros Spend Big for Hader and Altuve

he checkbook was open for the Houston Astros during the off season after their ALCS loss to the Texas Rangers in 2023. They acquired one of baseball's best relief pitchers, Josh Hader, to bolster their pitching staff which had lost three regular hurlers to free agency. And they locked up the man who may end his career remembered as Mr. Astro—José Altuve—with a five year contract extension that will take him to age 39.

The Hader signing was a surprise. Not only does it call for $95 million over five years, but the Astros won him by competing with other clubs for the hard throwing lefty. He now joins a bullpen featuring Ryan Pressly, José Abreu, Rafeal Montero and other contenders. While primarily a closer it was expected Hader would have help in the role with incumbent Pressly still around. The back end of the bullpen seemed to be ready to continue to be a strong feature of the staff.

The 30 year old Hader had a 1.28 earned run average and

33 saves for San Diego in 2023. His career save total, mostly for the Milwaukee Brewers, shows 165 saves in 190 chances over seven seasons.

A few weeks after Hader's signing the Astros worked out a deal to keep José Altuve on the team through the likely end of his career when he will be 39 years old. He will be paid $125 for those five seasons.

The club announced that the team, José and his agent Scott Boras had agreed on a five year contract extension that would run from 2025 through 2029. Altuve was already contracted to play in 2024.

The Astros starting second baseman, three time American League batting champion, 2017 AL MVP and career .307 hitter is most certainly assured of joining Craig Biggio and Jeff Bagwell as career Astros whose future will be in the Baseball Hall of Fame.

With the acquisition of Hader and the extension of Altuve owner Jim Crane was quoted as saying the goal of continuing to win championships remains with the Astros.

27

J.R. Richard Has a Stroke

Mike Scott and Roger Clemens in the NL and Dallas Keuchel and Justin Verlander in the AL won Cy Young Awards as Astros. Many Houston fans think J. R. Richard may have been on his way to winning the NL honor in 1980 before he suffered a stroke.

Richard knew something was wrong long before he was felled during a workout in the Astrodome on July 30. He was not with the team because he had been placed on the disabled list. He was on the list to rest his arm, which he described as being tired. Early medical examinations showed nothing physical and many were skeptical even though there was no reason to feel that way. Within a few days, a blood clot was found causing a blockage in a shoulder artery. Blood thinners and only light work was prescribed. He would take time to improve. Richard was having the best season of his major-league career. After his first 17 starts, his record was 10 – 4 with a 1.90 ERA. He had thrown four complete games with all being shutouts. In 113.2 innings, he had allowed only 65 hits. He had 119 strikeouts and had walked only 40 hitters.

At only 30 years old and coming off two straight 300+

strikeout seasons, Richard was in his prime. He had led the
NL with a 2.71 ERA in 1979 when he finished third in Cy Young
voting. From 1976 through 1979 he had won 20, 18, 18, and
18 games respectively. His season ERA was never higher than
2.97. And he led the league in strikeouts in both 1978 and 1979.
He was a dominant figure with his 6-foot, 8- inches, 222-pound
body working from the mound. Former teammate Jimmy
Wynn, who faced Richard after Wynn joined the Dodgers, said
that he felt confident enough facing J. R. that the first time
he did, he told Richard that if he hung him a slider he should
watch out. "I told him, 'If you hang that slider, I'm going to
take it out of here,'" remembered Wynn. "He hung one and I
hit it hard against the wall, but only got a double."

Wynn knew that Richard was intimidating to a lot of
hitters, but, probably because he knew him so well, he was
not to Wynn. "For me, he wasn't that scary, but for others
who looked at him—six-foot, eight- inches tall, one hell of a
slider, and a fastball near a hundred miles an hour, plus when
he wound up and threw, he looked already halfway to home
plate—I can imagine some fear."

In 1980, with his great season going, there was no reason
Richard would want to miss games unless something
was really wrong. As it turned out there was. The question
unanswered to this day is what triggered his stroke?

As Richard remembered in his book, Still Throwing Heat,
"I was inside the Astrodome doing a work-out so I could be in
some kind of shape when I came off the disabled list.

"All of a sudden, I felt a high-pitched tone ringing in my
left ear. And then I threw a couple more pitches and became
nauseated. A few minutes later, I threw a couple more pitches,
then the feeling got so bad I was losing my equilibrium. I went
down on the AstroTurf. I had a headache, some confusion
in my mind, and I felt weakness in my body. I didn't have
knowledge of anything going on."

An ambulance was ultimately called, but before it arrived,
Richard passed out. When he got to the hospital, surgery was

performed. A blood clot in his neck was removed. Doctors determined that the symptoms he had been feeling were from restricted blood flow. There were unfounded stories as to what may have brought on the actual clots that constricted blood flow, but no one knows for sure.

Astros team physician Dr. Harold Brelsford was concerned that a chiropractic manipulation J. R. received earlier on the day of the stroke might have been a factor. Chiropractor Dr. Jack Christie denied the theory and was later backed up by Dr. William Fields, a noted neurosurgeon. However, medical histories of strokes after chiropractic sessions have been recorded in more than a few cases and could not be ruled out. The only thing certain was the stroke ended J. R. Richard's career.

J. R. Richard never threw another pitch in the major leagues. He did make an exhibition game appearance for the Astros against Toronto on April 4, 1992. He went one inning and didn't allow a run or hit, but walked the bases full. He tried to make a comeback through the minor leagues that year and 1983, but simply was not even close to what he once was.

In 1980, the Astros made the postseason for the first time in franchise history. They lost in the postseason, but how good could that club have been in that postseason or following years had J. R. Richard not been felled early? And to what heights could Richard's career have reached?

He was already 30-years-old, so winning 300 games would not have been likely, but how many strikeouts could he have compiled? How many Cy Young Awards could he have grabbed? Larry Dierker was a teammate when he broke in and a broadcaster when his career ended. "I think at the end he was one of the top four or five pitchers in the NL. It would have been hard to project him to 300 wins even if he had never had the stroke because it took him so long to find the strike zone more consistently."

J. R. Richard wound up with a 107 – 71 career record with

a sparkling 3.15 ERA. He had 1439 strikeouts in 1606 innings pitched. That was in primarily just five and a half full seasons in the starting rotation. If he could have duplicated those five and a half years instead of having his stroke, he might have been a Hall of Fame candidate.

Astros Single-Season Pitching Strikeout Leaders		
Gerrit Cole	326	2019
J.R. Richard	313	1979
Mike Scott	306	1989
J.R. Richard	303	1978
Justin Verlander	300	2019
Justin Verlander	290	2018
Gerrit Cole	276	2018
Nolan Ryan	270	1987

28

Jeff Bagwell's 1994 Season: Astros Best Ever!

 eff Bagwell played 15 Hall of Fame seasons for the Houston Astros. He hit .297, had a .408 OBP, ripped 449 home runs, drove in 1529, and stole 202 bases.

When his career ended after the 2005 season, those were his career numbers. However, the single season that stands out the most and up to now remains the best season for any Houston hitter ever came in strike-shortened 1994.

In that season, Jeff played 110 games with 470 plate appearances. He hit a franchise record .368 to go with 39 home runs and 116 league leading RBIs. He also led the NL with 104 runs scored. His OBP was a whopping .451 with an astounding .750 SLG—both also leading the league. His biggest single game was against the Dodgers on June 24 in the Astrodome, when he crushed three home runs, including two in one inning. Bagwell hit 23 of his 39 home runs in the cavernous dead-air of the Astrodome. Despite hitting .368, Jeff was not a close challenger for the batting title. In 1994, Tony

Gwynn hit .394!

While the season was shortened by the labor stoppage that also wiped out the postseason that year, Bagwell would not have played more games anyway. On August 10, just before the stoppage was to begin, he was hit on his left hand by a pitch from Andy Benes and the fourth metacarpal bone was broken. His season was over.

If one wants to project what Bagwell's number might have been had he continued on the hitting pace he was on until August 10, it comes out to 56 home runs and 169 RBIs! Bagwell was voted unanimously as the NL MVP. Bagwell's greatest season came before he started extensive weight work to make himself even stronger. In 1994, the condition Bagwell was in was just right. No Astro player before or since has had a season like Jeff Bagwell did in 1994.

Astros Single-Season Home Run Leaders		
Jeff Bagwell	47	2000
Lance Berkman	45	2006
Richard Hidalgo	44	2000
Jeff Bagwell	43	1997
Jeff Bagwell	42	1999
Lance Berkman	42	2002
Jeff Bagwell	39	1994, 2001, 2003
Moisés Alou	38	1998

29

The Houston Astrodome: Eighth Wonder of the World

A stadium is one of the legends of Houston baseball history? Darn right it was, and frankly the original Yankee Stadium, Wrigley Field, and Fenway Park would fall in that class as well for their cities. But the Astrodome, admittedly missing the championship teams of the Yankees home, was far more architecturally and historically important than any of them.

When it was built and opened in 1965, it was the first enclosed air-conditioned stadium in the world large enough to host traditionally outdoor sports. The stadium was the dream of Houston legend Judge Roy Hofheinz.

The Astros were the first to play in such a building, which was also the first with luxury suites, multiple restaurants, padded seats, and ultimately artificial turf instead of grass.

The latter development was forced on the club after it was discovered the light coming into the building from the skylights was not sufficient to keep grass healthy. However, Hofheinz had suspected that might be a problem long before some roof panels were painted to lose their translucence to help fielders find baseballs hit in the air. He already had an idea some sort of artificial grass would be needed and soon was in touch with the Monsanto Corporation that had begun experiments with such a surface for use on playgrounds and areas that could not grow grass. Hofheinz also knew the Astrodome would be used for more than just "grass sports" like baseball and football.

In addition to baseball, the Harris County Domed Stadium, as it was officially known at first, staged rodeos, bloodless bullfights, heavyweight championship fights, the famed Billy Jean King vs Bobby Riggs "Battle of the Sexes" tennis match, the first nationally televised prime time college basketball game when number 1 UCLA fell to number 2 Houston in

Photo courtesy of Library of Congress

The Astrodome was called "The Eighth Wonder of the World."

front of over 52,000 fans. That crowd, by the way, was also the largest ever to witness a college basketball game at the time. Concerts were performed by some of the entertainment world's finest, from Judy Garland to Elvis Presley, and many stars in between. Billy Graham held a service; Evel Knievel jumped over some buses. Houston Cougar and Houston Oiler football; Texas high school football championships; All-star Games in baseball, football, and basketball; championship fights and wrestling exhibitions; conventions, including the Republican National Convention in 1980 and much more were all staged in the Astrodome. The Dome's last major use before plans were made to save it was hosting homeless families from New Orleans after Hurricane Katrina.

The Astrodome's Future

The Astrodome was very special and may be again. While it won't host the big sporting events, plans have been drawn up to renovate the building to give it a new life for decades to come.

But there are considerable problems. Mike Acosta, the founder of a group called Astrodome Reimagined, is also perhaps the greatest historian of the building ever. He has made models of the building from its past as well as many possibilities for its future. Getting the funding for one of these projects AND the political red tape cut are two significant road blocks.

According to Mike, the lease for the land where the Dome and NRG Stadium, home of the Houston Texans and other facilities used by the Houston Livestock Show and Rodeo is owned by Harris County. It is called NRG Park.

Any changes or improvements must be approves by the county and monies provieded essentially by the county. Therefore, private investors in any facility could not work independently but directly with the county. That includes the current lease holders, the Texans, and the Rodeo.

Unlike the Astros at Minute Maid Park downtown who can make renovations or improvements they pay for themselves in their lease with the City of Houston, the situation with Harris County at NRG park is more restrictive.

So while plans for renovation and re-use of the Astrodome can be made, getting action on them puts them on a "wish list" behind the current primary leaseholders.

In addition, while the Astrodome's status as a Texas State Historical Landmark keeps it from beingarbitrarily demolished, it also prevents some changes to it without approval.

For instance, a project proposed to bring the main floor to ground level by adding at least a couple of underground parking levels that would serve the Texans and the Rodeo... then making renovations above as part of a "New Astrodome" the required entry and exits for the parking could be in violation of changing the look of the landmark.

Just the same, Mike and his people keep working on ideas of bringing the structurally sound Astrodome back into use someday.

However, right now the "Eighth Wonder of the World" just sits — almost hauntingly empty.

Plans are still being discussed. Acosta and the many who want the Historical Landmark to continue to have real use aren't about to give up. But there are many rivers to cross and perhaps a lack of bridges right now.

30

Roy Hofheinz and the Other Three Founding Fathers

**W**hile the Astrodome was Judge Roy Hofheinz's baby and he served as the titular head of the Colt .45s and Astros in their early years, he had a lot of help. Craig Cullinan, George Kirksey, and Bob Smith partnered with Hofheinz to make Houston a major-league city. Smith and Hofheinz owned the most stock.

Kirksey and Cullinan did the groundwork even before the other two were involved. Kirksey, a journalist and promoter, kept the Houston name before the owners of teams in both leagues. Cullinan, a Texaco heir, had the money to help Kirksey make those contacts. Later when things were looking good for Houston, Hofheinz jumped in with both feet and had a lot to do with bringing in Smith, who had the deepest pockets and land available for a couple ballparks. The duo became leaders of the Houston Sports Association which would form the nucleus of the board of directors. From the beginning, Hofheinz's focus was finding a way to beat the Houston heat and humidity with an indoor stadium.

It was Kirksey with the original dream and Hofheinz with the pièce de résistance—the concept of building a covered, air-conditioned stadium for the new Houston team to use. Once the plan to go hard for a team was on, Hofheinz dedicated himself to reading every book he could on baseball. He wanted to show the owners he knew their sport and history.

Houston would have eventually been granted a franchise, but the city was able to get in on the first expansion thanks to Kirksey, Cullinan and the plans for a domed stadium. They had been putting Houston into the hopper as a relocation site for the St. Louis Cardinals and Philadelphia Athletics during the 1950s. The Cards were sold to Anheuser-Busch and stayed put. The A's elected to move to Kansas City instead of Houston.

When Houston was included in the proposed Continental League along with a new franchise in New York to replace the Dodgers and Giants who had left for California, everything accelerated. The AL expanded, calming government leaders in Washington who had lost their team to Minnesota by putting a new team in the nation's capital. They added a team in the Los Angeles area to get the AL on the West Coast to keep the NL from dominating the West.

The NL essentially took two teams that were possibly heading for the Continental League in Houston and New York. Had Kirksey and Cullinan not been pushing so hard to get Houston into Major League Baseball, that would not have happened at the time.

Then, when Hofheinz came up with his model for the domed stadium, Houston was a lock. The city would be the only truly new city in the expansion. MLB was already in Los Angeles and New York and had been in Washington before.

Hofheinz, formerly both the mayor of Houston and a judge, was the most colorful of the ownership group. According to some reports, he had visited the Coliseum in Rome and learned that it had been often covered with a shade-producing canvas cover during inclement or extra hot weather. That may have given him the inspiration for a modern domed stadium. Others say he was influenced by the birth of the covered air-conditioned shopping malls that were starting to appear around the country. In fact, that was what he was working on when the baseball project started. He dropped the shopping center project for others to finish.

Whatever the influence was, the planning and construction of the Domed Stadium was all Hofheinz. The judge even had living quarters for himself built into the right-field area. They included what might be expected, but also a couple bowling lanes, a Presidential suite for the ultimate visiting dignitary, a board room for meetings, private offices, and other rooms, like the circus room, the P. T. Barnum room, a children's play room, barber shop, and the famed Tipsy Tavern with a slanted floor.

The judge's circus and Barnum rooms may have been an indication of his future plans . Hofheinz would buy the Ringling Brothers-Barnum and Bailey Circus a few years after getting the baseball team started. He also was the man behind the development of Astro World, a top-notch amusement park across the street from the Dome.

The Hofheinz-Smith-Kirksey-Cullinan quartet would not agree on matters long. Once the team was up and running, perhaps the magic of the build was gone. The others were bought out and Hofheinz would ultimately take full control. But before being debilitated by a stroke, the Judge caused financial set-backs by his expansion of the Astrodomain complex and purchase of the circus . The Astros actually had to go into receivership and were owned by credit companies until John McMullen bought the team in 1979.

However, the "Big Four" should never be forgotten for their role in getting Major League Baseball to Houston and the construction of the Astrodome. They were all true legends.

31

Dr. John McMullen Buys the Astros

He knew very little about baseball, even though he had been a minority stockholder in the New York Yankees. He knew very little about Houston since he was a native New Yorker. However, he knew a good deal when he saw one. So, John McMullen, with PhD in Mechanical Engineering and a 15-year Naval career achieving rank of Commander, rounded up 25 fellow investors to buy controlling interest in the Houston Astros and what was known as Astrodomain. Why did he want a baseball team in Houston? He said he wanted to run the show because "there is nothing more minority than being a minority owner under George Steinbrenner." McMullen closed the deal in May 1979. His run had success on the field, but turmoil off.

The price for all of this was a below-market $19 million dollars plus debts still unpaid. He bought all this from the Ford Motor Credit Corporation who, along with others, had taken control of the team from original owner Roy Hofheinz several years before.

The team McMullen had bought was operating on a small budget, but, under manager Bill Virdon and President/GM Tal Smith, making inroads on the field. How much of that McMullen really knew is questionable. Smith, who had been running the whole show for the previous five years, would be dismissed by McMullen following the 1980 winning season, summing up the relationship.

"He knew very little about baseball, and he and I didn't see eye-to-eye on nearly every issue. Dave Smith had given up a home run in a game late in August 1980 at Shea Stadium to the Mets, and McMullen wanted to release the guy. As a team, we had little power and emphasized aggressive baserunning. Occasionally some runners get thrown out. He wanted to fire the coach."

If that sounds like someone else Smith once worked for, George Steinbrenner, Tal said the difference was that George would get over it.

Early on, McMullen ran afoul of some of his co-owners. The firing of Smith was what brought things to the fore. In November 1980, a suit was filed in Federal Court to oust McMullen as General Partner of the Astros. He held 34% of the franchise and, as the largest shareholder, held that title. Attorney Joe Jamail, one of the limited partners, filed the suit which accused McMullen of mismanagement that caused irreparable loss and damage.

While the furor started over firing Smith and replacing him with Al Rosen, the partners were also upset that McMullen had bought a $2.5 million plane to fly the ballclub without consulting the other owners first.

While no significant change resulted from the action, McMullen, in defending his firing of Smith, essentially said it was due to the team drawing too many fans as a result of the success Smith had a large hand in building. McMullen said Smith's contract had an attendance clause, and with 2.5 million attendance in 1980, he would be too expensive to keep. Very few fell for that excuse, but it helped explain why the Associated Press, in a story written July 25, 1982, described him as it did when the team was sold to Drayton McLane:

> *Drayton McLane Jr., who described himself as a wholesale grocer trying to learn baseball, eagerly announced Friday that he is buying the Houston Astros, ending the unpopular fourteen-year reign of John McMullen.*

McMullen and the man who would buy the team from him in 1993, Drayton McLane Jr., had one thing in common: neither of them knew much at all about baseball when they bought the Astros. McMullen didn't know what an RBI was. When he picked up a copy of The Sporting News and found it was full of baseball news, it was like he had discovered the new world.

The personalities of McMullen and McLane were drastically different, however, they both were at the helm during periods of Astro success. Starting in 1980, the Astros became a pennant race factor for the next decade. Sometimes it was in spite of McMullen and not thanks to him. While his object was to make money, he didn't talk about it much except when he complained of low season ticket sales or lack of support. One of his GMs, Bill Wood, recalled, "The guy never talked to me about money except one thing that stuck in my mind. The year we lost ninety-seven games, he said we made the most profit that year, more than several previous years."

That feeling was echoed by his players—that McMullen's real intent was to make money and not win games. The infamous nearly month-long road trip forced on the club for the 1992 Republican National Convention irked everyone who was affiliated with or followed the club. McMullen said he was doing it because the city wanted it and it could bring in a lot of money. Some of that would be coming to McMullen as lease-holder of the Astrodome, of course. The players knew that. The deal for the convention was made prior to 1992, but it was during that season that McMullen sold the Astros to Drayton McLane Jr.

Once McLane bought the team from McMullen and took over control in 1993, another good run started that lasted until the final years. The club may not have been as successful on the field during that period if McMullen were still owner.

McMullen was certainly not a total negative, far from it. McMullen was responsible for Yogi Berra spending time with the Astros as a coach. He was a New Jersey neighbor and close to Berra and Craig Biggio. He was popular with the players he developed a personal relationship with like Biggio. Others he barely knew.

John McMullen was never loved by Astro fans. He was an absentee owner who would too often blame Houston for not supporting the team enough. He also reportedly flirted with moving the team to Washington, D.C. in 1986, but would neither confirm nor deny it. He didn't always know the players on the team. Joe Sambito was Sam Bito as far as he knew for a time. Yet, while he owned the team, fans were treated to postseason teams in 1980, 1981, and 1986. The team fell off until 1989, when Craig Biggio debuted, and the club was a contender with 86 wins. However, it was not until the next owner took over that the club was able to put more back-to-back strong seasons together.

John McMullen bought the Astros when they, and Houston, needed him. He turned a profit on the deal after buying the operation for a reported $19 million in 1979 and selling it in 1993 for a reported $115 million to Drayton McLane Jr. McMullen retained some of the ancillary properties that he had originally purchased with the team, including the cable television network HSE, which carried both the Astros and Texas Rangers, and later sold them for greater profit.

His purchase of the club originally was very important to the franchise. Too few remembered that part of the McMullen legacy when he left. The negatives outweighed the positives for most fans.

32

1986 National League Championship Series

There has been a book written about just one game in this series. Jerry Izenberg called it The Greatest Game Ever Played. Even with the heroics in two games of the 2017 World Series, that title may yet hold up—at least for Mets fans. The Mets won the series four games to two to get to the World Series and meet the Red Sox. However, had the Astros been able to survive the "greatest game," they very well might have been the NL rep.

Why? Because Mike Scott, who had already totally controlled the Mets in two starts, was set to start Game Seven. The series never got there.

Scott won the series opening game, 1 – 0, over Doc Gooden who made one mistake. He gave up a solo home run to Glenn Davis. That was enough.

However, New York came back in Game Two to beat an ineffective Nolan Ryan and take the most one- sided game of the six, 5 – 1. The Mets had a two-run fourth and three-run fifth to secure the win.

Back in New York, the Mets took control with a 6 – 5 victory in the third game. Houston had a 5 – 4 lead until the bottom of the ninth when Lenny Dykstra hit a two-run walk-off homer off the Astros' Dave Smith.

In Game Four, the Astros tied the series with a 3 – 1 win behind Scott. Working on only three day's rest, Scott spun a three hitter. Alan Ashby's two-run and Dickie Thon's solo home run brought home the Astro runs.

A day of rain moved Game Five back a day. Although the Mets were held to only four hits, they outscored the Astros, 2 – 1, in twelve innings. A Gary Carter RBI single plated the walk-off winning run against reliever Charlie Kerfeld.

The Astros had lost a run when Craig Reynolds was called out to complete a double play and end the second inning, disallowing a run scored by Kevin Bass. If replay had been used in those days, Reynolds would have been called safe at first and Bass's run would have scored. The Astros had more chances to score during the game than the Mets, but never could get the big hit. The loss gave the Mets a 3 – 2 lead as the series shifted back to Houston.

Game Six was the one described in Izenberg's book. Given that the Astros scored three runs in the first inning in a series that had been lacking scoring, things were looking pretty good. In fact, going to the last inning Bob Knepper, was leading the Mets, 3 – 0. The Astros were one half inning from tying the series at three games each with Mike Scott ready to pitch the seventh game.

The Astros never got there. Knepper was apparently gassed. A triple by Lenny Dykstra, single by Mookie Wilson, and double by Keith Hernandez ended Knepper's day. With one out, the Astros lead, 3 – 2, and Hernandez at second, Dave Smith was called in. He was wild, walking both Gary Carter and Darryl Strawberry. Then, Ray Knight's sacrifice fly tied the game at 3 – 3.

It stayed that way through the 10th, 11th, 12th, and 13th innings. In the top of the 14th, the Mets broke the tie when Wally Backman singled off Aurelio Rodriguez to score Strawberry.

The game was not over yet. In the bottom of the inning, Billy Hatcher raised the roof at the Dome a couple feet when his high drive to deep left field reached the seats, making the score 4 – 4.

In the 16th, with the Astros deep into the bullpen, the Mets were able to score three times. A Strawberry double, Knight RBI single, two wild pitches, and a Dykstra single made it 7 – 4 Mets.

The Astros did not quit. They got two of the runs back on a walk to pinchhitter Davy Lopes, a single by Bill Doran, an RBI single by Hatcher, and a single by Glenn Davis to make it 7 – 6.

With the tying run in scoring position and the winning run on first base with two out, Kevin Bass came to the plate to hit against lefty Jesse Orosco. Bass was well-prepared for the at-bat. "He wasn't going to give me anything I wanted to hit. All I was going to get was nasty sliders down and in. It was kind of like I was going up there to swat flies," said Kevin after the game. "I'm not stupid. I knew what was coming."

Orosco threw five straight sliders. The count was 3 – 2. He threw a sixth. Bass missed it and the game and season for the Astros was over.

The Mets went on to beat the Boston Red Sox in the World Series. Some of the Astros may have been at home watching.

33

Astros Win First Postseason Game But Not Series in 1980

After the Astros got past the Dodgers in their one game playoff for the NL West title in 1980, they found themselves in the postseason for the first time in the franchise's 19-year history. The NLCS opened in Philadelphia and the Phillies behind ace Steve Carlton won the first game, 3 – 1.

It would be Game Two in which the Astros would have a postseason victory for the first time. The Astros won, 7 – 4, and it set the scene for perhaps the closest postseason series of all time. Houston's win took ten innings—the first of four straight extra-inning games before the Phillies would win in five games. The crowd at Veteran's Stadium for Game Two was a record 65,476, nearly all of them pulling for the Phillies to take a two-game-to-none lead before the series shifted to the

Astrodome.

As for the Astros' first postseason win, the teams were tied at 3 – 3, but the Phillies had a great shot to win in the last of the ninth. They loaded the bases off Houston reliever Frank LaCorte with one out. Bake McBride, Mike Schmidt, and Lonnie Smith all singled to load the bases. But LaCorte struck out Manny Trillo and got Garry Maddox on a foul popout to Dave Bergman at first base.

Then in the Astro tenth, the game was won. With one out and two on, José Cruz singled home Terry Puhl, who had led off the inning with a single. César Cedeño bounded into a fielder's choice and drove in a second run. Then Bergman, who had entered the game for Art Howe in the eighth, hit a triple into right field. Two more runs scored. The Astros had a 7 – 4 lead. Joaquin Andujar got the final outs in the last of the 10th, and the Astros had their first postseason victory. Afterward, it was noted that the three- hour, 34-minute game was the longest NLCS game ever. Needless to say, the game was played much faster in 1980!

Following Game Two, the Astros were upbeat. "We accomplished what we came for," said Houston second baseman Joe Morgan. "Of course we wanted to win both, but when you split on the road you have to be satisfied. It was typical that we kept battling. These guys have character. Before this series is over, everyone in America will know just who are the Houston Astros." Morgan went on with his postgame analysis for reporters, "You really could not tell who had the playoff experience tonight. Our guys showed plenty of poise. I think we are going to surprise people before this is over."

Astro manager Bill Virdon knew things were dicey in the last of the tenth when the Phillies had the tying run at the plate and the fans screaming. What was he thinking? "I wasn't thinking. I was praying!" The skipper was a bit more conservative in his view of the future than Morgan when asked if the Astros had the upper hand after a split in Philadelphia and a trip home to the Dome. "No, you are never in the driver's seat when you are playing a good baseball club and the Phillies are a good ballclub. We'll see what happens." The Astros would win Game Three in 11 innings, 1 – 0. Joe Niekro pitched ten shutout innings, but the win went to Dave Smith in relief after Denny Walling's game-winning walk-off sacrifice fly plated Rafael Landestoy. 44,443 fans had packed the Astrodome and went home very happy.

The happiness didn't last for Astro fans.

Although the next two games were also played in Houston, both went to Philadelphia to wrap up the series. Game Four was a 5 – 3 Philly win in ten innings. Greg Luzinski and Manny Trillo had back-to-back RBI doubles off Joe Sambito to take Philadelphia to the victory.

Finally came Game Five. Up to that time, Nolan Ryan, who started the game, had been death to foes when leading into the eighth. Not this time. The Astros took a 5 – 2 lead to the top of the eighth. Ryan was knocked out of the box after singles by Larry Bowa, Bob Boone, and Greg Gross loaded the bases. Then Pete Rose worked an RBI walk-off a 3 – 2 pitch. The score was 5 – 3 in favor of the Astros, but the bases were still loaded with no one out.

Joe Sambito entered the game and got pinch-hitter Keith Moreland to bounce into a force out, but it still scored the fourth run. Ken Forsch replaced Sambito and struck out Schmidt. Pinch-hitter Del Unser singled and the game was tied. Manny Trillo pushed the Phillies into a 7 – 5 lead after a two-run triple. The five-run eighth had moved the Phillies from three runs behind to two runs in front.

Yet, the Astros were not dead. Craig Reynolds and Terry Puhl both singled and, with both on base and two outs, Rafael Landestoy and José Cruz both singled to tie the game. The game went to the ninth tied, 7 – 7.

Frank LaCorte had to work around two baserunners in the top of the ninth, but the Phillies did not score. Dick Ruthven had an even easier time against the Astros in the last of the inning. They went down 1-2-3.

A two-out double by Garry Maddux in the top of the 10th plated Del Unser, who had doubled earlier in the inning. Philadelphia led, 8 – 7. They were three outs away from their first World Series appearance in 30 years.

They got there when Ruthven tossed his second straight 1-2-3 inning.

After the game, Philly third baseman Mike Schmidt was effusive in praise for his team during a post- game champagne celebration. "I saw stuff out there tonight that I couldn't believe. We had heart second to none. Both teams were digging for it. There was so much at stake. I can't believe we did it!"

Neither could the Astros and their fans.

34

Gerrit Cole Fans 16 Diamondbacks and Allows Only One Hit

After the Astros 2017 world championship season, general manager Jeff Luhnow knew to win again, the team could not stand pat. So, he worked out a trade with the Pittsburgh Pirates for right-handed pitcher Gerrit Cole. Luhnow had eyes on Cole during the previous season before he made the deal to acquire Justin Verlander. Luhnow sent a package of players to Pittsburgh for Cole during the offseason between 2017 and 2018. Cole didn't take long to make an impression. He teamed with Verlander, Dallas Keuchel, Lance McCullers Jr, and Charlie Morton. The Astros starting rotation was being ranked as one of the best of all time when Cole took the mound in Phoenix for an interleague game against the Arizona Diamondbacks on May 4, 2018.

What he did that night ranks among the most outstanding

pitching feats in Astro history. Totally dominating the Diamondbacks, Cole struck out a career-high 16 hitters while allowing only one hit—a fifth-inning double by Chris Owings. Throwing only 114 pitches in his complete-game victory, 82 of the pitches were strikes. The Astro offense provided Cole with eight runs of support in the eventual 8 – 0 victory. Yuli Gurriel had four hits in five at-bats while driving in three runs on two doubles. Carlos Correa also collected two doubles for three more RBIs.

Just how strong was Cole? The last three pitches he threw in the game were recorded as speeding to the plate at 98, 99, and 99 miles per hour each!

Gerrit Cole was a good pitcher for the Pittsburgh Pirates, but he—like Charlie Morton, Brad Peacock, and Dallas Keuchel—all became better pitchers in Houston with Brent Strom as pitching coach. The oldest active pitching coach at 70 and former lefthander, noted parenthetically as the second pitcher ever to undergo Tommy John surgery during his playing days, has a simple philosophy on pitching that is tailored to fit his pitchers. His philosophy is to use the four seam (no sinking and usually best) fastball and not to be afraid to pitch up in the zone. Then, after getting ahead in the count, bury hard sliders or curves on the edges of the strike zone. He preaches using "hard" pitches and not "teasers." Hitters have less time to react to hard stuff and, even if the pitch is slightly off target, have more trouble than with slower velocity pitches that miss their mark. Soft contact and strikeouts are the goal. Gerrit Cole is a great example of making that plan work. His game on May 4, 2018 was the best. In two seasons with Houston before leaving for the New York Yankees as a free agent, Cole set a new season strikeout record with 326 and won 35 of 45 decisions.

35

Craig Biggio Back from Knee Surgery with Five Hits!

he Astros had opened Enron Field in 2000, but their new home did not provide more wins. After taking division titles in 1997, 1998, and 1999, the club had fallen under .500. They were exciting in setting a NL record with 249 home runs, but they gave up a ton of runs as well. They even lost their future Hall of Fame second baseman Craig Biggio to knee surgery after he was taken out on a double play pivot in Florida by future Astro Preston Wilson on August 1. When Craig went down, the team was already out of contention with a 40-66 record, 18 games out of first place.

During the offseason, strenuous workouts got Biggio back into top shape prior to the 2001 season. His work payed off big in the season's first game. On April 3 the Milwaukee Brewers visited Houston to open the season. Biggio felt good at the plate and was obviously seeing the ball well.

Hitting second in the lineup, Biggio ripped an 0 – 1 pitch

from the Brewers' Jimmy Haynes to right field for a single in his first at-bat.

In the third for his second at-bat, he cracked the first pitch from Haynes for a single to center. Hitting in the fourth with the Astros leading, 8 – 2, and facing reliever Will Cunnane, he singled to right field on a 1 – 2 pitch. Biggio was three for three.

And he wasn't finished. In the last of the seventh, leading off the inning against Valerio De Los Santos he singled to left on a 1 – 1 pitch. Thanks to the Astros adding more hits and runs in the frame to push the lead, 11 – 2, he was able to get one more at-bat.

In the bottom of the eighth, looking for his first five hit game ever, Biggio got it with a line drive single to center field on the first pitch off Curt Leskanic. Biggio opened the 2001 season with a five-for-five game after missing the last two months of 2000 following knee surgery and rehab. Biggio made note he was back. And he was back in a big way. As he told the media, "I'm glad to be back and playing again. After having it taken away from me last year, to get five hits is great. But I'm more happy we played well as a team and I was back in uniform." While five hits in a game was a new experience for Craig, up to this game he had compiled 24 games in which he had collected four hits prior to April 3, 2001.

Craig would finish 2001 with a .292 average to go with 20 home runs and 70 RBIs. The only noticeable change in his hitting numbers was that he no longer stole or attempted to steal as many bases as before but he still could hit.

It was also very ironic that Biggio had only one other five-hit game in his career on the night he reached 3000 career hits in 2007.

Stros Doubles Leaders	
Craig Biggio	668
Jeff Bagwell	488
José Altuve	400
Lance Berkman	375
César Cedeño	343
José Cruz	335
Bob Watson	241
Alex Bregman	235
Jimmy Wynn	228
Terry Puhl	226
Ken Caminiti	204

36

Bringing Nolan Ryan Home

he Astros first postseason action came in 1980, and it was likely not a coincidence that was also the first season long time Alvin resident Nolan Ryan was wearing an Astro uniform.

He began his career playing parts of all of five seasons with the New York Mets. Mostly he was a staff pitcher. Until 1970, his fourth season, he had appeared more out of the bullpen than as a starter. His record with New York was 29 – 38 with a 3.58 ERA. He was not on a Hall of Fame track at all. So the Mets traded him to the California Angels in the AL. He was one of four players sent west for shortstop Jim Fregosi. In the normal rotation regularly for the first time, Ryan blossomed. He still could be wild in 1972, leading the AL in both walks and wild pitches, but he was able to lead his league in strikeouts for the first time. Before his career ended, he would lead the league eleven times. In 1972 with the Angels, he fanned 329 hitters. He would strike-out 300 or more six times, including 301 for the Texas Rangers in 1989 when he was 42 years old! With the Angels, Ryan became a star. Year in and year out for 8 years, he was the hardest pitcher to hit in the AL. Not only did he throw a record-tying four no-hitters, the league's batting average against him was annually minuscule.

Still, after the 1979 season, when he would be a free agent, the Angels elected not to offer the 33-year- old a new multiyear contract felt to be suitable.

The Astros had a new owner, John McMullen, who was ready to take a chance, spend some money, make his team better, and win over the fans. McMullen offered Ryan's agent, Dick Moss, a four-year contract calling for one-million dollars a year. The contract was historic, making Ryan the first million- dollar-a-season player.

"We certainly feel it is historic, but it is a fleeting honor. We feel there are ten players in the leagues that, before their careers are over, will be more highly paid, but Nolan certainly has reached the pinnacle of his profession," said Moss at the signing.

While McMullen took credit for bringing Nolan Ryan back home for the 1980 season, Tal Smith had tried to work out a trade with the Angels for the Express before McMullen bought the club.

"I had tried to make a trade for Nolan for two years. I thought I had a deal at the 1978 winter meetings. Angel GM Buzzie Bavasi and I had worked out a multiplayer deal. I thought we had the makings of a deal, but when the meetings were closing, I couldn't find Buzzie. So, the deal never happened," recalls Smith.

"When Ryan became a free agent after the 1979 season and McMullen was in charge, he wanted to take over and left me out of it. I can understand wanting to make a splash with a million dollar offer, but that was way over market by several hundred thousand dollars. It became a real problem and cost the club a lot more," added Smith. "We had J. R. Richard under a new contract for only two hundred thousand. His agent was livid. He had a point. At that stage, Richard was the more effective pitcher and was younger. Nolan was coming off two only slightly above-average seasons with the Angels. He was a drawing card, but we had to do something."

What the Astros did was to invest J. R. with the incentive bonuses that were part of his contract. That resulted in his receiving more than $700-thousand in 1980.

Nolan was almost a local kid. While born in Refugio, he grew up in suburban Alvin, located only about 30 miles from the Astrodome. After his success with the Angels, bringing him home was a major story all over the country, and certainly a major story for Nolan. "I thought about this for many years. As a ballplayer growing up in Alvin, it was always something I wanted to do. What's more important, though, was for my family and for me to play close to home."

At the time, there was criticism of McMullen's move and not just for the price. Hard to believe, but some thought Ryan was injury prone.

"For some reason, I have a reputation for being injured a lot. Really, in my fifteen-year career, I've had only two arm problems. In 1975, I had some bone chips removed, which almost every pitcher in the league will have at some time or another, and this year I tore some muscle fiber in my elbow," pointed out Ryan. "That mended after a couple of weeks and right now my arm feels as good as ever. But once you have some arm injuries people think you are finished." Ryan would not retire until 1993. After signing with the Astros, he would pitch for 14 more seasons!

Ryan joined a rotation with the Astros that included J. R. Richard, Joe Niekro, and Ken Forsch. Niekro would have the highest ERA at just 3.55. He would also win the most games, going 20 – 12. Ryan would be very tough to hit, but his won-lost record was not outstanding, as he was only 11 – 10 despite a 3.35 ERA. He gave up only 205 hits in 233.2 innings pitched.

The Astros' lack of hitting (and the advantage of having the Astrodome as the home field) affected pitchers positively even if they didn't get as much run support as they would have preferred. Yet, the Astros were severely handicapped by the loss of J. R. Richard to a stroke in late July. He would never recover to play another game in the major leagues. Ryan came in just before the Astros would really need him. Furthermore, starting in 1980, when the Astros made the postseason for the first time, he was a key member of two more postseason teams during his nine-year Astro career. In his second Astro season in 1981, Nolan set a record by throwing his fifth no-hitter when he beat the Dodgers on September 27, 5 – 0, his only no-hitter in the NL. He pitched six more in the AL, four with the Angels and his last two with the Texas Rangers. Individually as an Astro, Ryan would win 106 games, lose 94, and carry a 3.13 ERA during that span. He would lead the NL in strikeouts twice, despite being limited by GM Dick Wagner to a pitch count in the 100 range for several seasons.

As an Angel, Ryan had pitched until he was out of gas. After a new weakness in his elbow was diagnosed, Wagner wanted to be more cautious. Ryan missed some starts and pitched fewer innings. When healthy, he was the same Nolan Ryan. He led the NL in ERA twice, and in in 1987, his 2.76 was best in the league yet his record was only 8 – 16! Poor Astro hitting in his starts was a major contributor. No ERA champ before or after has had such a discrepancy between won-lost record and ERA in the league.

A great disappointment for Houston fans was Ryan wearing a Texas Ranger cap into the Hall of Fame. He did play more years in Houston than anywhere else, but became a true legend with Texas where he won his 300th game, pitched two no-hitters, and set the final career strikeout record with 5714.

Frankly, the Angels was the team with which Ryan became Nolan Ryan and would have been a strong candidate to put a cap on the plaque, but former owner Gene Autry, with whom Nolan was very close, had died. And the Rangers were very smart in signing Nolan to a post-career contract. Plus, it was the Astros that had let Ryan go. That pretty much eliminated them. The Rangers rescued Nolan, and he gave them even more than they could have expected.

Nolan Ryan Box Stats Over 27 Years					
	Mets	Angels	Astros	Rangers	Totals
Years	5	8	9	5	27
Wins	29	138	106	51	324
Losses	38	121	94	39	292
ERA	3.58	3.07	3.13	3.43	3.19
Strikeouts	493	2416	1866	939	5714
Walks	344	1302	796	353	2795
No-Hitters	0	4	1	2	7

37

Ryan Exhibition Start for Texas Sells Out the Dome

 ow much did Houston love Nolan Ryan? Well, when he came back to the Astrodome to start an exhibition game for the Texas Rangers in 1993, the building was totally full. The announced attendance was 53,657 for a game that had no bearing on anything. Neither team had big seasons in 1992 nor expected them in 1993. Nolan Ryan was the selling point.

The game was promoted as a good-bye to Nolan. After a good first season in Arlington with the Rangers in 1989, when he won 16 games and led the AL with 301 strikeouts, injuries had started to cost him some mound time in 1990. By 1992, at 45-years-old, Nolan knew it was about time to hang up his spikes. He announced that 1993 would be his final season.

So, the game at the Astrodome was arranged. Ryan pitched six innings in his Houston swan song. He only struck out one and gave up four runs and ten hits. Even, so 53,657 strong were there to see him throw his final pitch in Houston.

Besides the incredible crowd on hand to see him pitch a final time in Houston, what were the highlights of the game from the dead pan Nolan? "My sacrifice bunt was the highlight of the night for me. That and my popup!" Those were Ryan's first at-bats since he left the NL for the AL Rangers in 1989.

More seriously, Ryan said afterward, "It was a special night and the fans are what made it special. It's hard to describe, but you remember those special feelings like tonight. It was special for the fans to give me an ovation like that. But this game was also a lot of pressure and I'm glad it's over."

Ryan's first regular season start that season was fine. He was the winner versus Boston six days later by going six innings, allowing four hits and one unearned run while striking out five. Texas won, 3 – 1. Nolan would be sidelined much of the year before throwing his final pitch at Seattle on September 22 when his right elbow ligament gave out during the 807th game of his major-league career.

It was a tough way to end his illustrious career. However, his last game in Houston back on April 3 was one to remember for the love 53,657 Houston fans showed for the future Hall of Famer and strikeout king.

38

Dickie Thon's Tragic Beaning

he history of baseball has a lot of "what might have been" stories. For the Houston Astros, there are a couple that come to mind immediately. What if J. R. Richard had not had a stroke, and what if Dickie Thon had not been beaned?

In both cases, the incidents may have kept the Houston Astros from winning a pennant and World Series.

Dickie Thon, in 1983, had the best season at shortstop for any Houston player up to that point, and arguably the best in team annals until the arrival of Carlos Correa.

Thon, while playing home games in the pitcher-friendly Astrodome, hit 20 home runs, drove in 79 runs, and batted .286 in 154 games. He also stole 37 bases in 45 tries. He was on the All-Star team, won the Silver Slugger Award as the NL's top offensive shortstop, and finished seventh in the MVP vote. He was only 25 years old.

There is little question that his acquisition in a trade from the Angels for pitcher Ken Forsch on April 1, 1981 might be remembered as one of the team's best if an incident in early 1984 had not happened. Thon played off the bench in 1981, but by 1982 he was the Astros' regular shortstop.

Through the first five games of 1984, Thon was hitting

.353. Then the Astros faced the New York Mets on April 8. A pitch by Mike Torrez got away high and inside. The pitch hit Thon around his left eye and broke the orbital bone, forever affecting his vision in his left eye and his depth perception. The first diagnosis revealed a tripod fracture of the interior orbital rim. There was no brain damage from the beaning, but Thon, who never lost consciousness, suffered blurred vision for some time due to retinal damage caused by the force of the pitch.

While Torrez was never popular in Houston again, he was apologetic from the start. "Please tell his family I hope everything is okay." Torrez said he pitched outside to Thon when striking him out earlier, "so I wanted to start him inside" in the third inning.

"He started out over the plate thinking I was going outside again, and my fastball just took off," continued Torrez. "He didn't have time to get out of the way."

Thon didn't give up. After missing the rest of 1984, he came back in 1985, but was not the same. He had to make adjustments to be able to pick up the ball while hitting. Thus, he was slower to the ball, and the most obvious effect was loss of power. His last season as a semiregular was in 1986 when he played in 106 games, but hit just .248 with only three home runs. The potential superstar from before the eye injury was gone. He was released during spring training 1987. He actually walked out after starting with no-hits in eight at-bats and after committing three errors. His career in Houston was over and maybe even over for good.

To his credit, Thon didn't quit and continued to figure out how to play with essentially one and a half eyes. He had stops in Philadelphia, San Diego, Texas, and Milwaukee was able to hang around for 15 seasons. He learned how to make contact with a less powerful swing, although he did have a solid 1989 season with the Phillies during which he hit .271 with 15 homers and 60 RBIs. Generally, he was an average shortstop for his post-Houston seasons. He could have been so much more.

39

Oswalt's Near Electrocution May Have Saved Career

he Astros second-winningest pitcher, Roy Oswalt, may never have become a major-league pitcher in the first place due to a serious accident that could have killed him.

During the latter stages of the 1999 season pitching for the Class A Michigan Battle Cats, Roy had to contend with a very sore upper shoulder. He had gone 13 – 4, but with a high 4.64 ERA. He struggled late in the year. In fact, Roy told ESPN columnist Alan Schwarz, "My shoulder felt like it was torn. It hurt so much [that] I couldn't sleep at night. I had to take six Advil to go to sleep."

At 21-years-old, Roy had not yet pitched above the Class A level. If he didn't show well in the spring, he could be headed toward another year on that level, or even released due to being damaged goods. After the season, he told his wife he had to call a doctor. Something had to be seriously wrong.

Before he set up an appointment, he continued doing the things he normally did during the offseason in small Weir,

Mississippi. That meant chores around the country home, including making sure all his farm vehicles were in good shape.

Roy was checking the spark plug wires, and when he touched one of them, the truck started. That sent current flowing through Oswalt's body. As a result, the muscle in his hand tightened and he couldn't let go of the wire or the vehicle! Bolts of electricity had essentially glued him to the truck. "I was holding on to that wire for what seemed like two days but was probably less than a minute. Finally, my foot slipped off the bumper and I was thrown off."

Oswalt said that once he was no longer being used as an electrical circuit, he was okay. He had no ill effects, but he did have a good one.

"I went in the house and told my wife, 'You're never going to believe what happened.' And I told her the story and that my shoulder doesn't hurt as much."

As it turned out, about a week later Roy couldn't feel any pain at all. He never felt any pain again. The suggested explanation for what happened was the electrical surge may have broken loose scar tissue in his shoulder which had been causing the pain. No one knows for sure.

The next season Roy had a good spring training then started at high Class A Kissimmee before being elevated to AA Round Rock, where he was 11 – 4 with a 1.94 ERA in 19 games. His elevation had been planned for just one start. Nolan Ryan, who was co-owner of the Round Rock franchise, was impressed and urged the Astros to keep him there. Ryan knew what he was asking for. By 2001, Oswalt was a major leaguer and remained one through 2013. His Astro career featured 143 wins, trailing franchise leader Joe Niekro by just one. Overall, Roy was 163 – 102, 3.36, for 13 seasons, also playing in Philadelphia, Texas, and Colorado in addition to his 10 seasons with Houston. But it took a big jolt to get him going.

Astros Career Pitching Wins Leaders	
Joe Niekro	144 over 11 years
Roy Oswalt	143 over 10 years
Larry Dierker	137 over 13 years
Mike Scott	110 over 9 years
J.R. Richard	107 over 10 years
Nolan Ryan	106 over 9 years
Don Wilson	104 over 9 years
Shane Reynolds	103 over 11 years

40

Drafting Lance Berkman

Lance Berkman may have been the best draft pick the Houston baseball team has ever made in the first round when they didn't have the first choice overall. Certainly, the selection of Carlos Correa may ultimately be the best choice the team ever made, but his career needs more time and he was in a different situation than Berkman. Virtually everyone in baseball had Correa as a very high choice. The status of Berkman was more fluid. When he was selected as the 16th pick in the first round, however, it was very popular in Houston and in the Astros draft room. The Astros had only hoped he would still be around then. The fans, did too, because they knew him. He had played three years for Rice University just a few miles from the Astrodome. A switch-hitter, the New Braunfels, Texas, native almost fell into Rice's lap as well. Berkman wanted to play for the University of Texas, but the Longhorns did not pursue him. Rice was lucky as the Astros would be a few years later.

Astros GM Gerry Hunsicker said, "We believe Lance Berkman was the premier hitter in this year's draft and are fortunate he was available at the sixteenth pick. He is the best hitting prospect we have drafted in some time. A switch-hitter with power is a rare commodity [that] you just can't pass up."

Berkman didn't have to sign with the Astros. He could have returned to Rice for his senior year, but that was always unlikely. He had not been an Astros fan most of his life. "Growing up I was kind of a Yankees fan, but when I went to play at Rice, the dome was just two minutes from my apartment, so I did become a pretty big fan," Lance told the media.

As a first round pick it was nearly certain Berkman would sign with the Astros and forgo his senior season, which he did. But what a college career Lance Berkman had!

During his junior and final season at Rice, Berkman hit .431 with 41 home runs and 134 RBIs during the much shorter college season. Playing both the outfield and first base, Berkman was honored as a first team All-American and the National Player of the Year. Even so, Lance wasn't the top pick in the 1997 draft. He wasn't even the first Rice player chosen! That honor went to 100+ mph fire-balling pitcher Matt Anderson, who was taken by the Detroit Tigers. Six players selected ahead of Lance became All- Stars in the major leagues, but no one had a better career than Berkman. The six included J. D. Drew, Troy Glaus, Jason Grilli, Vernon Wells, Michael Cuddyer, and Jon Garland. From his debut season in 1999, Lance was on postseason teams six of his first seven seasons. In 2001, he led the NL with 55 doubles while hitting .331.

The next season, he hit 42 home runs and led the league with 128 RBIs. He hit 45 home runs and drove in 136 while hitting .315 in 2006. As late as 2008, when he was 32 years old, he again led the NL with 46 doubles while hitting 29 home runs, driving in 106 runs, and batting .312.

When Lance wrapped up his career after stops with the Yankees, Cardinals, and Rangers, his record showed an outstanding career .406 OBP including a .410 mark during his twelve Houston seasons.

While Lance was never a World Series champion in Houston, he won a ring with the 2011 Cardinals following his last good season. He had hit .301 with a .412 OBP, slugged 31 homers and drove in 94 runs in 145 games. Then in that World Series, he hit .423 with a .516 OBP while clubbing a homer and driving in five runs.

Berkman's career wasn't extremely long, but it was extremely effective. Many will argue that as a natural hitting talent, Houston has never had one better.

Yet Berkman wound up playing the first twelve years of his 15 year career in a Houston uniform. He had a .293 average as an Astro, with 326 of his 366 home runs, and was the toughest out in the Houston lineup over six postseason series. Lance hit .320 with six home runs and 26 RBIs while playing in 29 Astro postseason games.

In the four-game sweep by the White Sox in the 2005 World Series, Lance hit .385 with six RBIs in four games. Lance was one Astro not kept in check by Chicago pitching.

Photo courtesy of Photo Mojo

Biggio and Bagwell added a key third "Killer B"with Lance Berkman.

When Lance left the Astros in a trade to the Yankees in 2010, he was a victim of the future sale of the team and the effort by outgoing owner Drayton McLane Jr. to clear the deck of higher-salaried veterans to build from scratch.

This was too bad for Astro fans, who would have liked to see the very popular Berkman play his whole career in Houston. But Berkman was having the worst season of his career when he was dealt. Hitting only .245, he had 13 homers and 49 RBIs before going to the Yankees for pitcher Mark Melancon and infielder Jimmy Paredes on July 31 at the trade deadline.

Lance Berkman will always be remembered as a key member of the famed "Killer B's" headlined by Craig Biggio and Jeff Bagwell, and featuring others like Derek Bell, Sean Berry, Geoff Blum, and anyone else whose name started with a "B."

Lance didn't last as long as Biggio or Bagwell, but his total numbers were better than all the rest, and he might have been the best natural hitter ever to wear a Houston uniform.

41

Berkman Grand Slam and Ausmus Solo Set Up Burke

uring Lance Berkman's outstanding career with the Astros, if one at-bat stands out, it had to occur in the same 18-inning game that Chris Burke would win with a home run. Lance had a home run that, had he not come through, Burke would have had no chance!

It was October 9, 2005. Houston led the best of five 2005 NLDS series two games to one. A victory would send the Astros to the NLCS vs the St. Louis Cardinals. A loss would require both teams fly back to Atlanta for a deciding game. Houston did not want that.

However, it looked likely as the game moved to the bottom of the eighth with Atlanta leading six to one. But the Astros were not dead yet.

Brad Ausmus led off, walking on a 3 – 2 pitch. Eric Bruntlett then singled on a 1 – 2 pitch. The Braves replaced starting pitcher Tim Hudson with hard-throwing Kyle Farnsworth. The first hitter he faced was Craig Biggio, who bounced into a force play at third.

Luke Scott entered the game to pinch-hit for Willy Taveras. During the at-bat, the Astros pulled off a double steal with Bruntlett stealing third and Biggio second.

Whether the double steal unnerved Farnsworth or not, he wound up walking Scott on a 3 – 2 pitch. The bases were filled for Lance Berkman with one out. Atlanta still led, 6 – 1. Not for long. On the third pitch he saw, Berkman drove the ball out of the playing field for a grand slam. The Braves lead was only 6 – 5.

That was as close as Houston would come in the eighth, but in the top of the ninth, Chad Qualls retired the Braves in order. That set up heroics by two unlikely stars.

The first was catcher Brad Ausmus. Ausmus was, at this stage of his career, a weak hitter. He had hit just three home runs in 134 games and 387 at-bats during the 2005 season. He came up against Farnsworth with two and no one on base. However, Farnsworth made a big mistake be falling behind on the count to Ausmus two balls and no strikes.

Hitting off Farnsworth and his fastball, which often touched 100 miles an hour, was no cinch. But Ausmus was quite sure that, with the count in his favor, he would have to look for nothing but that pitch. He was right and was able to make solid contact. When the ball hit the bat, it was a very well-hit line drive heading toward the wall in left-center field. The only question was whether it would be high enough to make it into home run territory or be a two-base hit.

The ball ricocheted off the wall, but high enough to be a home run! The Astros had comeback from a 6 – 1 deficit by scoring five over the eighth and ninth. Then came extra innings.

The extra innings turned into a full game-length nine more before Chris Burke's winning homer in the eighth. Yet, Lance Berkman had a hand in it—by being replaced by pinch runner Burke after Lance had hit a double in the tenth.

There were a lot of fans second guessing manager Phil Garner for replacing Berkman when the game wound up going on and on and on—especially when his spot in the batting order, filled by Burke, came up in the 18th.

As Joe Garagiola once titled one of his books, Baseball is a Funny Game. Berkman had hit a key grand slam in the eighth. Ten innings later, the man in his spot in the batting order won the same game.

Most Important Astro Home Runs in Houston Postseason History
Yordan Alvarez vs Philidelphis 2022 World Series
Yordan Alvarez vs Seattle 2022 ALDS
Jeremy Peña vs Seattle 2022 ALDS
Chris Burke vs Atlanta 2005 NLDS
Jeff Kent vs St. Louis 2004 NLCS
Brad Ausmus vs Atlanta 2005 NLDS
Lance Berkman vs Atlanta 2005 NLDS

42

McLane's Ownership Run Superb Until the End

hen Drayton McLane Jr. bought the Houston Astros from John McMullen on November 9, 1992, he was the second straight Astro owner to come into baseball knowing very little about the game. He was one of several who had toyed with buying the club, including a consortium headed by Bob and Ken Aspromonte. There was even a contact with Nolan Ryan about being part of a buying group. Ryan was still a player with the Rangers, however, and his involvement was not possible.

McLain was originally part of a group of Houston and Texas businessmen who were trying to put together a deal for the club. The original group included Ben Love as leader. He was the ex-chairman of Texas Commerce Bancshares. Others included son Jeff Love, Gerald Hines, George Fontaine, Charles Duncan, Robert Onstead, and McLane. As, one by one, each dropped out and other potential bidders were either short of funds or the will to continue, McLane took charge. That was a Drayton McLane trademark.

One of the wealthiest men in the state as the second-largest stockholder in Walmart and president of McLane Company, Inc., McLane made his mark in the grocery distribution business started by his father as a small operation out of Temple, Texas. The purchase price for the Houston Astros Baseball Club and Astrodome USA was reportedly $115 million. Astros management was mainly kept in place after the sale. Manager Art Howe knew it would be a learning experience for all. He recalled in the book Houston to Cooperstown:The Houston Astros' Biggio & Bagwell Years," I remember we lost the first three games of the year and he came into my office and asked, 'What's wrong?' He was used to football. You lose two or three in a row in football and the season's done. I just said, 'We've got 159 more to go, and I think we're going to lose three in a row a few times.'" The Astros would lose three or more in a row ten more times that season.

McLane also did another McMullen-like thing. He went after a couple successful local pitchers to join the team at great expense. He brought in both former NL Cy Young Award-winner Doug Drabek, and ex- Texas Longhorn star Greg Swindell. Both had their moments but did not live up to their contracts. Still, McLane tried.

McLane was a very positive person. He would visit the clubhouse and talk with the players before nearly every home game. Chatting with the manager was also a regular ritual. Most of his players and managers got along very well with him, but privately sometimes wished he wasn't always around trying to give pep talks. He was a strong leader and definitely not an absentee one. He had a condo in downtown Houston, and his private plane got him between his home in Temple and Houston in no time. He had a hand in everything but let those he had in charge run things—with a few exceptions. McLane brought Tal Smith back to be Astro team president of baseball operations and had one of baseball's first top female executives in Pam Gardner in charge of the business side.

He let those already in place do their jobs while evaluating instead of sweeping a broom through the offices right after taking over. Like any boss, he would make decisions not popular with everyone, but he usually had the fans in mind and was the most personable owner any Houston professional sports franchise had ever had. Few can argue with the success of the team during his run until a sale was in the future.

From the takeover of the Astros for the 1993 season through 2011, the Astros won 1556 games, lost 1456, and had a .517 winning percentage. To put those seasons in perspective, the all-time franchise winning percentage didn't pass .500 till 2019.

In addition to having the best string of victories, the Astros under McLane's ownership were in the postseason six times, including the team's first World Series visit in 2005 as NL champions. They also finished second in their division six times but fell short of the wild card. During McLane's years in charge, the team was almost always in contention. That was the story until the end of 2008, when McLane decided to sell the club.

He had a deal in place with Jim Crane in 2008, but when the stock market fell, so did the deal. The negotiations had been very private and the public never knew until later. From that point on, however, the word was out that McLane would entertain offers.

In the meantime, the edict for the top management with the Astros was to cut costs to prep for a sale. As Tal Smith, Astro team president for baseball operations then put it, "At the end of 2008, the philosophy to build the team changed when the sale to Jim Crane fell through. It was the first time we knew selling the club was on his mind."

"Drayton became emotionally tied to selling the team. That is when we started down-sizing," remembered Smith. "We were directed to cut the payroll as much as we could. In the next couple years, Roy Oswalt, Lance Berkman, Hunter

Pence, and Michael Bourn were all traded to get value before their free agent years since the Astros would not be bidding to retain them." GM Ed Wade was forced to use his wiles to make the team as good as he could for as little as he could. Players like Kazuo Matsui, Miguel Tejada, Jason Michaels, Darin Erstad, Brian Moehler, Russ Ortiz, Brett Myers, and Aaron Boone passed through years after their peak.

A few minor-league products like third baseman Chris Johnson, shortstop Tommy Manzella, pitcher Bud Norris, and Brett Wallace all got looks. The last good season under McLane rule was 2008, when the club finished, 86 – 76, and were in contention for a wild-card spot into the last week.

After that, it was over. McLane started appearing at fewer games. In 2011, the franchise lost over 100 games for the first time ever. The departure of the last top players, Hunter Pence and Michael Bourn, happened that year. Pence was traded mid-game, Bourn later.

The sale to Jim Crane was announced, but it would not be until November that it would be finalized and the Drayton McLane era would be over.

McLane did well, financially and on the field, as long as he was trying. He bought the club for $115 million in 1992 and sold them for something between $610 and $680 million in 2011. The figure was disputed and it was reported Crane got a rebate from Major League Baseball since he was forced to move from the preferred National to American League. There were also some law suits over the value of a regional sports network formed with Comcast and the Astros and Rockets to replace longtime partner Fox Sports Houston. Nearly half of the total price was for the proposed television network. The final sale price is thus in question. However, whatever it was, Drayton McLane came out making a significant profit.

While his stewardship at the end was not impressive, the bulk of his reign was the best long-term success story in Houston baseball history up to that point.

Top Ownership Records				
	Jim Crane	Drayton McLane	John McMullan	Team Total
Years	13	19	13	61
Wins	1080	1556	1040	4921
Losses	817	1457	1014	4892
W/L Percentage	.569	.517	.506	.501
Post Seasons	8	6	3	17
World Series	4**	1	0	5

**Won World Series twice

— 43 —

Altuve Hits Three Home Runs vs Red Sox in 2017 ALDS

Into the 2019 baseball season a Houston Astro player had hit three home runs in one game 13 times. But no one ever hit three in one game in a more important game than José Altuve in 2017. His came in the postseason, and it set the tone for the whole postseason where the home run was going to rule.

Altuve, had hit 24 home runs during the regular season for the second straight season. He hit his first in the postseason in the first inning of the ALDS vs Boston on October 5 after Alex Bregman had launched one off Red Sox ace Chris Sale. He hit his second home run, also off Sale in the fifth. That pushed the Astros lead to 5 – 2, and in the last of the seventh he hit his third to end the game, 8 – 2, in a Houston series-opening victory.

Hitting three home runs in a game, even for a hitter as good as Joe Altuve, was unexpected, but manager A. J. Hinch said that what good hitters can do. "He's the best hitter in the league in a league of really, really good hitters. And to watch him have a day like today is a great reward for the work that's put in to not only be a good hitter who gets hits, but be a good hitter who produces runs, and that's not easy to do at this level," Hinch was quoted by Houston Chronicle writer Jake Kaplan after the game.

The Astros went on to win the series three games to one and move on to face the Yankees in the ALCS.

Altuve became the 10th different Astro to hit three homers in a game. Glenn Davis did it twice and Jeff Bagwell three times during their careers. Jimmy Wynn did it first against the Giants in 1967 and Carlos Lee had done it most recently before Altuve back in 2007. Others on the list include Lee May, Vinny Castilla, Lance Berkman, Richard Hidalgo, and Morgan Ensberg. Altuve would hit three in a game again in 2023 during a series against the Rangers in Arlington. He actually hit four straight including one in his last at bat in the previous game setting a Houston record. Following the 2023 postseason, Altuve was nnumber two all-time in postseason home runs, trailing only Manny Ramirez by a small margin.

Astros MVP Awards	
Jeff Bagwell	1994 NL
José Altuve	2017 AL

44

Carlos Beltrán Eight Postseason Home Runs 2004

Ranking as one of the Astros top three midseason trades ever (Randy Johnson and Justin Verlander were the others), Carlos Beltrán took a while to show his true skills, but in the 2004 postseason, he was the best ever.

During the 90 games with the Astros after being acquired from Kansas City, Carlos hit only .258 but added 23 home runs, drove in 53 runs, and stole 28 bases in 28 attempts.

Then came the postseason. In the first five game series with the Braves, which the Astros won, Beltrán hit .455 with four home runs and nine RBIs. Then in the next seven game series against St. Louis, he hit .417 with four more homers and five RBIs. Over all he hit eight home runs in 12 games, which set a record. However, the Cards won the NLCS, and Beltrán's season was over.

Beltrán's post season record was later broken. Randy Arozarena of the Tampa Bay Rays hit 10 in 2020. He played more games as the Rays went to the seventh game of the

World Series. He had seven through the same rounds Beltrán had played. Tying Beltrán's total was Corey Seager of the 2020 Dodgers, and Nelson Cruz of the 2011 Rangers who also went to seven games in the World Series. Barry Bonds rounds out the 8 HR hitters. He did it in 2002 with the Giants who also played to the seventh game of the World Series.

While it lasted Beltrán was more than human. As Craig Biggio told MLB.com years later, "There's some guys who wear a Superman shirt, but he WAS Superman. Anyone who was part of that, that saw it, watched it—every ball he hit was hard. Every out he made was hard. It was one of the most incredible hitting experiences I've seen in my life for that time of year and the numbers he put up."

Alas, Beltrán had no chance to add to his totals in up to seven more games. He also had no chance to add to his Astro legacy while in his prime as he moved to the New York Mets the next season as a free agent. Many Astro fans were crushed when his agent Scot Boras got him the deal with New York, and for the rest of his career when he played in Houston in another uniform Beltrán heard "boos" from the crowd.

All ended well, of course. He rejoined the Astros in 2017 to serve as a veteran presence and sometime designated hitter. He was part of the World Series champions and was on a championship team for the only time in his career. He then retired.

The Astros really wanted to re-sign Carlos Beltrán after the 2004 season. However, owner Drayton McLane's efforts were thwarted by Beltrán's agent Scott Boras, who was calling all the shots. As McLane told me in the book *Houston to Cooperstown*, "They had an unannounced deal with the Mets, and I kept talking with Scott Boras and making offers. He let me keep talking, but he had already made a deal with the Mets. Boras absolutely wanted to take him to New York for more endorsement dollars, but the Yankees weren't interested."

McLane felt Beltrán was more of a Houston-market player, but he was never able to get to Beltrán directly. "I tried very hard to convince Boras that Houston was a better fit. I met with Boras twice personally, but he would never let me talk directly with Beltrán. I even got Carlos's number directly from either Jeff or Craig and left word I'd be willing to fly anywhere to talk with him directly, but he was totally dominated by his agent." The relationship between Boras and the Astros was limited for years, with the club reluctant to even deal with any players he represented.

45

Kent Sends Fans to the Streets with Walk-Off HR in 2004

**hen** Jeff Kent signed to play with the Astros in 2003, his acquisition moved future Hall of Famer Craig Biggio from second base to the outfield. Offensively, getting Kent into the lineup was a good move. In two seasons Kent hit .293 with 49 home runs and 200 RBIs. While his postseason numbers did not approach those of Carlos Beltrán, he hit the single most important home run for the Astros in their history up to that time.

It was October 18, 2004. A full house at Minute Maid Park was cheering to help push the Astros into what was hoped to be a commanding advantage in the best-of-seven NLCS series. The winner of the series would get to the World Series, where the Astros had yet to appear.

As the game moved into the ninth, pitching had dominated. Woody Williams had pitched seven scoreless innings, allowing only one hit for St. Louis. Meanwhile, the

Astros' Brandon Backe went eight shutout frames, also surrendering only one hit.

By the ninth the bullpens had taken over and kept the game scoreless. Then came the last of the ninth.

Carlos Beltrán led off with a single. Then Jeff Bagwell flied out to center field. Beltrán then stole second base, which left first base open. The Cards intentionally walked Lance Berkman hoping Kent could be induced to hit into a double play.

Instead Kent seized the moment. As he later said, "I knew I was going to get something good early in the count. I wanted to drive the ball deep and not hard on the ground. I was used to having the hitter in front of me walked intentionally since I had hit behind Barry Bonds so long in San Francisco."

Kent hit the first pitch from Jason Isringhausen. And he really hit it. With the roof at Minute Maid Park open, it seemed to just disappear. The three-run game-winning homer gave the Astros a 3 – 2 lead in the series.

Until the 2017 World Series Game Five, Minute Maid Park was never louder. Downtown Houston was never livelier either as fans hit the streets after the game celebrating. Jeff Kent showed emotion, which he rarely did, approaching home plate to officially record the homer. Fans were certain this was the year. Only one win in two tries and the Astros would be in the Series.

It was the Cardinals that would defend their home turf, win the next two games and move into the Series.

The home run would be the last Kent would hit in an Astro uniform. He was gone after the season when the Astros passed on his contract option year, perhaps a move to free more money to re-sign Carlos Beltrán, which failed. For years Kent was upset about not being invited back as he told MLB. com's Brian McTaggart, "The team went to the World Series the year after I left, and I was pretty bitter about that. The time I was in Houston was, albeit short, was pretty great."

The time in Houston may have been short, but the memory

of his big home run will be remembered for a long, long time.

To Reporters and Fans, Kent was an Enigma

Jeff Kent hated to do the typical pregame show or postgame one-on-one interviews on radio or television. Since I did a lot of them that limited our conversations during his two seasons with Houston. However, I gave him credit; he was up front about it. I had introduced myself in the spring 2003, and he said he preferred not to do them. I said, "What if you hit a walk-off home run?" He said he would still rather someone else be selected. I respected that desire and never bothered him. We could still get postgame sound from his clubhouse comments from the comfort of his chair after games. However, after the 2004 postseason, he was willing to come out of the clubhouse to a live television position to talk about the game just played. A producer went into the clubhouse, asked Jeff, and out he came to talk with me after two or three games. I was never sure exactly why he changed his attitude, but surmised that his apparently sour demeanor was not winning over owner Drayton McLane and that Kent had an option year on his contract for 2005. The Astros didn't pick up his option anyway. From a team standpoint, that was probably not a good move.

46

Justin Verlander Traded to Astros at the Last Minute - Twice!

**W**hen the Astros make a trade to beat the deadline, their record has been excellent. Randy Johnson, Carlos Beltrán, and Justin Verlander being brought in at or near the deadline made major contributions to the club. Verlander, however, has the longest lasting value. Johnson and Beltrán wound up as "rent-a- players" since they became free agents after the season and elected to sign elsewhere.

And they did it with Verlander twice! After signing with the Mets as a free agent following the 2022 season he was reacquired by the Astros on August 1, 2023 to help them down the stretch again…as he was in 2017 when they won their first World Series.

In 2017 Verlander still had two seasons left on his

Photo courtesy of Keith Allison

Justin Verlander put the 2017 Astros over the top.

contract. That meant a lot. The 34-year-old joined the Astros for the final month of the 2017 season. He had passed through waivers with a contract clause allowing him to pick where he could be traded, keeping some suitors away. He wanted to go to a team that could win but was also reluctant to leave Detroit where he had played his whole thirteen-year career. As recently at 2014, the Tigers had been a contender, but the immediate future did not look as bright.

As a Tiger, Verlander had been a first-round draft pick, an AL MVP and Cy Young Award winner, the author of two no-hitters, and a number of other near-no-no's.

The Astros had looked into acquiring Verlander before the regular trading deadline, but at that time the

Tiger's demands were too high, and Verlander was not ready to accept a deal.

But Astro GM Jeff Luhnow, perhaps being egged on a bit by members of the team, most vocally pitcher Dallas Keuchel, resumed an effort to get Verlander into a Houston uniform in time to be eligible for the expected postseason. Keuchel had expressed dismay that the club had not made a move for pitching help prior to the trading deadline. While the Astros has been leading the American League West all season, they had not played well in August, and their pitching staff had been stretched by injuries. The bullpen had been especially overworked. Getting Verlander proved to be a morale as well as physical boost for the team.

The deal went right down to the wire. The trade details had to be at the Major League Baseball offices by midnight. The Tigers and Astros had agreed to the terms. However, Verlander, with a right of refusal, had to approve it.

A phone call from Keuchel to Verlander may have clinched the deal. The paperwork was online and in the MLB office with seconds to spare. Verlander would be an Astro in exchange for minor leaguers Franklin Perez, Jake Rogers, and Daz Cameron, whom the Tigers hoped would be part of a franchise rebuild.

Verlander was an immediate hit in Houston. During September he was 5 – 0 as the Astros rolled to the AL West title. Then in the postseason he won two games in the opening ALDS series with the Red Sox. His first win was as the starter in the opening game. The second was after pitching over two innings of relief to close out the series clincher in Game Four.

The next series against the Yankees would get the winner into the World Series. Verlander started and won Game Two 2 – 1 while striking out thirteen in a 124-pitch complete-game victory. A bottom of the ninth RBI double by Carlos Correa brought in the winning run.

Verlander was the winning pitcher in Game Six to keep the Astros alive and even the best of seven at three games each. The Astros would advance to the World Series with a win in Game Seven the next day. Verlander was named ALCS MVP after posting a 2 – 0 record combined with an 0.56 ERA while striking out 21 in 16 innings pitched.

Though he lost his only decision in the World Series, his

mates were up to the task. For the full postseason Verlander was 4 – 1 with a 2.21 ERA and a miniscule .177 batting average against. For Verlander's Astro time in 2017, he was 9 – 1. A very timely trade, and with two more years left on his contract, the best midseason trade in Astro history.

As it turned out rotator cuff surgery cost him two seasons, but he did pitch his third career no hitter in Toronto in 2019 and won a third Cy Young Award, second in Houston in 2022 after returning to action.

He left for the New York Mets as a free agent in 2023 at age 40, but was back in Houston half way through the season as the Mets started to tear down their under achieving club.

47

Randy Johnson Trade Made 1998 Astros the Team to Beat

When Astro GM Gerry Hunsicker acquired left-handed starting pitcher Randy Johnson at the trade deadline in 1998, many thought that was the last piece in a Houston puzzle that had all the pieces in place to get to the World Series.

It didn't turn out that way, and the Astros couldn't sign Johnson to a contract to stick around, but until the acquisition of Justin Verlander in 2017, it rivaled only the signing of Carlos Beltrán in 2004 as the club's biggest midseason trade ever.

Johnson had been wrapping up a stint playing in Seattle with a very lack luster start to his "lame duck" season. He was coming to the end of his contract with the Mariners and it was known they would not be able to bid on the level he and his agent were expecting when the contract ran out. So, he was very tradeable.

The Astros were interested, along with those who were felt to be more likely to land the big guy like the Yankees, Red Sox, Dodgers and all the other big money clubs. Johnson professed excitement when he was acquired by Houston.

"I'll be excited to put on my new uniform tomorrow," said Johnson after arriving at the Astros hotel in Pittsburgh. "I can't walk on water. I can't spread the Red Sea, but every time I go out I expect to win."

The 6-feet, 10-inches, 230-pound Johnson had been 20 – 4 with a 2.28 ERA for the Mariners in 1997, showing he was fully recovered from an injury-plagued 1996. But with free agency looming, he got off to a mediocre start in 1998. In 23 starts, he was only 9 – 10 with a 4.33 ERA. Then after he joined the Astros, he proved there was nothing physically wrong with him when he went 10 – 1 with a 1.28 ERA in 11 starts. Four of those starts were complete-game shutouts.

After Randy made his first Astro appearance, a 6 – 2 win in Pittsburgh, Houston was 67 – 44 and led the National League Central by four and a half games.

By the time the season was over, the Astros had won a then-franchise record 102 games and took the division title by 13 games. Although their 102 – 60 record was not the best in the league (Atlanta had a 106 – 56 record), with their strong finish and Johnson leading the rotation, they were strong favorites to win it all.

Then came perhaps the greatest disappointment in Houston baseball up to that point. They lost the best of five first round in the NLDS to the San Diego Padres. The upset was not really as huge as Astro fans felt. The Padres had compiled a 98 – 64 record and won the National League West by nine and a half games. The Astros didn't lose to the Padres, though, as much as they did to one pitcher and one superb pitching staff. Kevin Brown and his mates were too much to handle.

Johnson pitched well in the opener, but Brown was better. The Padres won 2 – 1 at the Astrodome. Houston was held to only four hits. Brown allowed only two in eight innings. The only Astro run was unearned off closer Trevor Hoffman in the ninth. Johnson also pitched eight innings but left the game trailing 2 – 0. A sacrifice fly by Jim Leyritz and solo homer by Greg Vaughn did the damage.

With the Astros on the verge of elimination in Game Four, Johnson started again. He pitched well, but the Astros again offered no offensive support in losing the game and series to Sterling Hitchcock and the Padres. Johnson allowed only two runs—just one of them earned—and only three hits in six innings. The Astro bullpen let four more runs score and San Diego won the game, 6 – 1.

While Johnson would move on the Arizona to play for the Diamondbacks and win a World Series while there, he admitted at his Hall of Fame induction the 1998 that Astros might have been the best team he ever played for. They just were outplayed in the postseason and never reached their potential.

Johnson did while an Astro, however. He was very, very good.

48

Ken Johnson Tosses No-Hitter but Loses Game

he rarest feat in baseball is pitching a no-hitter, but not winning the game. And in 1964, in the last season the Houston Major League Baseball team would be called the Colt .45s, a right-hander named Ken Johnson did it. While there have been five games in history where a team allowed no-hits and still lost, Johnson is the only pitcher to throw a complete-game no-hitter and lose.

Pitching a no-hitter is quite an achievement, but not really all that rare. Heading into the 2024 season, there had been 322 no-hitters thrown in major league history. The Houston Astros pitchers had thrown 16 no-hitters themselves. The Dodgers (both Brooklyn and Los Angeles) have the most with 26, but the San Diego Padres are the only team in MLB history to never have a pitcher throw a no-hitter.

Johnson's no-hitter was the second in franchise history and one of two pitched when the club was still known as the Houston Colt .45s. Don Nottebart had no-hit the Reds on May

17, 1963, 1 – 0. Johnson's would have the same final score, but he was the loser in the game on April 23, 1964.

Johnson's game was scoreless until the top of the ninth. With one out, Pete Rose tried to beat out a bunt. Johnson was able to field it but rushed a throw wildly, and Rose was safe going all the way to second base. Chico Ruiz slapped a ball off Johnson's shin, but third baseman Bob Aspromonte was able to make the play to first. Rose moved to third with two out. The next hitter, Vada Pinson, pulled a ball to second baseman Nellie Fox and, when Fox booted the ball, Rose scored the only run of the game.

While only 5,426 fans were in the seats for that game, it was never forgotten by future Hall of Famer Fox. After the game he told Johnson he was sorry for his error, but Johnson told him, "It was my fault. I put the runner [Rose] on or we'd be out of the inning." When the media got to Johnson, he realized what had happened immediately, "I guess that will put me in baseball history! What a way to get into the book."

Johnson who used a knuckleball among his assortment included a fastball, curve, and change from many different angles was "on" the whole game. Still the superb outing was not a fluke. While his 13-year major-league career finished with a 91 – 106 record, his 3.46 career ERA was good. And he had four nice seasons with a subpar Houston club holding a spot in the starting rotation and winning eleven games twice.

Johnson had come to the Colt .45s in the expansion draft from the Reds prior to the 1962 season. He would leave Houston in a trade to the Milwaukee Braves on May 23, 1965 with Jim Beauchamp for outfielder Lee Maye. That season would be Johnson's best overall as he won 16 games. He would have three more seasons with 13, 14, and 13 wins respectively with the Braves in Atlanta through 1968.

Ken Johnson was handy pitcher to have, while not a star. Yet he is in the baseball record book all by himself in losing a complete-game no-hitter!

49

Nolan Ryan Throws Record Fifth No-Hitter

**W**hile Nolan Ryan was spending nine seasons in an Astro uniform, the team made the postseason for the first time and then appeared in three of them. He became the strikeout king and the first to fan 4000. He also led the NL in ERA twice. Yet, on September 26, 1981, Nolan achieved his greatest feat. He broke the tie with Sandy Koufax and became the first pitcher in baseball history to throw five no-hitters. His catcher that day, Alan Ashby, would be the fifth different catcher to handle a Ryan no-hitter.

In addition to the four no-hitters Ryan pitched for the Angels during his eight seasons in the Los Angeles area, his final career totals would include seven no-hitters, 12 one hitters, and 18 two-hitters.

It was something fans anticipated every start Ryan had much of his career. Fans knew they had a chance to see something special. On that afternoon in 1981, with NBC-TV airing the game between the Astros and Dodgers nationally, fans DID see something special.

The game was important, too. Houston led the Reds by a game and a half in the National League West for the season's second half. That was the season that was cut into two halves as a result of a midseason work stoppage. There were only eight games left.

Going into the game, Ryan had thrown four no-hitters and seven one-hitters in his career, but had not thrown a no-hitter for six years. Ryan was a different pitcher by 1981. He had improved his curve and was toying with a change. During most of his Angel career, he was a fireballer who threw an occasional curve. It was a major pitch.

"I really didn't feel like I had good velocity today, but I got ahead with my curveball. The key was my curveball. You can't win with one pitch. It doesn't matter how fast you can throw, but with a curve they have to think about the breaking ball," Ryan told the media after the game.

The victory would be Ryan's tenth, raising his record to 10 – 5 to go with a league-leading 1.74 ERA. He struck out 11 but was wild at times with walks and a wild pitch.

He walked Steve Garvey to lead off the second. Then Garvey stole second and moved to third on a wild pitch after Ryan had struck out Pedro Guerra and Mike Scioscia. Ryan got the third out when Ron Roenicke popped out.

In the third, a walk, two strikeouts, and another walk brought Dusty Baker up, but he grounded out.

By the ninth inning with the Astros comfortably on top, the crowd was thinking no-hitter. Ryan knew the Dodgers didn't have any hits the whole game, but didn't think about a no-hitter until the seventh. He thought fate might be on his side when Terry Puhl made a one-handed running catch on a line-drive hit by Scioscia to cut off an extra-base hit in that inning.

In the top of the ninth, Ryan struck out pinch-hitting Reggie Smith to open the inning. Then he got Ken Landreaux to groundout to Denny Walling at first base. Then he got Baker to bounce one to Art Howe at third. His throw across the diamond for the out completed the no-hitter. Ryan was the first pitcher ever to throw five of them.

Ryan said after the game, "It's hard to believe I got the no-hitter. It's the one thing I wanted [to break the tie with Koufax]. I've had a shot for a long time. At my age [34] I thought I wouldn't get it. I don't have the stamina I used to have. I didn't challenge guys in the later innings."

The irony of THAT comment is obvious. Not only did Nolan pitch twelve more seasons, retiring at 46, but he also threw two more no-hitters while a Texas Ranger at the end of his career.

But for Astro fans those were just padding. He set the record in a Houston uniform on September 26, 1981. As for his catcher that day, Alan Ashby, this was his second no-hitter in a Houston uniform. He had caught a no-hitter by Ken Forsch earlier and would catch Mike Scott's pennant-clinching no-hitter in 1986.

Nolan Ryan No-Hitters
May 15, 1973   Angels vs Royals   3-0
July 15, 1973   Angels vs Tigers   6-0
Sept. 28, 1974   Angels vs Twins   6-0
June 1, 1975   Angels vs Orioles   1-0
Sept. 26, 1981   Astros vs Dodgers   5-0
June 11, 1990   Rangers vs A's   5-0
May 1, 1991   Rangers vs Blue Jays   3-1

50

Verlander No-Hits Blue Jays in Toronto

Justin Verlander had thrown two no-hitters while with the Detroit Tigers. And while he was a superb pitcher still while hurling for the Houston Astros another no-hitter was a long shot. He was just past his mid 30s and was involved in the game of pitch counts so common.

But then came September 1, 2019 in Toronto. He joined a small company of three time no hit pitchers when be blanked the Blue Jays 2-0. (There are only six of them headed by Nolan Ryan who had seven and Sandy Koufax who threw four. Cy Young, Bob Feller and an early baseballer named Larry Corcoran had thrown three. On this day Verlander would join that list.)

It was not easy, although one early walk to Cavan Biggio was all that kept him from a perfect game. Yet, when your team is not scoring any runs the pressure is on just to keep things even.

"I've been so close to a third one so many times and it just doesn't happen," Verlander recalled after the game. "And, tonight, Abraham Toro comes through with a huge homer to give us a run. And it was only fitting he would field the last ball and get the final out."

The homer by Toro didn't come till the top of the ninth off Toronto reliever Ken Giles.

Verlander threw 120 pitches in the game. At that point only seven pitcher in all of major league baseball had thrown that many that season. It was a total Verlander had reached 63 times in his career but not since his Detroit days.

The no-hitter may have been the deciding factor in the Cy Young voting that year between Justin and team mate Gerritt Cole who had a Cy Young season of his own, but finished behind Verlander in the final voting.

51

Astros No-Hit Seattle with Four Arms in 2019

**W**hen baseball let starting pitchers pitch they had quite a number of no hitters pitched by starters. But in recent years having one pitcher go all the way has been upstaged by multi-pitcher heroics. The first by the Astros was against the Yankees in New York in 2003. Six pitchers teamed up.

Then between 2019 and 2022 they did the multiple pitcher thing three more times. The fewest to team up was versus Seattle at Minute Maid Park on August 3, 2019. This no hitters could have not been more unexpected.

The Astros starting pitcher, Aaron Sanchez, had only been with the team for three days after having been acquired from Toronto and had lost his last thirteen decisions. But he went a strong six innings. It didn't hurt that the Astro bats were raking Mariner pitching making Sanchez' job more comfortable.

After Sanchez (who entered the game with a 3-14 6.07 with Toronto) the Astros brought in Will Harris in the seventh.

He walked a hitter but allowed no hits. Neither did Joe Biagini in the eighth and Chris Devenski in the ninth. Only Harris did not come to Houston in the trade with Toronto.

Martin Maldonado was behind the plate. He had re-joined the Astros at the trading deadling from the Cubs.

Offensively, Michael Brantley drove in four runs for Houston on three hits. José Altuve hit the only homer as the pitching staff got nine run support.

Sanchez could not have been happier, "What a fun night. For me, I was coming in here trying to make

an impression. This is awesome. You can't write it up any better than that!"

It was the Houston franchise's 12th no hitter in history. There would be more.

52

Alex Bregman Wins All-Star Game MVP 2018

As defending world champions, the 2018 Houston Astros had a full contingent of personnel part of the AL All Star team. Six players were selected with José Altuve getting a starting job at second base after receiving the most votes of any player. Also on the club were pitchers Justin Verlander, Gerrit Cole, and Charlie Morton along with outfielder George Springer and third baseman Alex Bregman.

Verlander and Cole were not slated to play due to the timing of their last regular season appearances, but the other four would and wound up distinguishing themselves. Altuve had a single in the third and final of his at-bats. Morton pitched two innings. He was good for most except two pitches that were located over the fence.

It would be Springer and Bregman that would especially shine. Springer singled in his first at-bat. Bregman was not so fortunate. That is, until the game got to the 10th inning.

With the game tied, 5 – 5, Bregman led off the inning against Los Angeles Dodger reliever Ross Stripling. On Stripling's fifth pitch with the count 2 – 2, Bregman ripped a ball into the stands in left field. The AL had retaken the lead, 6 – 5. While teammate George Springer would follow with a back-to-back home run, and the AL would add an eighth run it was Bregman's tiebreaker that earned him the game's MVP award.

The game itself deserved another footnote. There were a record 10 home runs hit in the game along with another record 25 strikeouts. All or nothing baseball was front and center for the 2018 game with Astro Alex Bregman the star of stars.

Bregman was not a novice to being involved in game-winning hits in 2018. He had four during the regular season which included two very strange ones.

On June 18 vs. Tampa Bay, his one-out two-run double off Rays reliever Sergio Romo plated the tying and winning runs in the last of the ninth for a Houston win, 5 – 4. Then five days later on June 23, in the last of the tenth inning, he hit a high popup a few feet inside the first baseline less than ten feet from home plate in a 3 – 3 tie with two out and Derrick Fisher running on the pitch. Kansas City first baseman Eric Hosmer overran the ball which fell behind him as Fisher crossed the plate.

A more conventional walk-off by Bregman won the June 27 game vs. Toronto when his two-run homer off Ryan Tepera in the last of the ninth carried the Astros to a 7 – 6 victory.

There was one more game-winner by Bregman in 2018 that was even stranger than the popup-overrun by Eric Hosmer. And it didn't even go as far. With the game tied at 5 – 5 in the last of the eleventh inning on July 10 and one out, Bregman swung over the top of a pitch and dribbled it no more than five feet in front of the plate. Oakland catcher Jonathan Lucroy picked up the ball and tried to tag Bregman but missed and then threw the ball toward first. The ball never got there; it nicked Bregman's helmet and bounced away as young Kyle Tucker crossed the plate for a Houston win, 6 – 5.

53

Jeff Bagwell Hits Milestone with 400th Home Run

Only one player has ever hit 400 or more home runs while wearing a Houston uniform. That man is Hall of Famer Jeff Bagwell who wound up his 15-year career with 449 long balls—all as an Astro.

Jeff's first home run was on April 15, 1991 in Atlanta off lefty Kent Mercker. The run gave the Astros the lead in the ninth. Jeff, who had not shown home run power in the minor leagues, would wind up with 15 homers in his first NL season. He had only two home runs until May 5 when he came to the plate in Pittsburgh as a pinch-hitter. He hit a pitch from Bob Kipper than showed he would be hitting for real power. The ball was lofted into the upper deck in left-center field. Measured at 456 feet, it was only the ninth ball ever hit into the upper deck of 22-year old Three Rivers Stadium. Many observers said it was the longest of all of them.

For Jeff, knowing it was only his third major-league home run was modest, "I never saw it. You hit three homers a year like I do and pitchers don't like it if you start watching them. That doesn't look too good. I asked somebody when I got back in the dugout, and he told me where it went."

Jeff proved he was not a three-homer-a-year man quickly. On July 20, 2003, he hit his 400th!

It was his second home run of the game, both off Cincinnati's Danny Graves at Great American Ballpark. After adding a run to the Astros lead with number 399 in the top of the fourth, Bagwell faced Graves again in the sixth. With two outs and leading the count two balls and a strike, Jeff lofted a ball high and deep toward left-center field for milestone home run number 400.

Jeff would hit 49 more home runs in his career that was hampered and finally cut short by chronic shoulder injuries. But he is a Hall of Fame player, and the only Astro to hit 400 or more home runs in an Astro uniform.

Astros Home Run Leaders (200 or More)	
Jeff Bagwell	449 over 15 years
Lance Berkman	326 over 12 years
Craig Biggio	291 over 20 years
Jim Wynn	223 over 11 years
José Altuve	209 over 13 years

54

Biggio and Berkman Go Back2Back Twice: First Astro Duo

I t was a great thrill for Astro fans to see Alex Bregman and George Springer go back-to-back with home runs to win the 2018 MLB All-Star Game, but two Astros from the past had pulled it off twice in the same regular-season game in 2005. July 25, the Astros hosted the Phillies at Minute Maid Park. Craig Biggio and Lance Berkman touched Philly pitchers as a tandem. In the bottom of the first inning, Biggio homered to left field off Philly starter Cory Lidle. Next up: Lance Berkman pounded a ball to the center field area that was also "over and out!" The Astros led 2 – 0. Then the next time each came to the plate, they repeated the act. That was in the third inning. With the Astros still leading 2 – 0 and Willy Taveras on base, Biggio slammed another homer to left into the Crawford Boxes. Then the next hitter, Berkman, finished the second Biggio-Berkman back-to-back with a homer to right. That gave the Astros a 5 – 0 lead in a game that would ultimately wind up as a Houston win, 7 – 1, for starting pitcher Andy Pettitte.

The victory also kept Houston a half-game ahead of Philadelphia in the wild-card standings. Houston would ultimately hold off the Phillies for the NL Wild Card and parlay it into the city's first championship in the NL and a World Series berth. Biggio and Bagwell may be the most remembered duo in Astro history, but on this night it was Biggio and Berkman that did something never done before in Houston baseball history.

It would not be until 2023 when two Astros duplicated the feat again. Mauricio Dubon and José Altuve did it. The interesting thing was Dubon was hitting ninth and Altuve lead off. The number nine hitter and leadoff man had never hit back to back homers twice in the history of baseball.

55

Eddie Mathews Hits 500th Home Run as an Astro

Eddie Mathews's career is loaded with trivia questions. For example, he played with the Braves in three different cities: Boston, Milwaukee, and Atlanta. He played for three franchises: Braves, Astros, and Tigers. He hit 493 home runs as a Brave, but he hit the second-most in a Houston uniform, including his greatest milestone home run, number 500.

Eddie started the 1967 season in Houston and remained with the Astros until just before the trading deadline when he moved on to Detroit. His first homer for the Astros was against Mel Queen in Cincinnati's Crosley Field on April 14. His most satisfying homer had to be the one he hit off former Colt .45 pitcher, Bob Bruce, pitching for Mathews's former team, the Braves, on June 17. That one, number 498, broke a 3 – 3 tie in the last of the ninth and gave the Astros a walk-off win. Mathews never forgot the Braves had let him go.

Number 500, his seventh of the 1967 season, would come

EDDIE MATHEWS HITS 500TH HOME RUN

in San Francisco on July 14. Jimmy Wynn and Rusty Staub were aboard, and the Astros were trailing the Giants, 4 – 3. He hit it in the top of the sixth off future Hall of Famer Juan Marichal. Future Ford Frick Award winning announcer Harry Kalas, father of future Astro TV voice, Todd Kalas, had the radio call that day.

And what did Mathews say after the game? "I wish it would have come against the Braves," he told the media. Then he got more reflective on hitting number 500. "Don't ask me how many I hope to hit. It was tough enough to get this one. I was trying to hit it in Philadelphia and then against Chicago but didn't. When I got to San Francisco, I thought I would forget about it and just swing the bat."

While Mathews had not had great success against Marichal in the past, he had collected some hits against him. "He has a good screwball to left-handed hitters, but I hit a fastball," said Eddie. Next up on the homer list was Mel Ott at 511. "Don't start that stuff already. I'd like to pass Ott, and I think with any luck I can this season. No matter how many homers you hit, someone else comes along to pass you."

Mathews added it was good he got to number 500 while still on the road with the wind blowing out. "If I had hit that ball in the Astrodome, I would still be running!"

Of the ten homers Mathews would hit as an Astro, three came off future Hall of Fame pitchers, Gaylord Perry, Tom Seaver, and Marichal.

On August 17, 1967 Mathews was traded for two players to be named later (ultimately, Leo Marentette and Fred Gladding). He would hit 512 home runs in his career, just getting past Ott by one, and be elected to the Hall of Fame. While he will always be remembered for his years with the Braves, he hit his biggest milestone home run while a Houston Astro.

56

Larry Dierker Named Houston Astros Manager

I t was probably the greatest surprise for Houston Astro fans ever. After the 1996 season, when the Astros had finished second again but lost ground in the won-lost column with just an 82 – 80 record, it was decided Terry Collins's run as manager had gone long enough. A change was needed. But who?

Veteran manager Jim Fregosi's name had come up in the media. So had the possible elevation of coach Matt Galante, who had some veteran player support. But the team's upper management had a unique idea. How about asking former pitcher and longtime broadcaster Larry Dierker if he might like the job?

Dierker was approached and thought it over. While he loved his TV and radio work, he knew he would never get a chance to run a major-league club and to put some of his theories on how to work with a team and implement those theories into games. "When I was offered this job, I said it was like being given the opportunity to go to the moon," Dierker said. "I knew there might be risks, but who would not want to go on that ride?"

The Astros kept everything very secret, but on October 4, 1996, it was secret no more. With the media gathered at the Astrodome, Dierker stepped into the room. As owner Drayton McLane recalled, "We kept Larry in the next room and [team president] Tal Smith, [GM] Gerry Hunsicker, and I took our places. Then we brought in Larry. I looked at the faces in the room. Milo Hamilton [Houston's lead play-by-play announcer and Larry's longtime on-air partner] was shocked and did not look happy."

Actually, what Dierker talked about on the air with Milo was the inspiration for making him manager. He had never managed or coached but played in the major leagues for more than a decade for several managers. Plus, he was a real student of the game's history as well as how it was played—and managed. He often expressed opinions different than what was conventional in the game played in 1996. He wanted less reliance on the bullpen and more from starting pitchers. He wanted managers to do less and set a style he wanted and let the players handle it. Longtime baseball men, Smith and Hunsicker liked what they were hearing.

Did hiring Dierker work? Before the pressures of failing in the postseason finally forced a mutual separation after the 2001 season, the Astros had their best stretch of seasons in their history. They won division titles and made the playoffs four of the five years he was in charge. His regular season record of 448 – 362 remains the second-best percentage of victories (.553) of any multiyear Astro manager. His win total—in just five seasons—ranks behind only Bill Virdon in Houston history, and Virdon managed in eight seasons. A. J. Hinch, who guided the Astros to 101 wins and the 2017 World Series then added 103 more regular season wins in 2018, went past Dierker's won-lost percentage at .577 and has a very good chance to best Dierker's win total. Larry, however, will rank high in Astro managerial stats and success for a long time. His hiring in 2014 was a very good one, but not as much as it was a surprise.

Houston Manager Won-Lost Percentage				
AJ Hinch	2015-2019	481	329	.594 * **
Dusty Baker	2020-2023	320	225	.586 * **
Larry Dierker	1999-2001	735	348	.556
Terry Collins	1994-1996	224	197	.532
Phil Garner	2004-2007	277	252	.524 *
Hal Lanier	1986-1988	254	232	.523
Jimy Williams	2002-2004	215	197	.522
Bob Lillis	1982-1985	276	261	.514
Bill Virdon	1975-1982	544	522	.510
Leo Durocher	1972-1973	98	95	.508
Cecil Cooper	2007-2009	171	170	.501
Harry Walker	1968-1972	355	353	.501
Art Howe	1989-1993	392	418	.484

* Took teams to the World Series
** Won World Series

57

Don Wilson: Houston's No-Hitter Man

here is only one pitcher to ever pitch two hitters in a Houston uniform, and it is not Nolan Ryan. Don Wilson had the honor with his first being the first no-hitter pitched in the Houston Astrodome.

That first no-hitter came on June 18, 1967 against the Atlanta Braves. He dominated Hank Aaron's team by striking out 15 hitters—including Aaron himself on three pitches for the final out. According to teammate Jimmy Wynn, the way Wilson handled Aaron that night was the highlight for Don. He disliked Aaron a great deal. Jimmy doesn't really know why. Another former mate, Larry Dierker thinks he knows. "I think when he got mad he could be scary. He really took it as a challenge and worked himself up to get out the best."

That first no-hitter was only one highlight of his first full major-league season. He also had a streak of 29 straight scoreless innings.

The next season he had games striking out 16 and then 18

Cincinnati Reds. He really didn't ever like the Reds. The rivalry reached the pinnacle in 1969. In three straight games in that season, Cincinnati had beaten the Astros by scores of 11 – 5, 14 – 0, and 10 – 0. Wilson was so mad at the way the Reds played that he visited their clubhouse after the 14 – 0 game.

"They were ahead fourteen to nothing. Johnny Bench was still calling for curves on three and one counts. Pete Rose was still running for extra bases. They weren't satisfied to win, they wanted to make us look ridiculous. In the dugout, they were laughing at us. They were even sticking their tongues out and turning their caps around backward—making fun of us. You just don't do that in my book. Nobody is going to do that to our club and get away with it," Wilson told Houston Chronicle sports writer John Wilson.

The season before, Don Wilson had shown the Reds what he already thought of them with those big strikeout games. He would have to put them down again.

The show was set with an unusual opening act. On Wednesday April 30, 1969, Reds pitcher Jim Maloney kept the Astros in check by no-hitting them. That was the night before Wilson would have his next start against Cincinnati. The Astros had lost eight straight.

There was only one way to top or at least equal that act. So, Wilson threw a no-hitter himself. Before the game, when Jimmy Wynn and his roommate Joe Morgan arrived at the clubhouse, others were wondering where Wilson was.

"When Joe and I walked up, we knew what was happening. He was holed up in a secluded spot thinking and concentrating on what he had to do. He went out and pitched a no-hitter himself," Wynn remembered.

Of the 27 outs recorded by Wilson, only one was a groundball. He had 13 strikeouts and 13 flies and popups. According to Larry Dierker, that was Wilson's style. "He had a natural sailing fastball. It was his natural fastball. He wasn't trying to throw a cutter. It was just about the best pitch you could have. Guys would swing and miss all the time, and when they did hit it, they usually hit popups and soft fly balls to the opposite field."

It was not an easy finish. Pitching with a lead, 4 – 0, he went to 3 – 2 on three hitters he faced in both the eighth and ninth inning and walked a couple. He even lost an out when his catcher Don Bryant dropped a foul ball. In the ninth, he struck out Tony Perez and got Johnny Bench on a fly to center. Earlier he had hit Bench with a pitch, which most felt was done on purpose. Wilson was hit by a pitch himself and had to avoid two other pitches during the game. This was closer to a gang fight than a baseball game that night. With two out, he walked Fred Whitfield but got future Astro Tommy Helms for the final out on a popout caught by Doug Rader at third.

Wilson had his second no-hitter, but the action wasn't over. While Astro teammates rushed to the mound to congratulate him, Don was not smiling. He was looking toward the Reds dugout and started that way for some mayhem. Fortunately, as he pointed out later, his teammates stopped him. "I was pretty far out. I'm glad the boys stopped me. I hate to think what might have happened had they let me go after them."

As manager Harry Walker said after the game, "He pitched like he had a personal grudge with every member of the Cincinnati team. He wouldn't talk to anyone on the bench. The guys were afraid to go near him. They left him alone."

After the game Wilson admitted, "There were a couple of times my legs were shaking so much I had to step off the mound. I never wanted anything so bad in all my life as to pitch that no-hitter."

If pitching the second of back-to-back no-hitters was not enough of a special memory, the time he had a chance for a third no-hitter but was pulled from the game was perhaps even more noteworthy.

On September 4, 1974, Wilson had held the Reds hitless through eight innings, but he had been wild and was trailing 2 – 1. An error by shortstop Roger Metzger had allowed both runs to score. So as the Astros came to bat in the last of the eighth, manager Preston Gomez lifted Wilson for a pinch-hitter, but it didn't help. Not only did the Reds hold on for the 2 – 1 win, but did get a hit in the ninth off reliever Mike Cosgrove. Gomez had made the move before. In 1970 while managing San Diego, he pulled starter Clay Kirby who had not allowed a hit but was trailing, 1 – 0, to the Mets after eight innings. The Mets wound up winning, 3 – 0.

Longtime Astro fans who remember Wilson agree that, when he was at his best, he was one of the toughest pitchers in baseball. His no-hit, high-strikeout games and career 3.15 ERA would attest to that.

58

Death of Don Wilson

here are two player numbers retired with the Houston Astros that are special. The two players both died in the middle of their career while wearing Houston uniforms. Number 32 is for pitcher Jim Umbricht. He suffered and succumbed to cancer when the team was still the Colt .45s. His career was just getting started.

The other number retired for a player who died while playing for Houston is the number 40 of Don Wilson. His career was in full swing when he was found dead in his garage from carbon monoxide poisoning on January 5, 1975. He was a month away from his 30th birthday.

Wilson was at his physical peak and was one of the toughest pitchers for hitters to deal with in the NL. His record of 104 – 92 was compiled in just eight full seasons. His career ERA was an outstanding 3.15. He won 16 games twice, 15 games once, and had double-figure victories in every season. He threw 78 complete games and 20 shutouts in 245 career starts. He also authored two no-hitters.

Wilson was a workhorse. He had overcome chest pains (never fully diagnosed) as far back as 1968. He suffered elbow tendinitis in 1970 and had to spend some time on the disabled list. He was outspoken and was fined for disparaging remarks directed at manager Leo Durocher in 1973. Wilson was not always easy to get along with. Sometimes his teammates were not sure how he would react to situations. As Jimmy Wynn put it, "Don Wilson was the type of player you didn't know what was in his heart or on his mind from the start until the game ended."

Tal Smith concurred, "That's a good description. He could be very personable, articulate, and intelligent. Other times he could be sullen and withdrawn, and what was the reason for that? Whether it was a split personality or something else, I don't know. He was a real enigma, but a superb talent."

"With the Astros, his problem was consistency. When he was on, he was as good as anyone in the league. We didn't get that every game. He may have had some things that maybe affected his concentration, but he had a great arm," remembered Tal.

Fellow pitcher Larry Dierker was effusive in praise, "I thought he was as overpowering as any pitcher we had at times, including J. R. Richard and Nolan Ryan. But he didn't bring that stuff to the mound every start. It seemed like it all depended on his emotional state."

Wilson had proved his durability with a start at Texas League Amarillo that Smith won't forget. In those days, game reports were filed in by minor-league managers and usually mailed. When Tal picked up one from his manager at Amarillo, Morris Medlock "Buddy" Hancken, he was distressed. "I picked up a phone because I was livid," said Tal. The report said Wilson had thrown something like 220 pitches! "Hancken explained that [Wilson] was throwing great, and [Hancken] had asked him how he felt several times, and he wanted to go back out there, so Buddy let him."

Smith remembers that, after he left the Astros to work for the Yankees in the early 1970s, George Steinbrenner, Yankee owner, wanted to talk about Wilson in a possible trade. Tal said, "It was not my idea. It had come from other people, and they obviously came to me since I had worked with Wilson. The issue at hand was Wilson for Mel Stottlemyre. Obviously, it did not happen."

Had Wilson not died, the deal would have been good for New York. Stottlemyre's career ended by natural causes the same year Wilson's did, after 1974. In 1973, Wilson was 11 – 16 with a 3.20 ERA.

Stottlemyre with New York was 16 – 16 with a 3.07 ERA. However, in 1974 Stottlemyre pitched his last season and was 6 – 7 with a 3.58 ERA while Wilson was 11 – 13, 3.20 in Houston. Wilson was three years younger. Stottlemyre later served as the Astros pitching coach for two seasons in the early 1990s.

When Wilson was found dead in his garage on the morning of January 6, 1975 the circumstances were suspect. Tragically one of his children, sleeping in a room above the garage, also died, and another had been affected. Wilson and his wife reportedly had a stable relationship, although she had a swollen jaw that was never fully explained. Many thought it possible an altercation between the two had resulted in his wife's swollen jaw, possibly exacerbated by alcohol use, and Wilson went to sit in his car with the radio on to cool off. Because the weather that night was dipping into the upper 40s, it is not impossible to think the garage door was closed and car heater was on with the engine running. A basic mistake, but not impossible to theorize if he was mentally impaired. Because his body was found to have a high alcohol content, some suspected he may have passed out before succumbing to the carbon monoxide.

None of his teammates could find any reason to believe he would have or had any reason to commit suicide. Some of his closest teammates questioned the investigation results which officially ruled Wilson's death an accident and the case closed one month after he died.

59

J.R. Towles and Yuli Gurriel Drive in Eight Runs in One Game

Justin Richard Towles, always known as just J. R. Towles was a major catching prospect in the Houston Astros system when he made his major-league debut late in 2007. In just 14 games and 40 at-bats, he hit .375 with a homer and twelve RBIs.

He drove in eight of those runs in one game, which set a Houston Astros franchise record that was not equaled for fourteen years!

In St. Louis, during the 153rd game of the season for the Astros, but only Towles's sixth, the Astros ultimately pounded out 23 hits and 18 runs. Towles had a major part.

With two out in the top of the second, J. R. singled home two runs off Cardinal starter Braden Looper.

The score was still only 2 – 0 when Towles came up in

the fourth with two more runners in scoring position, and he singled again to bring them both home. The Astros led, 4 – 0, and Towles had driven in all four.

In the sixth inning, Towles faced Looper for the third time. He drove in another run with an opposite- field double. The Astros led, 5 – 0, all thanks to J. R. Towles.

At this point, the rest of the team started to roll. While the red-hot Towles was hit by a pitch, no doubt to see if he could be cooled off, in the seventh,, the Astros added five runs and led 10 – 0 to the bottom of the seventh.

In the eighth, Towles would walk with the bases loaded for his sixth RBI and eventually score as part of a six run explosion, making the count Houston, 16 – 0.

Towles would get one more at-bat. In the ninth with the Cardinals out of pitchers, former Houston farmhand and infielder Aaron Miles entered the game on the mound.

Cody Ransom led off with a walk. Towles, who was 3 – 3 and had been on base five times with six RBIs, upped those numbers to 4 – 4, six times on base, and eight RBIs when he took the first pitch from Miles over the left-field wall.

The Astros won the game, 18 – 1, and Towles had set a club record.

If he wasn't already in that position before, Towles looked like he would be the person to take over behind the plate in 2008. Brad Ausmus was moved into a back-up role to serve as a mentor for Towles, but Towles struggled handling pitchers and, more importantly, solving major-league pitching as a hitter with the job given to him in the spring. Ausmus wound up taking over the job as J. R. finished the season with a .137 batting average and only 4 homers and 16 RBIs in 54 games.

Towles had other chances to come around the next three seasons, but never could produce on the level needed. His defense suffered at times as well. He was a free agent for 2012 and had minor-league shots with Minnesota, St. Louis, Los Angeles, and Texas in ensuing years. He never made it back.

But on September 20, 2007, J. R. Towles was the best hitter

in baseball.

His record was not equaled until Yuli Gurriel was with the club. And Gurriel did it with only a two hit game. However, he started against the Colorado Rockies with a three run first inning home run. He hit a sacrifice fly in the third and cleared the bases with a double in the fourth. That gave him seven runs batted in. He got number eight with a run scoring ground out in the sixth.

Perhaps not as spectacular as how Towles did it, but just as productive. And like the Astros one sided win when Towles brought home eight Gurriel's feat was part of a 14-3 win over the Rockies at Minute Maid Park. The magic day was August 7, 2019

60

For One Season, Mitch Meluskey: Best Hitting Catcher

.R. Towles had the best single game for an Astro catcher ever, but Mitch Meluskey had the best single season at the plate for any Houston backstop. The pitchers caught up to Towles while a shoulder injury and immaturity did Meluskey in.

The Astros had won division titles in 1997, 1998, and 1999, but were hardly solid at all positions. Although Brad Ausmus had done a great job defensively and handling pitchers in 1997 and 1998. He even hit .269 the latter season. But the team had a better-hitting catcher on the roster, Tony Eusebio, and a young guy in the minors who it was hoped would win the job. Both got chances to play after an edict came down from owner Drayton McLane Jr. to find ways to pare the payroll. Despite Ausmus' importance, with the two others around, after the 1998 season, he was sent back to Detroit, the team the Astros had acquired him from in 1996. As Tal Smith remembered, Brad and his owner didn't mesh well. Much of it stemmed from the dry humor of Ausmus. "Drayton could never understand it," said Smith. "When Ausmus would see Drayton in the locker room, he might ask him why he was paid so much? He would be so self-deprecating with his humor Drayton might ask me later, 'He just doesn't have any confidence in himself.' That was certainly not the case, but Drayton would take what he said seriously."

The Astros felt the higher priced Ausmus could be replaced by the stronger-hitting Tony Eusebio in 1999 or even better by their minor-league catching phenom who might be ready. That player was Mitch Meluskey. Mitch did win the job out of spring training and started the season, but Eusebio was needed early on. Meluskey suffered the first of his shoulder injuries. Both catchers ultimately proved that, at that position, there is a lot more to success than batting average or power hitting.

Eusebio did fine offensively in 1999. The Astros won their third straight division title. However, with the club moving into the new Enron Field in 2000, it was time to see what the switch-hitting kid catcher could do. He had won the starting job for 1999, but no one really saw him that year. The shoulder problem ultimately would be his physical downfall.

Meluskey had started his professional career in the Cleveland system and was not on a fast-track before he was part of a four-player minor-league deal in early 1995 that sent him to the Astro farm system. He immediately started to show the bat that would get him to the major leagues.

In 1996 he hit .317 splitting time between A and AA levels. Then in 1997, not only did he hit .303 but added 17 home runs splitting time between AA and AAA.

In 1998 Mitch marked himself as Houston's next catcher when he hit .353 with 17 more homers in AAA. He even got eight at-bats in the major leagues with the Astros at the end of the year.

Mitch might have taken over in 1999 with Eusebio never getting his chance had he not suffered the major shoulder injury. Mitch had made the 1999 Astros out of spring training but went on the disabled list after only ten games. He underwent surgery for right shoulder laxity. He was on the disabled list from April 26 and never played again in 1999.

Meluskey healed well enough to win the job again in 2000 and showed the hitting ability he has shown in his last two minor-league seasons. He hit .300 with 14 home runs and 69 RBIs. Defensively he threw out 24% of base stealers. While under the league average of 32%, his offensive skills placed him fifth in Rookie of the Year voting.

With Meluskey, however, his numbers didn't tell enough of the story. He was a 26-year-old rookie who broke all the rules of comportment. His relations with veteran players were poor. His work habits were below what was expected from major-league players. He was immature and cocky. He had a batting cage altercation with veteran Matt Mieske after Mitch arrived late for his turn and tried to jump in front of the vet. A punch or two was thrown before the teammates were separated.

Meluskey's relationships with his pitchers was unacceptable, and despite his hitting skills, he was put on the trade block. The Astros wanted Brad Ausmus back and were able to swap Meluskey along with pitcher Chris Holt and outfielder Roger Cedeño to the Tigers for Ausmus and pitchers Doug Brocail and Nelson Cruz. Astro manager Larry Dierker had to be tactful when asked by Tiger manager Phil Garner about Meluskey. He emphasized Mitch's ability to hit as a switch-hitter. Defensive and leadership problems were down played as much as possible.

Meluskey reinjured his shoulder with the Tigers and missed the entire 2001 season on the disabled list. He played in only eight games with Detroit in 2002 and was released.

Meluskey kept trying to get his shoulder and attitude in place, but the shoulder problem became chronic. He had a look with Oakland and even signed as a free agent with the Astros in late 2003 after a strong minor-league season with the bat, but he was not the offensive player he showed in 2000 and his shoulder was shot. Mitch Meluskey's career was over at only 29 years old.

Personality problems aside, it was a balky shoulder that ended the career of the single-season best offensive catcher the Astros ever had. Mitch Meluskey became just a foot note instead of a star.

61

César Cedeño
Had All the Tools

here has likely never been a player to wear a Houston uniform with more tools to become a star major- league player than César Cedeño. Others have built bigger numbers, and some current Astros may surpass Cedeño in the hearts of fans, but one of his former managers, Hall of Famer Leo Durocher, compared Cedeño to Willie Mays.

César never approached Willie's career numbers, but how about what he DID do?

The native of the Dominican Republic broke into the major leagues with the Astros on June 20, 1970. He was 19 years old.

In 90 games that first year, he hit .310 with 7 home runs and 42 RBIs. He also stole 17 bases in 21 attempts. Defensively, he ultimately moved Houston's longtime power hitting Jimmy Wynn from center field to left to give Cedeño more room to roam. According to Jimmy, that was not what César wanted. "He did not want to play center field. He wanted to play right field like his idol, Roberto Clemente."

Just looking at numbers, Cedeño's batting average and Wynn's power is the offensive separation. OBP in Houston seasons had Wynn at .362 and Cedeño at .351. Even the modern practice of adding SLG and OBP is close. Wynn at .806 and

Cedeño at .805. Both were fast, but César stole more bases and still is the Astros career leader. And he had a batting overage more than thirty points higher. Wynn had seasons with as many at 37 and 33 home runs. He stole as many as 43 bases. Cedeño never hit more than 26 homers but stole 50 or more bases six times with a high of 61. Cedeño led the NL in doubles twice with 40 in 1971 and 39 in 1972. Wynn had 30 or more doubles only twice.

Cedeño couldn't wear the uniform of his idol because, when he broke in, veteran teammate Norm Miller had it. By the time Greg Gross took it over in 1973, Cedeño had made a name for himself with number 28. So, while the club put him in center field when he preferred right, he couldn't even emulate his idol by wearing his number 21 either.

Cedeño's first full season in 1971 wasn't quite as impressive from a numbers standpoint, with his average falling to .264, but he led the NL with 40 doubles.

In 1973 and 1974, Cedeño had Hall of Fame track seasons. He hit .320 each year. He stole 55 and 56 bases and hit 22 and 25 home runs. He had 39 and 35 doubles, leading the league again with the 39 in 1972. He was so good that the Astrodome was called by some "César's Palace." Leo Durocher's exact quote was, "At twenty-two, Cedeño is as good or better than Willie was at the same age. I don't know whether he can keep this up for twenty years, and I'm not saying he will be better than Mays. No way anybody can be better than Mays. But I will say this kid has a chance to be as good. And that's saying a lot."

Larry Dierker: "I don't think he could have been as good as Mays or Hank Aaron. He didn't have as high an OBP because he didn't walk much. Still, when I look at his numbers I am surprised they weren't better because they don't jive with my image of watching him play."

However, in 1974 at only 23 years old and despite driving in 102 runs while hitting 26 home runs, Cedeño started to decline.

The "can't-miss" future Hall of Famer played in the major leagues until age 35 in 1986, but at his best was just a good player.

Not an All-Star or main player on his teams, just a solid pro.

Cedeño's career ended with a 17-year log of a .285 batting average, 199 home runs, and 976 RBIs. He stole 550 bases including 487 in Houston which is still the franchise record. He won five straight Gold Gloves, but all in his first seven seasons. He was in four All-Star Games, but none after he was 25 years old. Those who saw him or played with him had the highest praise. Tal Smith: "He was outstanding. He was the greatest talent I think the franchise has had. I thought he was destined for the Hall of Fame."

What happened to this Willie Mays clone?

His decline may have started due to a tragic incident that happened after his second .320 season in 1973. Cedeño was involved in a domestic incident with his 19-year old girlfriend. The two were apparently drinking and playing with a gun in their native Puerto Rico. The gun went off and the girl was killed. César was charged with involuntary manslaughter but was released after 20 days in jail.

For the next several seasons, many fans would not let him forget the incident while he was on the field. He was no longer looked at as anything but a flawed star. And his star began to dim. Dealing with the signs in the stands and words directed at him likely had an effect in his play, but former teammate Bob Watson thinks it also indirectly caused Cedeño to alter his hitting style. In 1974 he hit 26 homers and drove in over 100 runs, but his batting average dropped from .320 to .264. Watson was quoted in a story by David Schoenfield in 2012 about that. "He was so young and so proud that I think he tried extra hard to prove to everyone that it [the fan reaction] did not bother him. He altered his swing trying to hit homers. After that, pitchers made adjustments, and he could never readjust himself." Dierker said César's personality was different, too, "He was never the same. He was a carefree kid before the shooting, and he wasn't so carefree after."

Of course, injuries cannot be discounted for the fall of Cedeño. He hurt his knee in winter ball after the 1972 season.

The injury didn't affect him in 1973 apparently, but within four seasons he was playing on two bad knees and ankles. That took away most of his base stealing. The Astrodome had moved the fences back in 1977 and was a hard place to hit for power.

Still, despite a torn knee ligament in 1978, hepatitis in 1979, and a broken ankle in the 1980 NLCS, Cedeño was not washed up at all. He just wasn't a star any longer. Sadly, he had completed one of his best seasons in 1980 by hitting .308 while stealing 48 bases.

After the broken ankle in the Philadelphia postseason series, Cedeño no longer had the speed. As he recalled, "I broke my right ankle, and it was one of the toughest things of my career. I hit a groundball to shortstop and tried to beat out a double play. At the last moment, I jumped and landed on the outside part of the bag with my body leaning forward. That's what caused my ankle to break. It was a painful moment."

He was only 30 years old and the rest of his career was downhill. Moving to Cincinnati in a trade for Ray Knight after the 1981 season, he would have only one more year as an everyday regular player. Larry Dierker was not surprised he lasted, however, "His talent was still valuable enough. Almost every major league team would have played him some after he left the Astros. He was still good enough. He just wasn't sensational anymore."

With the Reds in 1982, he hit .289 with eight homers and 57 RBIs. He stole 16 bases and was caught 11 times. The super-prospect César Cedeño was gone.

Though he may never have achieved the promise he first showed for a number of reasons, Cedeño lasted for all or parts of 17 seasons. He will always be remembered by long time Astro fans for what "might have been."

Astros Stolen Base Leaders			
César Cedeño	487	Joe Morgan	219
Craig Biggio	414	Terry Puhl	217
José Altuve	293	Jeff Bagwell	202
José Cruz	288		

62

Houston's First Major League Game was a Win!

verything has to start somewhere, and Major League Baseball in Houston started on April 10, 1962 at the infamous Colt Stadium. The ballpark had been built hurriedly on the property that would house the Harris County Domed Stadium (Astrodome), but not until 1965.

So, the Colt .45s had to endure hot humid summers complete with helicopter sized mosquitos for night games.

For the first game, conditions were great. Of course, it was only April!

The new Colt .45s were facing the Chicago Cubs in a battle of teams with similar skill levels. In fact, the Colt .45s would finish the 1962 season two spots higher in the NL standings than the 10th place Cubs.

On opening day Houston sent veteran lefty Bobby Shantz to the mound. While Shantz was on the downhill side of his career, he had won an AL Cy Young Award just a few seasons earlier. The Cubs' opening-day starter was Don Cardwell.

Chicago's lineup featured four future Hall of Famers in Lou Brock, Ernie Banks, Billy Williams, and Ron Santo. Houston's lineup had none.

There were 25,271 fans on-hand at the new temporary ballpark. Houston scored in the bottom of the first inning as Bob Aspromonte singled and came home on a triple by Al Spangler. In the third, the 45s scored three more. Aspromonte and Spangler both came home on the first ever Houston home run, a three-run shot by Roman Mejias. Houston would get another run home to make it 5 – 0, Houston, after three innings.

Meanwhile Bobby Shantz was keeping the Cubs at bay until Banks hit the first home run in Houston by a visiting player to make the score 5 – 1 in the seventh.

The Colt .45s were not done with their offensive show, however. Singles by Spangler, Mejias, Norm Larker, and Jim Pendleton opened the seventh to add two more runs. Later a single by Joey Amalfitano brought home another and the Colt .45s led, 8 – 1.

The Cubs added a second run on a sacrifice fly by Brock in the top of the eighth. Chicago was finished scoring for the day, but Houston was not.

Aspromonte and Spangler rode home on another Mejias

homer in the last of the eighth and the Colt .45s rolled on to an 11 – 2 first game-win.

Shantz got the win and, following the ovation received from the crowd, said, "I had been reminded that this was an historic occasion."

And so it was—Houston had not just joined Major League Baseball, but had a win to prove it. The Astros would wind up sweeping the Cubs, but would come back down to earth and finish the season, 64 – 96. That was good for eighth place, which was better than the Mets and Cubs.

The conditions at Houston Colt .45s games during the summer months were often atrocious. From mid- June to early September, the temperature and humidity often competed for top billing. Then, there was the sun during the day and the salt-marsh mosquitos at night. Colt Stadium was constructed for use only until the Harris County Domed Stadium next door was ready. It took three years and the .45s had to play outdoors until 1965. It was once said that even Ernie Banks never uttered his famous line, "Let's play two," when the Cubs were in the town during the summer heat. Outfielder Carl Warwick points out, "That whole area had been a swamp originally. When they dug a hole in the ground for the Dome, every mosquito in town found it."

Players would run through the outfield and find their socks covered with mosquitoes. It was especially bad right after a rain shower had come through in the late afternoon. The stands and field were routinely fogged before the players started working out and the fans were let in. It didn't help much.

With the heat, humidity, and mosquitos, it was not surprising that, when Rusty Staub was asked about Colt Stadium in Robert Reed's book Colt .45s, replied with "I don't care about what ballpark they talk about as being the hottest place on the face of the earth, Colt Stadium was it. There was just no relief, no place to hide. It was the hottest stadium that ever existed."

63

The Astros Sign Andy Pettitte and Roger Clemens

The Houston Astros had finished in second place in the National League Central in both 2002 and 2003. But neither finishes carried a strong enough record to get the team into the postseason as a wild card. In Larry Dierker's last season as skipper in 2001, the club was 93 – 69, but continued struggles in the postseason resulted in Dierker agreeing to be "retired." The new manager was veteran Jimy Williams. In 2002 the Astros were 84 – 78. No regular hit .300, and only Lance Berkman and Jeff Bagwell had really solid seasons. Berkman hit .292 with 42 homers and 128 RBIs. Bagwell had a .291 average with 31 homers and 98 RBIs.

The pitching staff had two solid starters in Roy Oswalt (19 – 9, 3.01) and Wade Miller (15 – 4, 3.28). The bullpen was strong and carried the staff.

In 2003, the team earned another second place, but was

Andy Pettitte in 2004. Nolan Ryan greeted him at the plate.

again not good enough, with an 87 – 75 record, to earn the postseason. The Houston offense was better, with six players hitting ten or more homers led by Bagwell with 39, Richard Hidalgo with 28, and both Lance Berkman and Morgan Ensberg hitting 25. Jeff Kent, acquired in the offseason for a two-year-with-option free agent contract, hit 22 homers, drove in 93 runs, and hit .297

Again, the bullpen was the strongest part of the pitching. Oswalt started only 21 games due to injury and was 10 – 5 with a 2.97 ERA. No other starter had an ERA under Tim Redding's 3.68. But Billy Wagner saved 44 games and the back end of the pen—Octavio Dotel, Brad Lidge, and Wagner—was the best in baseball.

To get the Astros over the hump and back in the postseason, they needed to improve the starting rotation. Obtaining both Andy Pettitte and Roger Clemens was well ahead of what anyone could expect, but they pulled it off.

It didn't take place without controversy first. Ace reliever Wagner had publicly reprimanded team management for not doing enough to make the club a winner. He felt they were not willing to spend enough to fill the holes the club had, even though they had been edged out by the Cubs by only one game for the NLC division title.

The first thing that happened was Wagner was traded on November 3, 2003 to the Phillies for three young pitchers. Then less than two weeks later, the Astros shocked the baseball world—most notably the New York Yankees—when they signed Yankee free-agent pitcher Andy Pettitte to come home. Pettitte had grown up in nearby Deer Park, and his family still lived there, but he had been nothing but a Yankee. No longer. He would join Roy Oswalt in a new Houston rotation in 2004.

Almost as soon as Pettitte signed on, a groundswell began to bring in yet another Yankee who lived in the Houston area. How about convincing the 41-year-old just-retired Roger Clemens to again team with Pettitte in their home town?

Owner Drayton McLane Jr. started laying out the charm. He even drove to the Clemens home unannounced and left a baseball-themed Christmas ornament as a gift.

On January 19, 2004 the Astros and the six-time AL Cy Young Award winner announced Roger would play for two more years and had also agreed to a ten-year personal services contract after that.

Astro fans were ecstatic. The owner and management were very happy. And why not? Season ticket inquiries and orders were coming in at a faster rate than ever. The phones never stopped ringing in the Astro offices. Just as important, all the players on the team started looking forward to 2004. They saw big winning in the future.

As history records, the Astros, with one of their strongest teams ever, got off to a mediocre start, were never in contention for first place in the central division, had to change managers from Jimy Williams to Phil Garner at the All-Star break, but finished very strong and made the postseason as a wild card with a 92 – 70 record. They also added Carlos Beltrán just before midseason, and he played in 90 games plus the postseason.

Pettitte pitched through elbow pain much of the season and finally had to go on the disabled list in mid- August. Clemens was a wonder. He would win 18, lose 4, carry a 2.98 ERA, and win a NL Cy Young Award.

The Astros never won a World Series with Pettitte and Clemens, but in 2005, with Pettitte healthy, the Astros made it to the World Series for the first time in franchise history. Bringing in Andy and Roger for 2004 made it happen.

64

Bob Watson Breaks a Barrier as Astro GM

During the early years of the Houston Astros, Bob Watson was one of the team's top hitters. In parts or all of 14 seasons with the Astros, Bob hit .297 with 139 home runs and 782 RBIs. For a 19-year career overall, he hit .295, spending time with the Red Sox, Yankees, and Braves. One of his biggest and most unusual moments came in 1975 when he was credited with scoring Major League Baseball's one- millionth run. In the first game of a doubleheader with San Francisco, he was on second base when Milt May hit a home run. However, since word was out that 999,999 runs had been scored up to that second Watson ran full speed to get to home plate. He was given credit for edging Cincinnati's Dave Conception for the honor which brought him a lifetime supply of Tootsie Roll candy.

As good as he was, what happened with him after his playing career was over may have been more significant.

He got into team management first as a hitting coach with the Oakland A's, then as assistant GM and later GM of the Astros. He served in that role in 1994 and 1995. He became the second African- American to hold a GM's position (after Bill Lucas in Atlanta). Moving to the New York Yankees, he became the first African-American GM to lead a World Series Champion in 1996.

From 1998 through 2010, Watson held an executive position within Major League Baseball.

65

Don Nottebart Pitches First Houston No-Hitter

Though most of its franchise history, Houston has been best known for its pitching. Certainly, having names like Nolan Ryan, Roger Clemens, Randy Johnson, Don Sutton, Roy Oswalt, Joe Niekro, Justin Verlander, Mike Scott, J. R. Richard, Larry Dierker, Don Wilson, and Dallas Keuchel spend time on the mound adds to that respect, but others have earned respect as well.

A journeyman pitcher named Don Nottebart won't be forgotten thanks to his timing. He pitched the first no-hitter by a Houston hurler.

Nottebart wound up a nine-year major-league career with the Brewers, Astros, Reds, Yankees, and Cubs with a 36 – 51 record and 3.65 ERA in 296 games. His no-hit season with Houston would be the best he would have. He finished 1963, 11 – 8, with a superb 3.17 ERA.

His, and the franchise's special night, came on May 17, 1963, when the future Astros were still known as the Houston

Colt .45s. The veteran right-hander was on the mound at Colt Stadium facing the Philadelphia Phillies. Nottebart gave up an unearned run in the 4 – 1 victory, and said after the game he didn't even use his full arsenal of pitches. As he told the Houston Chronicle's Olen Clements after the game, "I didn't throw a curve all night. I could hear Gene Mauch [Philadelphia's manager] yelling from the dugout, 'You'll never make it Nottebart, you'll never make it,' and that gave me an extra push."

Actually Nottebart didn't need to be needled by Mauch that he had a no-hitter going. His own catcher, John Bateman, let him know. When Bateman saw his pitcher looking a bit perplexed on the mound, he ran out and said, "Hey, Notty, you've got a no-hitter going!" While that broke all of baseball's rules of superstition, it also relaxed Nottebart. Bateman had been coming out to the mound all night with less than encouraging thoughts. As Nottebart said after the game, "All night he'd been coming out and telling me that my fastball was dead or my slider was hanging. I just told him I knew. Just get back behind the plate and hold your glove up."

Nottebart may have not thrown a curve, and all his other stuff might have not impressed his catcher, but he did shut up Mauch with a slurvy slider, changeup, and fastball. He struck out eight and walked three.

His hitting support came initially from Carl Warwick who homered in the first and added a triple and two singles. The Philadelphia run scored as a result of shoddy defensive play and a sacrifice fly by Don Hoak.

Played before 8,223 fans that Friday night in just two hours and twelve minutes, the victory did little except keep the Colt .45s out of the cellar in the NL, but did put the night in the history books as a Houston first. And, as is often said, "You can only have one first." For no-hitters, this was it.

Astros No Hitters				
	Date	Win/Loss	Score	Opponent
Don Nottebart	2/17/63	W	4 – 1	Philidelphia Phillies
Ken Johnson	4/23/64	L	0 – 1	Cincinnati Reds
Don Wilson	6/18/67	W	2 – 0	Atlanta Braves
Don Wilson	5/1/69	W	4 – 0	Cincy Reds
Larry Dierker	7/9/76	W	6 – 0	Montreal Expos
Ken Forsch	4/7/79	W	6 – 0	Atlanta Braves
Nolan Ryan	9/26/81	W	5 – 0	LA Dodgers
Mike Scott	9/25/86	W	2 – 0	San Francisco Giants
Darryl Kile	9/8/93	W	7 – 1	NY Mets
Roy Oswalt, Peter Munro, Kirk Saarloos, Brad Lidge, Octavio Dotel, Billy Wagner	6/11/03	W-Munro	8 – 0	NY Yankees
Mike Fiers	8/21/15	W	3 – 0	LA Dodgeres
Aaron Sanchez, Will Harris, Joe Biagino, Chris Devenski	8/3/19	W-Aaron Sanchez	8 – 0	Seattle Mariners
Justin Verlander	9/1/19	W	2 – 0	Toronto BJays
Christian Javier, Hector Neris, Ryan Pressly	6/25/22	W-Javier	3 – 0	NY Yankees
Christian Javier, Bryan Abreu, Rafael Montero, Ryan Pressley	11/2/22	W-Javier	5 – 0	Philadelphia Phillies
Framber Valdez	8/1/23	W	2 – 0	Cleveland Guardians

66

Moisés Alou Falls Off a Treadmill

f Moisés Alou's career in Houston had been longer than three years, he would no doubt be remembered more as one of the best hitters ever to wear an Astro uniform.

Even in his relatively short term with the club, he was anyway. In fact, his .331 batting average as an Astro is solidly on top of the Houston list. He had 1551 plate appearances over the period from 1998 through 2001.

What hurt his memory the most was the 1999 season. He didn't play a single game due to an offseason freak injury. He tore the anterior cruciate ligament in his left knee when he was thrown from a treadmill. He might have made it back before the season was over, but he ran over his son while riding a bicycle. His son was unharmed, but Alou's knee injury was aggravated. The 1999 season was the second full season of his professional career he had missed. In 1991 while with Montreal, he was sidelined with a broken ankle. While he came back after missing that season, he had lost a good deal of the speed that was part of his game before. No longer a candidate to play center field he moved to a corner spot and made his major contributions with his bat.

He did very well there. Drafted by the Pirates as the second pick of the first round in 1986 out of Canada College in California, he was dealt to the Montreal Expos late in 1990 after five years in the Pirate farm system where he had started slowly but was just starting to come around in 1988 and 1989.

Moisés was the son of longtime major-league star and manager Felipe Alou. His uncles included Matty Alou and Jesús Alou. Jesús had manned left field for the Astros twenty years earlier.

For his career in the major leagues, which passed through Pittsburgh, Montreal, Florida, Houston, Chicago (Cubs), San Francisco, and New York (Mets), he played 17 seasons and had a career .303 batting average. He had 2134 hits, 332 home runs, and 1287 RBIs.

Sadly, injuries cost him a large number of games, likely keeping him from becoming a Hall of Famer. He only played more than 150 games four seasons of his 17, and six seasons appeared in less than 100 games. But he could hit. An average of well over .300 was not unusual. He hit .312, .355, and .331 in three seasons with Houston. However, there was that missing 1999 season between the .312 and the .355. His batting eye had not been hurt by the missing season, and the Astros did win their third straight division title even without him that year.

In three active Astro seasons, Alou never failed to drive in 100 runs or hit fewer than 27 home runs. His biggest home run season was surprisingly in his first season with the team when it still played in the Astrodome. Alou hit 38 home runs, drove in 124, and hit .312 as the Astros won a club-record 102 games in 1998.

In the first year of then Enron Field (now Minute Maid Park), he hit 30 home runs, drove in 114, and hit .355. He was part of the NL record-setting Astro team that launched 249 home runs.

Then, as his contract ran out after 2001 following a .331, 27 – 108 season, he moved on.

He signed as a free agent with the Cubs for 2002. He was good for Chicago and even clubbed a career- high 39 homers in Chicago in 2004, but his batting average in Chicago was only .283. He moved on as a free agent to the Giants and later the Mets, finally retiring at 41 after the 2008 season.

Moisés Alou had been on a World Series winner in Florida in 1997, but arguably was the best he would ever be during his three seasons in Houston. Fans only wonder what might have been had he stayed off the treadmill and bike and had been available in 1999. The man could really hit!

67

Astros Spin Six-Pitcher No-Hitter at Yanks in 2003

Until 2003 the Houston Astros had never played a game in either Yankee Stadium or Fenway Park. Being in the NL was the main reason, and once interleague play was instituted, it took that long for the Astros to head East.

When they finally visited the original Yankee Stadium and Fenway, they lost four of six games, but they left their mark.

It was on June 11. The Yankees had won the series opener the night before, 5 – 3, but tonight Astro ace Roy Oswalt would be on the mound. Luck was not on his side. In the first inning, Oswalt felt a twinge in his groin and had to leave the game. Manager Jimy Williams would have to go to his strong pen very early.

Peter Munro, who had been a spot starter, was given enough time to get warm and entered the game. He was a little wild with three walks, but was able to last two and two-thirds innings while the Astro hitters scored four runs. Kirk Saarloos got the third out in the fourth and worked a hitless fifth inning. Manager Williams decided to go to his "big three" in the pen an inning earlier than usual. Brad Lidge worked both the sixth and seventh. He was very sharp throwing 15 strikes in his 23 total pitches.

In the eighth inning Octavio Dotel was called in. Before he took the mound, the Astros hitters had added two more runs, and Houston led, 6 – 0. In his inning of work Dotel struck out four hitters! Alfonso Soriano had swung and missed on a bad pitch for strike three and made it to first on the wild pitch. But Dotel had struck out Juan Rivera to open the frame and closed it with strikeouts of Derek Jeter and Jason Giambi.

The Astros added two more runs in the top of the ninth and led, 8 – 0. So why was ace closer Billy Wagner coming in to pitch the last of the ninth? Manager Jimy Williams knew; Yankee owner George Steinbrenner thought he knew. But Astro second baseman Jeff Kent didn't have a clue.

Wagner and his 100-mile-an-hour fastball struck out both Jorge Posada and Bubba Trammel to open the ninth. Then on the first pitch to Hideki Matsui, an easy groundball went Jeff Bagwell's way at first base. Game over! Six Houston Astro pitchers had combined for a no-hit game! It was a feat never achieved in the major leagues before.

With the Astros celebrating as they came off the field, Jeff Kent had no idea why. Surely his teammates didn't think beating the Yankees in a regular season game was that a big deal. Then Jeff finally figured it out. Oh, a no-hitter. That makes a difference.

Meanwhile Yankee owner George Steinbrenner thought Jimy Williams was piling on by using ace closer Wagner with an 8 – 0 lead. George figured it was a grudge Williams had against the Yanks from his days managing the archrival Boston Red Sox. As for Williams, all he would say is the Astros had a chance to make history, and Wagner was rested.

It was a great night in Astros baseball history, and even Steinbrenner recognized it by sending six bottles of champagne to the Astro clubhouse in honor of the feat.

68

Aspromonte Keeps a Promise Three Times!

The Houston Colt .45s original third baseman, Bob Aspromonte, achieved a feat when the franchise was young that may never be duplicated. He was asked by a young fan to hit a home run for him and he did it on three separate occasions.

In 1962 he visited a young fan in a local hospital being treated after losing his sight from a nearby lightning strike at his home in Arkansas. Billy Bradley was the youngster's name, and he had been following the Colt .45s on the radio. He asked Bob if he would hit a homer in the game that night. Bob, never a big home run hitter, said he would try. And he did hit one.

A year later, after Bob and Billy had kept in touch through letters, Billy was back in Houston for follow up treatment. There was a game that night. Same request, and Aspromonte did even better. He hit a grand slam!

Finally in 1964, Billy had regained some sight and was present at Colt Stadium on July 26. The media and team knew the story. So, when Aspromonte did it for a third time with a first-inning grand slam, there were tears in the eyes of many. After Bob crossed home plate, the game was stopped so he and Billy could embrace and Billy could be presented the ball.

The story didn't end there. A year or so later, Billy had regained enough of his sight to play baseball again. One day Aspromonte received an envelope in the mail that contained a newspaper clipping. The clipping told the story of Billy Bradley pitching a no-hitter in a youth league game. Attached was a note: "This one's for you, Bob!"

69

Jeff Bagwell Fulfilled a Dying Youngster's Wish

I t was August 28, 2002, at Minute Maid Park. The Astros were hosting the San Diego Padres that night. Among the fans on hand was longtime backer Marty Cunningham, who was with a family from New Mexico that was in Houston while son, 11-year old Stephen Rael, was being treated for cancer at M. D. Anderson Hospital. Marty arranged for Stephen, who had already lost a leg to osteosarcoma and was also fighting multiple tumors in his lungs and near his heart, to be down on the field before the game to meet some of the players.

Team chaplain Gene Pemberton was there, and one of the players he brought over to meet Stephen was Jeff Bagwell. As Stephen put it to Houston Chronicle reporter Michael Murphy after the game, "It was cool. Jeff is my favorite player and for me to meet him was just great. I got so excited. I couldn't stop talking."

When the pair were getting acquainted it was Pemberton who suggested to Bagwell, after Jeff asked what he could do for the boy, assuming he might like an autographed ball or bat, that "You should try to hit a home run for him." At that point Bagwell said, "I'm going to try, but I'm not Babe Ruth."

In the fifth inning Bagwell came to the plate facing Padre pitcher Mike Bynum. The Astros trailed by a run. The count went to 2 – 2, and on the next pitch Jeff hit it well over the left-field wall. The game was tied, but it was far more important than that.

As Stephen's mother recalled, "Stephen just started screaming and yelling when the ball went out. He kept yelling, 'That's for me! That's for me!'"

He told his mom that he felt a very warm feeling through his body. She said Stephen looked up at her and said, "Mom, that [feeling] is an angel coming to visit me. That's the angel

Jerry Coli: Dreamstime

Jeff Bagwell hit one for a youngster.

who's going to cure me of my cancer."

It was the greatest moment of Stephen Rael's life, especially when, while Bagwell was rounding the bases, he looked up to where Stephen and his family were sitting and made a subtle point toward them. They knew that Jeff knew.

The only thing that would have made this story better would have been had an angel really been there and Stephen Rael beaten cancer. Sadly, he did not. But for a short period, Jeff Bagwell made him feel on top of the world. That has to count for something.

70

George Springer Becomes First Six for Six Astro

Astro outfielder George Springer had been named the 2017 World Series MVP, a multiple All Star—who even homered in the 2018 game, but something that happened earlier in the 2018 season put his name on top in the Astro record books. He came to the plate six times and got six hits.

The game was on May 7, 2018 at the Oakland Coliseum. Going into the game, Springer, more noted for power than batting average, was hitting .264 at game time. When the Astros 16 – 2 rout of the Athletics was over, Springer was hitting .292. All it took was having a six-for-six game at the plate. He became the first Houston player ever to be perfect with as many as six hits in a nine-inning game.

Springer's big game started with a double in the first inning. In the second inning, he crushed a 462-foot, three-run homer. In the fourth, he singled. His next two at-bats featured infield singles in both the fifth and seventh innings, and then, in the seventh, a strong single up the middle.

After the game, the team's top hitter and three-time AL batting champion José Altuve was in awe. He even gave his teammate a bow after he hit that seventh inning single. Altuve had never had more than a four-for-four game, even with all his successes. He knew George had done something very special.

Houston Single-Season Batting Leaders		
Jeff Bagwell	.368	1994
Moisés Alou	.355	2000
José Altuve	.346*	2017
José Altuve	.341*	2014
José Altuve	.338*	2016
Derek Bell	.334	1995
Rusty Staub	.333	1967
Moisés Alou	.331	2001
Lance Berkman	.331	2001
Craig Biggio	.325	1998
Carl Everett	.325	1999
Yuli Gurriel	.319*	2021

* AL Batting Champion

71

Astros Trail 11-0 Early, But Come Back to Win

**E**very season the phrase "The games never over until the last man is out," is repeated hundreds of times—usually when one team falls behind early by a number of runs.

While it is technically true since baseball is played without a game length clock, large comebacks rarely carry through to victory. But it does happen sometimes.

For the Houston Astros it happened on July 18, 1994 at the Astrodome. On that night against the St. Louis Cardinals, the Astros trailed, 11 – 0, after just three innings. They closed the deficit to 11 – 4 by the sixth inning. Then they exploded for 11 runs in that frame to take a 15 – 11 lead which would hold on for most of the final score.

The Cards scored their first three before an out had been registered in the top of the opening inning. A Gregg Jefferies two-run homer ended starter Brian Williams's game. Another run came in off reliever Tom Edens, and it was 7 – 0 St. Louis after two innings.

In the third inning, a double, triple, and three more singles off Edens made it 11 – 0.

The Astros scored two in the fourth and added two more in the fifth. A Jeff Bagwell solo homer contributed. The score was 11 – 4, St. Louis, and stayed that way until the bottom of the sixth.

The Astros exploded. Craig Biggio started things with a walk. Pinch-hitter Kevin Bass brought Biggio home with a double. After a pitching change, Bagwell popped out. But Ken Caminiti walked. Luis Gonzalez singled home a run. James Mouton was hit by a pitch. Tony Eusebio walked with the bases loaded to bring in a run. The Cards changed pitchers again, but Roger Cedeño greeted the new pitcher with a two-run single.

The Astros were within two runs, and Mike Felder tied things with a two-run game-tying triple. Houston was not finished yet. Biggio beat out a roller to third, but Felder had to stay put. Never mind as Bass's single broke the tie. Another Cardinal pitching change, and Biggio stole second base. Bagwell walked to reload the bases. Caminiti ripped a single to left that scored two. Houston led, 14 – 11. The eleven-run inning concluded after James Mouton hit a sacrifice fly to score Bagwell. The score was in favor of the Astros, 15 – 11.

Doug Jones came in to pitch for Houston. He gave up a run in the top of the ninth, but that was all the Cardinals would get. Their comeback failed after the Astros had wiped out an eleven run deficit. They won, 15 – 12.

72

Astros Trailed by Six in 8th, but Rallied to Win in 2017

efore Houston's major-league baseball team played a game in Minnesota on May 29, 2017, they had never won a game in which they trailed by six or more runs when entering the eighth inning. Houston was 0 – 659!

Not only did that change, but the Astros equaled a team record set in 1994 by scoring eleven runs in one inning. They did it in the eighth!

Going into the eighth inning that game, Minnesota led, 8 – 2.

While a rally that large was unexpected, that THIS team did it was not. The Astros entered the contest with the best record in baseball and the largest division lead. Since opening day they had not looked back. The comeback was done the 2017 Astros way.

The refused to play the scoreboard. They refused to give up at-bats. They just played.

Josh Reddick walked to open the inning, then José Altuve

José Altuve had three of the Astros' 18 hits.

was hit by a pitch. Carlos Correa singled to score Reddick. Then Carlos Beltrán topped a ball to third. He beat it out for a hit. Brian McCann was retired on a pop fly, but Marwin Gonzalez singled to drive in two runs. Twin reliever Craig Breslow replaced Ryan Pressly on the mound.

Alex Bregman greeted Breslow with a single that loaded the bases. Evan Gattis hit a groundball, but Minnesota could not turn a double play. A run scored with Gattis safe at first with two out. The Astros were within two runs at 8 – 6 and George Springer to the plate when rain forced a ten-minute delay.

After the shower passed, the Astro hot run had not cooled. Springer singled scoring Gonzalez and the Astros were within a run. Reddick then doubled to bring home two and put Houston on top, 8 – 7. With Altuve at the plate, new pitcher Matt Belisle balked, sending Reddick into scoring position. Altuve didn't leave him there when he singled to bring Reddick home. Carlos Correa walked, and Carlos Beltrán capped the inning with a three run homer. Houston led, 13 – 8, after an eleven-run eighth.

The Astros still weren't done in the game. In the top of the ninth, they added three more on a two-run homer from Alex Bregman and a groundout RBI by Carlos Correa.

Houston had 16 runs on 18 hits. Carlos Beltrán had four hits while José Altuve and Carlos Correa had three each. Beltrán and Correa each drove in three runs. In the big eighth inning, fourteen players had come to the plate, and they scored seven of the eleven runs after there were two outs.

73

J.R. Richard Fans 15 in First Start

When James Rodney Richard made his major-league debut as a starting pitcher in the major leagues, his potential was obvious from the start. As a September call-up from the AAA Oklahoma City 89ers, he made his first start at just 21 years old on September 5, 1971 against the San Francisco Giants in the second game of a doubleheader played at Candlestick Park in San Francisco.

The Giants lineup had a few starters being given the second game off, but Willie Mays was there, playing first base for one of the rare times in his career. Bobby Bonds was in right field. The Astros lineup featured Jesús Alou, Joe Morgan, César Cedeño, Denis Menke, and John Mayberry.

In the last of the first inning, with Richard making his starting debut, things did not begin well. He had to face six hitters and give up two runs on a two-out double by Al Gallagher before he got Chris Speier on a groundout to end the inning. Richard's highlight was a strikeout of Willie Mays, the only K he would record in the frame.

In the last of the second, he walked a hitter, but gave up

no-hits or runs. He struck out pitcher Jim Willoughby for his second of the game.

The game moved to the third with the Astros still trailing 2 – 0. They rallied against Willoughby. With two out, Alou tripled and Morgan walked before the "twin Césars," Geronimo and Cedeño, both singled to tie the game at 2 – 2.

That may have stimulated Richard. He struck out the side, Tito Fuentes, Mays, and Bonds, in the bottom of the third.

The Astros took the lead in the top of the fourth after a leadoff single by John Mayberry and a Larry Howard single made it Houston, 3 – 2.

Richard didn't strike out anyone in a four-hitter fourth. Then the "twin Césars" did it again in the fifth. After a walk and stolen base by Joe Morgan, César Geronimo doubled him home. Then César Cedeño singled to score Geronimo. Houston led, 5 – 2.

Richard struck out two more in the last of the fifth, including Willie Mays for the third time.

In the sixth he struck out Bonds and Jimmy Rosario as the Astros held their lead, 5 – 2. In the bottom of the seventh, Richard caught Dick Dietz looking for a strikeout to open the inning.

In the eighth inning Mays avoided being fanned four times when he opened the inning with a walk. The Giants scored on a two-out error by Menke at third, and J. R. was in trouble until he struck out pinch- hitter Fran Healy to end the threat. He had struck out Gallagher earlier, and after eight innings Richard had 12 strikeouts.

The Astros went down in order in the top of the night, and Richard went back to the mound looking to nail down the game, 5 – 3. To say he did it is an understatement. With victory in sight, J. R. was unstoppable. He struck out Dietz, Ken Henderson, and Hal Lanier in order to end the game.

The 15 strikeouts in a first start tied the major league record set by Karl Spooner of the Brooklyn Dodgers in late 1954. Richard had just two earned runs while surrendering seven hits. He walked only three.

Despite the impressive debut, Richard would take some time to develop the command and control to become the star pitcher he was between 1976 and 1980 when a stroke ended his career. Still, on September 5, 1971, he showed the baseball world what he would become.

74

Jimmy Wynn's Homecoming Tape Measure Blast

immy Wynn was the first power hitter for the Houston Major League Baseball franchise. His career started with the Houston Colt .45s in 1963 and extended until 1977 with the Milwaukee Brewers. In Houston he was dubbed the "Toy Cannon" by sports writer John Wilson for Jimmy's power hitting from a relative small (5-foot, 9-inch, 160 pound) body. He was a Houston star from the start until 1973, when he was traded to the Dodgers for Claude Osteen and a minor leaguer. However, eleven of his 15 major- league seasons were in Houston uniforms.

Until Jeff Bagwell came along, Wynn held all the Houston home run records. He hit 291 in his career and 223 as an Astro.

He had two very memorable homers. The first was in his own home town.

It was on June 11, 1967 at Cincinnati's old Crosley Field. That was where Jimmy as a youth had seen countless games since he only lived a few blocks away. Reds stars like Frank Robinson and Vada Pinson had often helped him get past the gates. Wynn was originally signed by the hometown team. He was a graduate of Taft High School and attended Central State University in Wilberforce, Ohio, before signing with the Reds as an amateur free agent in 1962. However, after the 1962 season, he was drafted by the new Houston Colt .45s in the first-year draft.

By 1967 Wynn was an established star in the NL. In fact, despite playing home games in the cavernous Astrodome, he would battle the great Hank Aaron for the NL home run title down to the wire. Jimmy tells the story that what he did registered with Aaron. "He called me after he tied me with 37 and said he wasn't going to play the season's final games. The Commissioner got word of that and said he had to play or he would be fined. So, he played and hit two more," Wynn recalled in 2018. Aaron would win, 39 – 37, but Jimmy said Aaron called him the real champ that year. Hank was well aware how much harder it was to hit homers playing in the Astrodome than Atlanta's Fulton County Stadium. The total Jimmy registered at only 25 years old would wind up his career high and remain the most any Astro hitter would achieve in a season until Jeff Bagwell cracked 39 in 1994.

Still, there is little doubt that the home run Jimmy hit on that June day in Cincinnati will never be forgotten. In came in the second game of a doubleheader. The Astros had won the opener, 7 – 1. The second game was tied at 1 – 1 when Jimmy came to the plate to face right-hander Sammy Ellis. On the second pitch Wynn hit the ball right on the nose. As Jimmy told Bill McCurdy in the biography, Toy Cannon, "The ball took off from my bat on a high speeding arc to left field, changing quickly from ball size, to pea size to dot size as I watched it disappearing into the afternoon Cincinnati sky. No way has the ballpark held this one, I thought, so I began my trot at a respectable pace around the bases. Before I even reached first base, I heard a moaning rush of oohs and aahs, especially from the stadium seats that had a clear view of the area beyond Crosley Field."

The ball had soared over the big scoreboard in left-center field and didn't stop there. In landed on the I- 74 freeway that ran beyond the park. Then it took a high bounce and headed down a street that led directly to the neighborhood where Jimmy grew up.

While there is a television record of the ball clearing the scoreboard and bouncing on the freeway the rest of the story comes from those who claim that ball was found on Colrain Avenue. That was Jimmy Wynn's boyhood home street. He grew up in a house at 1917 Colrain!

Sadly, the length of travel for the ball was never measured, but it will always be remembered.

Jimmy says that if one of his managers, Harry Walker, had his way, there would have been a lot fewer homers. Walker who had won the NL batting title in the 1940s with a modified slap-and-run strategy. As a hitting coach in Pittsburgh, he took credit for turning Matty Alou into the 1966 batting champion with a .366 average that featured a lot of contact, but few homers and extra-base hits. Walker called it "pop and glide." It involved waiting as long as possible before swinging, which wasn't a new concept, but it also included hitting off the front foot and taking the pitch to the opposite field. Jimmy hit enough homers that he could usually ignore Walker, but others could not.

Wynn said his favorite manager was one of Houston's first—Lum Harris. "He had few rules. He told the players to be themselves, play hard, have fun, and win games," recalled Jimmy, "I think that is how you have to treat players over such a long season."

75

Rader and Wynn First to Hit the Dome's Upper Deck in 1970

 hree seasons after Jimmy Wynn had hit his mammoth home run in Cincinnati, both he and Doug Rader did something for the home fans.

On April 3, 1970, in an exhibition game against the Yankees before the season opened, Astro third baseman Doug Rader blasted a home run into the upper deck at the Astrodome where a ball had never gone before.

However, only nine days later in a regular season game, Jimmy Wynn did it too. His second homer of the game off the Atlanta Braves' Phil Niekro on April 12 landed in the same gold section (738C, row 6, seat 3) that Rader had found just a few seats away. Jimmy said, "I got a glimpse of both of my homers. The first was off a knuckleball which was not one of Niekro's best. The long one was off either a fastball or slider. When you hit a ball that hard, you've got to look." Jimmy wouldn't have to guess where he hit the ball in the future.

For years, the two seats where Rader and Wynn hit the first two balls that far were memorialized. Rader was known as the Red Rooster and that logo was painted on the seat where he ball landed. Jimmy's seat saw a toy cannon painted on—the nickname sportswriter John Wilson had hung on him years before.

76
Nolan Ryan Reaches 4,000 Strikeouts

When Nolan Ryan became baseball's all-time strikeout leader, he was a Houston Astro. As the 1982 season ended, he and Steve Carlton were battling to hold on to the top spot. There was a real question which hurler would be first to break the record. Brad Mills of the Montreal Expos became Nolan's 3509th strikeout on April 27, 1983, pushing him past long time record-holder Walter Johnson. Two weeks later Carlton would also best Johnson's old record, but never get close to Ryan again. Carlton finished his career with 4136 strikeouts. Following the 2018 season, that ranked third all-time, with one- time Astro Randy Johnson resting in second place with 4875.

Nolan's first major milestone strikeout—his 3000th—had come against César Geronimo of the Reds on July 4, 1980, also while an Astro. A footnote was that Geronimo had also been

Bob Gibson's 3000th victim in 1974.

Once Ryan passed Johnson, the next milestone was to become the first to 4000 whiffs. That occurred on July 11, 1985 against former Astro Danny Heep.

With six strikeouts through five innings against the New York Mets, Ryan faced the left-handed Heep leading off the sixth. Ryan wasted no time. He got Heep on three pitches with his strikeout pitch an overhand curve in the dirt that Heep could not lay off. The large crowd at the Astrodome immediately rose and showered Ryan with a standing ovation. Among those on hand was Baseball Commissioner Peter Ueberroth.

Coming into the game, Ryan had an 89 strikeout edge over Steve Carlton, who was on the disabled list at the time.

After Ryan fanned Heep for the milestone and the ovation died down, he wasn't finished. He struck out both Rafael Santana and Sid Fernandez to finish the inning with a flourish. He would strike out two more in the last inning he worked, the seventh, and finish the game with eleven strikeouts and 4004 for his career. Afterward the 38-year-old Ryan said, "The two keys for me are due to the fact that I've concentrated so many years on good mechanics of pitching and also I've concentrated on being as well- conditioned as possible."

Nolan Ryan was the first to 4000 and the only pitcher to 383.

That statement would be emphasized as Ryan pitched for eight more seasons, finally retiring after the 1993 season with 5714 strikeouts. His 5000th strikeout came in a Texas Ranger uniform in 1989 when he fanned Ricky Henderson.

When it was all over, Ryan would have played all or parts of 27 major-league seasons and six times striking out 300 or more, including the major-league record 383 with the Angels in 1983. He led his league in strikeouts eleven times while winning 324 games. He spread out his greatest moments between the Angels, Astros, and Rangers and striking out number 4000 was one of his great Astro memories.

77

Bob Bruce Tying a Record Never to be Broken

If records are made to be broken, some are made to be only tied. Houston Colt .45s pitcher Bob Bruce has one of those. On April 19, 1964, the lefty faced the Cardinals and struck out the side in the eighth inning. He did it only nine pitches. No one can ever do it better. Unfortunately, for the Colt .45s, the whole game was not that good. Bob Gibson kept Houston at bay and took a 6 – 1 victory. Just the same, Bruce put his name on a rather long line in the record books and no one can ever do better. Bob was pitching in relief of starter Don Nottebart, who had allowed the St. Louis runs. In two innings, Bruce recorded all six outs with strikeouts. He did allow one hit, a single to Johnny Lewis, leading off the top of the ninth.

Bruce was the first, but several other Houston pitchers have also done a nine-pitch, three strikeout inning. Pete Harnisch

Bob Bruce used only nine pitches to strike out the side.

in 1991, Mike Magnante in 1997, Randy Johnson in 1998, Shane Reynolds in 1999, and Brandon Backe in 2004 all completed the feat.

Sandy Koufax did it three times, and both Nolan Ryan and Randy Johnson twice, but neither of the former did it for Houston.

Pitchers have struck out more than three in an inning due to wild pitches or passed balls allowing the hitter to reach first. But that act takes the perfection out of the matter. Three strikeout on the nine pitches is the best that can be done.

78

Greatest Pitching Feat Against Astros and All-Time

On May 6, 1998, the Houston Astros were in Chicago to face the Cubs. They had their regular lineup in the game to face hard-throwing native Texan Kerry Wood. Wood pitched what many believe was the most dominant game in baseball history. Only a third-inning single by Ricky Gutiérrez kept Wood from throwing a perfect game no-hitter with 20 strikeouts!

When Derek Bell fanned to end the game, his 20th strikeout victim set the then-NL record and tied Roger Clemens major-league mark. Add that fact that there were no walks and only Gutiérrez reached base, and his feat almost became revered.

The Astro team he beat had a lineup that day featuring Craig Biggio, Derek Bell, Jeff Bagwell, Moisés Alou, Jack Howell, Dave Clark, Gutiérrez, Brad Ausmus, and pinch-hitter Bill Spiers. Houston would wind the season up by winning a then team-record 102 games.

79

Longest Shutout in MLB History at the Dome in '68

The Astrodome was famed for low-scoring pitchers' duels. The epitome happened on April 15, 1968, when the Astros and New York Mets played 23 innings with no runs. Finally, in the last of the 24th inning, Norm Miller scored when a grounder by Bob Aspromonte got past Mets shortstop Al Weis. Weis said, "It didn't take a bad hop. I just blew it. It went right through my legs."

The game lasted six hours, six minutes. The Astros Hal King and Mets Jerry Grote caught the whole game. It was a game to forget for Ron Swoboda and Tommy Agee of the Mets. Both were 0 – 10 at the plate. Aspromonte had the roughest game for an Astro. He was 0 – 9. The famed Astrodome scoreboard got into the act in last of the 22nd inning when it flashed, "The judge says he is ready for bed. Let's score a run!" Judge Roy Hofheinz, the Astros primary owner lived in an apartment built inside the right-field wall.

After about the 17th inning, said Astro outfielder Rusty

Staub, "Things got kind of funny." Astros coach Buddy Hancken was facing a crisis. "That was a three-package-of-chewing tobacco game. I just got one chaw left." A game to remember, but best only to read about and not to have witnessed or played in.

In 1989, the Astros and Dodgers played a 22-inning game at the Astrodome won by Houston, 5 – 4, on an RBI single from Rafael Ramirez off emergency pitcher Jeff Hamilton. The hit was deflected off the glove of emergency first baseman Fernando Valenzuela and scored Bill Doran. Hamilton was normally an infielder and Valenzuela usually a pitcher. The second part of this story is that both clubs played a 13- inning game the next day with Houston winning again, 7 – 6.

80

Berkman's Acrobatic Catch on Tal's Hill

When the Astros left the Astrodome for what was first known as Enron Field, the natural grass field with retractable roof in downtown Houston, one of the most unique features was in deep center field. At about the 400 foot mark, the field went from flat to a sloping terrace that stopped at the fence 436 feet away named "Tal's Hill" after the long time Astro executive who had several jobs from farm director to GM to president since the birth of the Colt .45s.

The hill was an homage to a number of similar hills in ballparks of yore. Most notably—and the last sloped outfield in baseball—Crosley Field in Cincinnati where Smith had broken into baseball in the 1950s was remembered.

Other parks had not been all flat. Wrigley Field in Chicago and Boston's Fenway Park once had very sharp rises before outfielders hit the outfield wall. At Fenway in left field it was called "Duffy's Cliff" because a Red Sox outfielder Hugh Duffy

Lance Berkman could hit and made many memorable plays.

became adept at handling the hill and still catching fly balls.

Another outfielder named Smead Jolley was infamous for never figuring it out. After being coached on how to go up the embankment and catch the ball, he had a game in which a batted ball went through his legs, and when he chased it down going up the hill, he fell as he tried to throw the ball to the infield. He made a wild throw and got three errors on the play. Afterward when asked about it he said, "I worked a lot on going up the hill, but never worked on coming down."

While that may be a humorous and at least roughly accurate story, both Crosley and Fenway's inclines were far different than the one constructed in Houston. Houston's Tal's Hill was so far from home plate it rarely was involved in play. But when it was, it could lead to some exciting moments.

Los Angeles Dodger outfielder Dave Roberts was remembered as handling the hill better than any outfielder ever to play it against the Astros one night. He had to actually go up the hill to catch three fly balls in the same game— probably the only time in the hill's life that had ever happened in the same game. Roberts made the catches as if he were running on flat ground. Very smooth.

Lance Berkman made a catch on the hill that lives in highlight videos and was one of the great, awkward and toughest catches those that saw it will never forget.

Berkman was essentially a first baseman who had to break in as an outfielder since future Hall of Famer Jeff Bagwell was at first. But he was, at worst, an average outfielder, and he carried a Hall of Fame skilled bat. So, on May 18, 2002, he was playing the outfield and stationed in center field against the Pirates. A ball by Pittsburgh outfielder Rob Mackowiak was really hit, heading toward the 436 foot wall and very high in the air. Berkman had time to climb the hill while keeping his eye on the ball. He started coming at it slightly from the right then looked up about three feet from the fence in the deepest part of the park, and with his number 27 fully in view, reached up and took the ball with both hands just before he hit the ground. As Milo Hamilton called it with partner Alan Ashby on radio, "High fly ball by Mackowiak . . . sends a high fly ball to center. Berkman back up on the terrace . . . and . . . did he hang on? I believe he did! He did! He did! He did! . . . Holy Toledo! What an unbelievable play! The ball was hit 430 feet if it was hit an inch. He went up the terrace . . . almost seemed like he was bending the wrong way . . . fell to the ground and the ball went into his glove!" Ashby added, "It was clearly the best play we have seen on the terrace at Astros Field."

After the catch, the crowd of 34,921 roared. Lance sat on the turf facing home plate with a wide grin on his hatless face. The catch was a classic.

81

Colt .45s Started Nine Rookies in One Game

uch was made about how the Houston Astros won 101 games and the World Series in 2017. They did it with a nucleus of very talented young players augmented with key veterans prior to and within the season.

However, building a team from scratch, which was nearly what the Astros did after three straight 100 loss seasons between 2011 and 2013, was nothing new in Houston. They tried to do it in the early years of the Colt .45s. The result wasn't there, but the effort was obvious.

It was never more obvious than on September 27, 1963, when the Colt .45s featured a nine-man lineup with nothing but rookies.

Starting pitcher Jay Dahl was the youngest at 17 years, nine months. The oldest was Jimmy Wynn who was just 21 years, six months.

The lineup included several players who would make a mark in the major leagues, but not all for the Houston franchise.

Dahl was the second choice to be the starting pitcher, but Larry Yellen begged off because the game was to be played on a Jewish holiday. Yellen would ultimately play in 14 major-league games with the Colt .45s with an 0 – 0 record and 6.23 ERA. Dahl's future was more tragic.

After suffering a back injury in 1964, which saw him play the outfield for a few games, he returned to the mound in Salisbury, North Carolina in 1965. After his first thirteen games he had a 6 – 1 record with two complete games, a shutout, and an ERA of 3.50. He had given up only 58 hits in 72 innings pitched while striking out 49. He was a bit wild with 46 walks, but was on his way back to Houston. In 25 minor- league games, 20 of them starts, he was 11 – 2 with a 2.50 ERA. He had given up 93 hits in 133 innings pitched with 122 strikeouts. He was a real prospect.

Then came the auto accident that ended his life before he reached his 20th birthday. He was in a car with fellow passenger Patricia Troutman that was driven by teammate Gary Marshall. They were coming home from dinner at a team booster's home on January 20, 1965. The car, travelling at a high speed, apparently hit a patch of sand on Lincolnton Road just outside Salisbury. The car went out of control and struck a tree. Troutman was killed instantly. Dahl died three hours later at a hospital. The driver, Marshall, survived but suffered a broken arm and leg and was blinded.

Marshall devoted his life to the ministry tending to the newly blinded. He died in 2006 at 62 years of age.

Dahl became a tragic baseball footnote: The youngest player to die after playing in the major leagues.

The rest of those in the Colt .45s All Rookie Lineup had baseball careers of note. Catcher Jerry Grote, a native Texan, made his fame as the backstop for the Mets in 1969 and 1973 when they won two World Series. He would be the Colt .45s catcher in 100 games in 1964, but only hit .181 and was traded to the Mets after a 1965 minor-league season at Oklahoma

City for Tom Parsons.

At first base was Rusty Staub. Rusty would have six solid seasons in Houston with both the Colt .45s and Astros. He played both first base and outfield. His best season was 1967, when he led the NL with 44 doubles and batted .333. After 1968 he was traded to Montreal and would play the next 17 seasons with the Expos, Mets, Tigers, and Texas.

The second baseman in the all-rookie game was Joe Morgan. He was the only member of the group that would be a future Hall of Famer. Unfortunately for Houston fans, what he did in Cincinnati, his second stop, would be where he would win those credentials. He actually spent more seasons (10) with Houston than with any other team, but he was at his best as a Red. Houston got him at the beginning and end of his 22-year career. His best Houston season was in 1965 when the Colt .45s became the Astros and moved into the Astrodome. Joe led the NL with 97 walks while hitting .271 to go with 14 homers, 40 RBIs, and 20 stolen bases. He would steal as many as 49 with Houston and hit as many as 15 home runs. His batting average was significantly higher during his Cincinnati years.

Shortstop Sonny Jackson was one of five starters in the game, not yet 20 years old. He would play for Houston through the 1967 season but was only a regular for his last two seasons. Then he moved on to Atlanta where he played for the Braves through 1974.

As a Houston player, Sonny played in only the all-rookie game in 1963, but when he came back for good in 1966 he was ready. He hit .292 and stole 14 bases. In Atlanta, his rep was defense first, hitting was bonus. He hung around on the AAA level with the Padres and White Sox before retiring and going into coaching in 1977.

Glenn Vaughan played third base in the all-rookie game. That season would mark his and eight other players' only major-league action. He hit .167, going five for 30. The next season, after a .270 2HR 44RBI season at AAA Oklahoma

City, his career ended at age 20. His life didn't however. Glenn, a Houston Lanier High School graduate, enrolled at the University of Houston. After graduating he spent his life working in insurance and real estate. He died of natural causes at age 60 in 2004.

In the Colt .45s' all-rookie outfield was Jimmy Wynn, who became one of the franchise's all-time home run leaders and longtime major-league star. He was flanked by Brock Davis in left field. Davis was the second-youngest starter behind Dahl. He would author a major-league career spanning six seasons with the Colt 45s, Cubs, and Brewers. While primarily a top-level minor-league star, his best major-league season was with the Cubs in 1971. In 106 games, he hit .256.

The right fielder had fame in the family, it just wasn't from Aaron Pointer. Aaron would only see action in 40 major-league games with the Colt .45s and Astros between 1963 and 1967. He was a key member of the club's AAA teams at Oklahoma City, however.

In Pointer's minimal major-league time, he hit just .208 with two home runs, 15 RBIs and two stolen bases.

However, his sisters were learning how to sing. The Pointer Sisters were one of the music world's top groups in the 1970s and 1980s. They started as a duet then added two more sisters as they grew of age. Hits such as "Slow Hand," and "I'm So Excited" were extremely popular for them. As time went on, some sisters moved on and were replaced by other relatives. Sadly, Aaron was never asked to join.

82

First Dark Days of Houston Baseball

**W**hile everything turned out great with the Houston Astros winning the 2017 World Series, there is little question the club was in the darkest period of its history from 2011 until 2015. The teams set records for losses during that period. However, it was not the first stretch of dark days in Houston. The first one threatened the very existence of the team in the city.

The Houston Astrodome was only a few years old when financial problems began to appear in the Roy Hofheinz empire. He had bought out his primary partner R. E. Bob Smith, and with members of his family, had almost dictatorial control over what he was building called Astrodomain. The deal included the baseball team and the lease on the Astrodome, a nearby hotel, the Astroworld amusement park, additional buildings on the Astrodome property such as the Astrohall and Astroarena, and even the Ringling Brothers, Barnum and Bailey Circus. The company also owned over 300 acres of prime land south of the city of Houston.

To buy all of that, the Judge had to secure a loan to cover

the debts accrued in buying and developing those properties. He secured one for $38 million from four banks and two major credit companies.

The original hope was that revenues from the Astros, circus, and rental of the Astrodome would be enough to cover the interest and principle on the loan. While all made money, it wasn't enough to cover the loan and run the operations. Ultimately over a period of years, it became too much, and even trying to sell parts of the Hofheinz empire was not enough. Partly, because the judge, who had been felled by a stroke early in the process (May 1970), was reluctant to sell.

He did work out a deal to sell his controlling interest in the Ringling Brothers, Barnum and Bailey Circus to the Mattel toy company for stock, but found later that unscrupulous operations within Mattel eventually resulted in the stock being nearly worthless. Hofheinz sued and won, but it was too late and too little to help enough.

New owners were sought. John Mecom, a Houstonian who owned the NFL New Orleans Saints was a candidate. Fears that the city might lose the Astros were first heard. Hofheinz, though in a weakened condition both physically and fiscally, said the Astros would not be leaving the Dome. Still, rumors were strong. Mecom ultimately dropped out for a number of reasons, and no other serious candidates were evident. Eventually, things began to be untenable, and by 1975 it was obvious to many observers that Hofheinz would soon have to relinquish control and sell out.

By the end of 1976, Hofheinz was no longer the primary owner. At first the creditors who assumed control of the operation kept Hofheinz on the board, but ultimately that "honorary" position was obvious. The family finally sold their stock, and when the four banks who were owed made settlements, the General Electric and Ford Credit corporations took over Astrodomain, including the Astros.

As a somewhat sad footnote, after Hofheinz had moved all his personal belongings and emptied the unique living quarters he had established in both the Astrodome and Astro Hotel, he wanted to rent a sky box to continue to support the team. The credit companies refused to allow him.

As one must realize while all this was going on, from roughly 1970 until September 23, 1976 when the sale to GE and Ford took place, the Astros were pretty much treading water in the NL. During that seven- year period, they never finished higher than third in the NL West, and usually were fourth or lower in the six-team division. They had only two .500-plus seasons (they were 84 – 69 in 1972 which was the best in team history to that point, and 82 – 80 the next year), and one .500 season (81 – 81 in 1974). Under managers Harry Walker, Leo Durocher, and Preston Gomez, the Astros were as good as they ever had been, but compared to their expansion partners the New York Mets, who had won two World Series by 1976, were still lacking. Attendance had dropped under one million in both 1975 (858,002) and 1976 (886,146). Attendance was never lower than that in any of the Astrodome years, and lowest in franchise history since they played outdoors as the Houston Colt .45s.

This should have been a period when the club would have been able to build a winner. Free agency did not become a factor until after 1976. The club had enough time, but for financial and perhaps management reasons, they were only mediocre. Spec Richardson was the guiding hand for much of that time. When Tal Smith was brought back in midseason of 1975 to replace Richardson, things started to turn. His first and perhaps most important move was hiring Bill Virdon to manage the team starting in 1976.

Off the field, the dark days weren't over. Doing "the best you can do for the least you can spend" was the unstated mantra. Smith had to find players to draft and sign that were affordable. The same went with building the Astros major-league club. Free agency came to Major League Baseball only a few months after he took over. That drastically started to change the cost of doing business.

The Astros went without a real owner until May 11, 1979 when John McMullen bought the club and remaining parts of Astrodomain for the bargain price of $19 million. Smith, with McMullen and his 25 limited partners backing him, built the Astros into a contender and division champion by 1980 and had the nucleus and system in place for more success from 1980 to 1986. Smith only saw 1979 and 1980 working for McMullen. Conflicts ended the relationship after the 1980 season.

Bill Virdon guided the Astros past their first "dark days."

83

The Second "Dark Ages" Were Part of a Plan

**W**hile the first Houston baseball dark ages in the 1970s was the result of financial mistakes, the second (from 2011 to 2015) was expected as part of a rebuilding plan. The Astros won the 2017 World Series and remained a power for years so it obviously worked.

Still it was a gamble. Nothing in sports is really a sure bet.

From about 2008, Astro owner Drayton McLane Jr. was looking to sell his team. He had owned the club since 1993. Neither of his two sons were interested in taking over the club, so to head off inheritance tax burdens, he was open to offers. He was not publicly selling out and never made any public acclamations the team was for sale. However, a good offer would make it happen.

As it turned out, he got an offer he could accept. A local Houston businessman named Jim Crane who had made his fortune primarily in the shipping industry made a bid. But when the nation's economic fortunes took dive in 2008, Crane

Drayton McLane owned the Astros during some good years.

backed out. McLane was not happy.

Still the club was unofficially back on the market, and one major decision McLane made was not to invest heavily in long-term contracts for veterans. In addition, he would instruct his staff to emphasize amateur scouting and farm system development. This would keep costs lower on the major-league level while hopefully still providing enough players for at least a representative team. Any new owner would not be buying a team with a number of long-term financial player-contract commitments. Some would also argue that it would mean that the price might be higher in sales negotiations since the new owner would not try to lower it to cover those existing contracts.

During the final McLane years, the last long-term high dollar contract the team signed was for outfielder Carlos Lee prior to the 2007 season. At the time, the Astros were only a season past their first World Series appearance, and it was hoped Lee's bat would be enough to boost the Astro offense back into the Series again. He did his part in 2007 by hitting .303 with 32 home runs and 119 RBIs. Even with Lance Berkman and Hunter Pence also having strong offensive seasons, the team finished only 73 – 89, primarily because only Roy Oswalt pitched well. The excitement in 2007 was Craig Biggio reaching 3000 hits before he retired after the season.

In 2008, the Astros surprisingly contended for a wild card and finished back over .500 at 86 – 75, but the team was essentially treading water. They were lacking deep pitching, and most acquisitions were moderately paid vets and not star players.

McLane and Crane also worked on their first deal in the 2008 season. In 2009 and 2010, McLane was quiet about selling the Astros, but his ears were open.

Finally, on November 21, 2010, Drayton McLane Jr. opened up and publicly announced the team was for sale. He wanted a local owner or ownership group but would listen to all.

In the meantime, Jim Crane had put in bids to buy a couple other clubs including the Chicago Cubs and Texas Rangers. Both clubs went local, so he looked at the Astros again.

As upset as McLane was with Crane when he pulled out of a tentative deal in 2008, offering large amounts of money can change things. This time the pair was able to work something out. The changeover took some time. A deal was announced in 2011, and finally, after MLB vetted the new owners, on November 17, 2011 the club had a new owner.

It had taken some time for approval since the amount of debt Crane would be assuming was higher than MLB preferred. Also, the many minority owners involved in the deal would have to be checked out. But when the vote was made, it was unanimous

Since the approval didn't come until so late in 2011, deep changes could not be made prior to the season beginning. The farm system and most staff positions stayed in place. The team would have a new President, general manager, manager, and staff, but trainers, broadcasters, media relations folk, and most sales positions would continue to be manned by the veterans. A new GM would not be in place until early December.

The biggest change was in philosophy. No longer would the Astros try to patch holes. They would invest heavily in scouting, drafting, and development. Young players would be the priority. Veterans would be moved out to make room for the kids which cut salary costs dramatically, but more was being spent on scouting. Money was also being spent in the analytic development of not only how the game should be played, but what players might be the best fit based on almost minutia-like statistics.

Even before the Crane group finished the purchase, the Astros had cleared the books by trading veterans Hunter Pence, Roy Oswalt, Lance Berkman, and Michael Bourn. They were all gone before 2012, the first season Crane took over.

Lack of experienced major-league players and perhaps even the feeling of uncertainty in the clubhouse contributed to the 2011 season resulting in something no Houston team had ever done. They lost over 100 games! The final record was 56 – 106.

The next season, 2012, was almost certain to be worse. The Astros were 55 – 107. The lineup still featured Lee for most of the year because his contract had not expired yet and no one wanted the slow- footed declining player in a trade. But it was also the second season for a young second baseman named José Altuve, a discovery from the previous regime. There was also a 23-year old utilityman named Marwin Gonzalez on the bench, and for sixteen games a lefty pitcher named Dallas Keuchel. The rest of the roster during the 2012 season was young players who may or may not make it and veteran "fillers" who had some skills, but not those of big-time winners.

Gonzalez turned into the new regime's first major acquisition although they didn't' know it at the time. He had been acquired from the Red Sox system on December 8 after the Red Sox had picked him from the Cubs system in the rule five draft the same day. Luhnow, just on the job, had asked the outgoing (they didn't all know it yet) scouting staff to pull off the deal at the winter meetings.

In 2013, the Astros hit bottom. For the third straight season they lost over 100 games. This time they set a team record going 51 – 111 and lost their last 15 games. Official attendance (actually tickets sold) was 1,651,883. Actual fans in seats was much lower. TV ratings recorded 0.0 on more than one occasion.

The TV thing was another problem. Followers of the

Astros were dropping faster than ladybugs on the windshield a speeding car. They weren't going to as many games and were watching even fewer. Portions of Texas that had been Astro hotbeds for decades like Austin and San Antonio were shifting toward the winning Texas Rangers. Astro baseball wasn't even available on television any longer. The new TV deal that McLane's men (along with the Houston Rockets) had negotiated to start in 2013 had financial problems from the start. The Astros claimed they weren't paid all year. And they were part owners of the network. In addition, Comcast had done a very poor job in selling the games to other cable and satellite companies. Only 40% of homes in Houston could see the games, and virtually no homes outside the city. All the coverage that the former network Fox Sports SW and Fox Sports Houston provided around the state and neighboring states was lost.

Maybe the low TV audience was a blessing. The Astros were absolutely awful. However, while the big team was bad, that meant higher picks in the amateur free agent draft. George Springer had been chosen in 2011. In later years players like Carlos Correa, Lance McCullers Jr., and Alex Bregman were all high picks. Houston did miss badly on pitcher Mark Appel, but at least traded him for other prospects. Appel never pitched for anyone in the major leagues.

The light at the end of the tunnel appeared in 2014. They were certainly not contenders but ended the 100-loss string at 70 – 92. Fans still weren't talking much Astros yet, but Altuve won the AL batting title, and nine players who would be on the Astros 25-man or expanded 40-man roster for the 2017 champions were with the team.

The curtain on the dark days finally lifted in 2015 when the Astros made the postseason for the first time since 2005. Club attendance improved as the record did. The Astros were 86 – 76 under manager A. J. Hinch. Dallas Keuchel won the AL Cy Young Award after a 20 – 8 record and 2.48-ERA season. They took out the Yankees in the wild-card game and then went to the wall with the Kansas City Royals in the next series.

While the Astros fell short of the postseason following an 84 – 78 record in 2016, they were only some tweaks away from a championship. More experience and adding some veteran presence did the trick. The Astros were a complete team.

As proven by the huge parade honoring the club after their 2017 World Series win, the dark ages were definitely over!

84

And How Good Has the Run Been?

nd how good have the Astros been from 2017 through 2023? Consider they are just a bit over .500 in the 62 years as a major league franchise (4921-4892 .501) But during the seven year run of ALCS appearances the team was 631-401. That was a winning percentage of .611. It included six American League West Division championships... the only loss coming in 2000 when the season was shortened to 60 games due to the Covid pandemic. Even so, that team which made the post season as a sub .500 wild card (29-31) took the ALCS to a seventh game before falling to Tampa Bay.

The Astros have averaged 100 victories in every full season during the run. Only twice not surpassing that number in a full season with 95 in 2021 and 90 in 2023. They set a team regular season record with 107 wins in 2019. That club lost in the World Series to the Nationals in seven World Series games. But they won a total of 117 games including postseason to set a record equaled by the 2022 World Series champion club.

In the 62 year franchise history Houston has been to five World Series with four of them in the last seven years. They have won six division titles. Only five were won in the first 55 years of the club.

How long can this run of success continue? The improvement of the competition in the division will have a lot to do with that. Plus the normal roster changes all clubs have to deal with on an annual basis.

Whatever the future—short term and long term holds... the Astros and fans have many pleasant memories from 2017 through 2023 that must be remembered.

85

John Paciorek: Most Perfect Ever

f one researches the name "Paciorek" in baseball records, a former outfielder named Tom Paciorek comes up most prominently. Tom, a native of Michigan, came to Houston to play football and baseball for the Houston Cougars and later had an 18-year major-league career with the Dodgers, Braves, Mariners, White Sox, Mets, and Rangers. Mostly a part-time player, his two biggest seasons were in Seattle. After he retired, he served as a White Sox telecaster for years.

But there was another Paciorek listed in the history books. His name was John, and he also played Major League Baseball. Also from Michigan and the University of Houston, John appeared in just one game, but recorded a statistical line that likely will never be duplicated.

His one game for the Houston Colt .45s on September 29, 1963, in front of a gathering of only 3899 in the season's last game, included three hits in three at-bats, two walks, four runs scored, and three batted in. He walked in the second inning with two out. He scored his first run when John Bateman followed with a two-run triple.

After three straight singles by Rusty Staub, Bob Aspromonte, and Ivan Murrell opened the last of the fourth, Paciorek singled to drive in two runs. Paciorek would later score on a sacrifice fly by Pete Runnels.

In the bottom of the fifth with the Colt .45s leading the Mets, 7 – 4, Aspromonte tripled and, with one out, Paciorek singled to left with Aspromonte scoring. A walk to John Bateman sent Paciorek to second, where he was driven in on a single by Bob Lillis.

In the sixth, Paciorek picked up his second walk, moved to second on a wild pitch, and came home on another Lillis single. The Colt .45s led, 12 – 4.

In the eighth inning, Paciorek made his fifth plate appearance and stayed perfect with a single to lead off the inning. He was stranded and the final score was Colt .45s 13, Mets 4. John Paciorek's magic day was done.

Others in baseball history have never played in the major leagues again with a 1.000 batting average, but no one has ever been as productive as John Paciorek in the only game he played.

The circumstances behind his short career centered on injury, but not immediately. Paciorek was invited to spring training in 1964 but performed poorly. He failed to make the Colt .45s and was sent to play first at Durham and later Statesville. But a persistent back problem, which had been diagnosed as a sciatic nerve injury during the previous season, got worse. Paciorek ultimately underwent spinal fusion surgery in 1964 which forced him to miss the rest of that year and all of 1965.

John returned to the minors in 1966 but hit only .193. The next season he was hitting only .104 in 32 games when he was released by Houston.

His best minor-league season took place after he was signed by the Cleveland organization for 1968— the same year younger brother Tom was starting his professional career in the Los Angeles system. At Reno and Rock Hill, John hit

.268 with 20 home runs and 73 RBIs in 95 games. But the next season at Waterbury in the Eastern League, John tore his Achilles tendon and his career ended at age 24.

While Tom Paciorek went on to have a long major-league life, John's one game in 1963 will likely last forever as the most productive one game "career" in major-league history.

86

Larry Yount Has No Stats, But Was in One Game

Perhaps the most disappointing line in the records of Major League Baseball is that of Larry Yount. His line lists one game with zeros in all other columns, and it wasn't because he was announced as a hitter and then a pinch-hitter was called. His story was worse and far more disappointing.

Yount was the older brother of future Hall of Famer Robin Yount. Larry was born in 1950 in Houston but grew up in California and was drafted by the Astros out of Taft High School in 1968. He had a strong arm and appeared in AAA at Oklahoma City part of 1968 despite less-than-impressive numbers.

In 1969 and 1970, he started to fulfill prospect status. He was 11 – 6 with an ERA of 2.27 in 21 games and 103 innings pitched at two stops in 1969 then was 12 – 8 with a 2.84 ERA at Columbus in AA in 1970.

Although his numbers were not as impressive back

at Columbus in 1971, he got the call to the Astros and was warming up in the bullpen on September 15. Yount had been one of the September call-ups on September 2 but had to serve a week long military stint before joining the team.

The Astros trailed the Atlanta Braves, 4 – 1, as the game entered the ninth inning, and Yount was summoned to come into the game. Larry later said his elbow didn't feel right in the bullpen, but he hoped stepping on his first major-league mound and the expected adrenaline rush would cover it. While taking his eight warm-up tosses, the elbow started to really hurt. He had to leave the game without actually throwing a pitch. Since he had been brought into the game before departing, it counted as an appearance.

In most cases, Larry Yount's day would have been only a minor footnote. He was only 21 years old. Surely, he would get more chances.

However, he would not. Yount came back in the spring and was one of the last players cut before the season. He stayed in the Houston organization until the end of 1973, but he was traded to Milwaukee during spring training the next year. He stayed in professional, albeit minor-league, baseball through 1975, but never had much success. From the time of his aborted appearance with Houston in 1971, his minor-league record was 16 – 42 with a 5.55 ERA.

Larry later became very successful in Arizona real estate and a long time trivia note in Astro baseball history. His brother Robin? He became a Hall of Famer inducted in 1999 with George Brett, Orlando Cepeda, and a guy named Nolan Ryan.

87

Jim Deshaies Fans First Eight Dodgers

Left-handed starting pitcher Jim Deshaies was a key member of the rotation in 1986 when the Astros came very close to the NL championship. That club lost in the postseason to the New York Mets, who would go on to win the club's second world title in beating the Boston Red Sox.

Deshaies was a high fastballing fly-ball pitcher who often kept hitters from getting the full wood on his moving pitches and then let the Astrodome air and distances do the rest. But one game against the Dodgers, he needed no help at all. He could have been pitching on a Little League field. He established a modern major-league record when he struck out the first eight hitters he faced.

On September 23, 1986, Deshaies and the Astros were closing in on clinching the National League West. Facing their top rival, Los Angeles, Deshaies was unhittable. He struck out Steve Sax, Reggie Williams, and Enos Cabell in the top of the first.

The Astros scored twice in the bottom on the inning, and when Deshaies took the mound in the second, it was 2 – 0. So, Deshaies struck out the next three: Pedro Guerrero, Alex Trevino, and Jeff Hamilton.

After six straight strikeouts, Deshaies was close to a record. Tom Seaver once struck out ten in a row, but not to start a game. Deshaies had a shot at being the first modern era pitcher to strike out the side the first three innings of a game.

Mickey Welch had struck out the first nine, but he did it when the game was much different in 1884. That was the first-year pitchers could throw directly overhand, and they were doing it from fifty feet.

Deshaies struck out the first two in the third, Dave Anderson and José Gonzalez. With his pitcher coming up next and already trailing 2 – 0, Dodger skipper Tommy Lasorda wanted to end the strikeout streak and get his pitcher out of the game.

He sent Larry "Lett" See to the plate to pinch-hit. Deshaies had numbers against Lett. In three previous meetings Jim had struck out him out twice, but this time. Lett flied out. Deshaies did have the modern record with eight in a row to start a game. His mark was tied by Mets pitcher Jacob DeGrom against the Marlins in 2014.

After the game Lasorda defended his use of pinch-hitter See. "I didn't send up a pinch-hitter to stop the string. I wanted to try and get some runs. Deshaies was exceptional; a major-league record wasn't it?"

As for Deshaies, he said his game strategy was simple. "I wanted to go out there and throw fastballs until I couldn't throw them anymore."

Steve Sax got the first Dodger hit with a single leading off the fourth. "You know it's going to end sometime," said Sax later, "He's got to lose something on the fastball."

That may have been the case, as Deshaies only struck out

two more hitters after his eight in a row, but he also allowed only one more hit, a single by Enos Cabell in the seventh, in his complete-game victory.

Deshaies's catcher Alan Ashby was close-mouthed during Jim's outing. "I didn't say a word to him. He is one of those rare pitchers who can throw up in the strike zone and get away with it. I wasn't going to say anything to mess that up."

88

Homer-Happy Games in 2000, 2019, 2022, & 2023

hen the Astros moved from the Astrodome to Enron Park for the 2000 season, things changed with Houston baseball almost immediately. Instead of being a strong pitcher's park, the new digs were made for hitters. The Astros had a solid power-hitting team in 1999 with half their games in the Astrodome. The team won its third straight NL Central title with 97 victories and hit 168 home runs.

Oh, but 2000 would be something else!

The Astros hit a NL record 249 home runs in 2000. They were good everywhere, with 114 of the home runs coming while on the road, but the 135 they hit at home eclipsed the franchise record of 82 home homers in a season. While the hitting was great, the pitchers were not and the club dropped under .500 and out of pennant contention. Even so, some of the individual games played that year were quite memorable.

On August 16, the Astros had six different players homer

in a home game. They were playing the Pittsburgh Pirates in front of over 30,000 fans. The game was scoreless until the last of the second when Lance Berkman opened the flood gates with a solo home run off Dan Serafini. After Brian Giles of the Pirates hit a two-run homer off Astro starter Scott Elarton in the top of the fourth, Jeff Bagwell cracked his 35th of the year in the last of the inning. Later in the same frame, Chris Truby hit a three-run shot and the Astros led, 5 – 2.

Two more two-run homers in the fifth for Houston. Tim Bogar and Moisés Alou with the honors. In the sixth, Julio Lugo hit the Astros sixth and final homer in the game.

It was the third game in 2000 that the Astros had hit six homers in one game, but the first in which they were hit by six different players.

The Pirates would add another for a total of eight in the game. Oh yes, Houston hung on to win, 11 – 10, in what would be somewhat typical of games played at Enron Field that first season.

Six homers in a game would tie an Astro franchise record for less than a month. They hit seven in a game on the road. The 2000 team hit homers everywhere. They got seven in a game at Chicago's Wrigley Field on September 9.

Amazingly the official wind direction was 12 miles an hour in from right-field. That is a bit misleading. The flags were blowing from right to left but that meant balls hit to left had help. The weather was also hot and a bit humid. As Cubs manager Don Baylor put it, "If you can't pitch inside, that's the kind of game you're going to have when the wind is blowing out." Cubs pitchers were over the heart of the plate too much, but Astros hurlers were much better. The Cubs never hit a ball further than the warning track all day.

The Astros won the game, 14 – 4, with normally light-hitting shortstop Tim Bogar being one of three Astros who hit two homers each. The others were Richard Hidalgo and Lance Berkman. Daryle Ward hit the franchise-record seventh in the seventh inning to complete the long-ball parade.

During and after the 2000 season, the Astros new home was often referred as Home Run Field or Ten Run Field instead of Enron Field. The sponsorship for the ballpark changed after the Enron Corporation was dissolved. However, before that, changes were made to reduce some of the easier home runs.

Most notably was a raise in the height of the wall in left field and left-center. The Astros also started playing more games with the roof closed than they had in 2000. Wind currents with the roof open often gave balls hit into the air an extra ride. Perhaps most important, however, was pitchers learning to take advantage of the park's huge 436 foot center-field distance better and get hitters to keep from pulling as many pitches.

Within two seasons, the park renamed Minute Maid Park was usually running right down the middle as a baseball home run haven. In 2000, however, it may have cost the Astros some wins, but sure made many losses thrill filled.

But the Astros were not hitting home runs...even after Enron Field became Minute Maid Park and the changes were made. It just took a few years.

On September 9, 2019 at Minute Maid Park against the Oakland A's the Astros had their second seven home run game. It saw the club hit six of them over a two inning period. Former Astro Mike Fiers, who was persona non grata to Astro fans after first revealing the team had used electronic methods to steal signs in home games in 2017 was touched for nine earned runs in his only full inning on the mound for the A's. After two innings the Astros had hit six homers: Alex Bregman, Yordan Alvarez, Robinson Chirinos, José Altuve, Michael Brantley and Alvarez again. They stayed on six thru the next innings until Chirinos hit his second of the game. That made it seven and tied the club record first set in 2000. The Astros won the game 15-0.

Their next notable effort came on the road in Boston on May 17, 2022. In that game they hit five home runs in one inning! It all came off the same starting pitcher for the Red

Sox, Jason Eovaldi. The bombers that inning included Yordan Alvarez, Kyle Tucker, Jeremy Peña, Michael Brantley and Yuli Gurriel. Houston won the game 13-4, but strangely did not hit another home the rest of the game after that second inning surge.

The next season, however, their team record seven in one game set in 2000 and equaled in 2019 was tied in a road game in Oakland. On Sunday, May 28th the club got long balls from Yordan Alvarez who hit two, Jake Meyers, Chas McCormick, José Altuve, Jeremy Peña and José Abreu.

Meyers' was the most important. His three run blast broke a 1-1 tie and gave the Astros the lead they would never relinquish in a 10-1 rout and series sweep of the A's.

But it was Abreu's poke that got over the fence in left that was the most memorable. After being acquired as a free agent in an off season signing the former White Sox slugger and AL MVP had not hit a single homer for the Astros. This was their 52nd game and many fans were quite impatient. When Abreu was rounding the bases, he broke into a sprint at second and never stopped running till he made a slide right before the dugout. His team-mates mobbed him. A very popular player with his team- mates they all seemed to be as relieved as Abreu and happy that he had finally hit a homer.

In his next at bat, though, the A's embarrassed by the late rout and Abreu's enthusiasm threw a pitch right in his direction. He was hit on the shoulder. While the Astro bench all rose and looked angrily in the A's direction nothing more occurred. They did not fully know Abreu's struggles up to that point. All Oakland knew was they were getting pounded again and thought he was showing them up.

89

Jeff Bagwell Passes Jimmy Wynn with Exclamation Point!

O n April 21, 1999, in his ninth season with the Astros, Jeff Bagwell passed Jimmy Wynn to become the franchises top career home run hitter. Wynn had hit 223 of his career, 290 home runs wearing a Houston uniform. Bagwell on that day not only tied Wynn for the all-time Houston mark, but broke it and added an extra homer to boot. When asked about breaking Wynn's team mark following the game, Jeff said, "I can't think of a more class act and better person than Jimmy Wynn. I always look at him with amazement."

Jeff hit three home runs in a 10 – 3 romp over the Cubs at Wrigley Field. The Wynn-tying homer came off Scott Sanders in the top of the first inning. In the top of the third with Houston leading, 1 – 0, Baggie became the team's all-time leader with his 224th homer. That home run came with two on and pushed the Houston lead to 3 – 0.

Finally, in the top of the seventh with the Astros leading, 5 – 2, he cracked his third homer of the day with a runner on. Bagwell's three homers on the day he passed Jimmy Wynn emphasized his spot as the greatest home run hitter in Houston history. He would finish his Hall of Fame career with 449 home runs—all in a Houston uniform.

Bagwell had been what was, for him, a homer slump before the game. His average was good at .372, but he had only hit one home run in 1999 before his big game. Manager Larry Dierker was happy to see the power show. "It's great to see Bagwell hit the long ball again. We're not amazed anymore because you see it so much, you come to expect it."

Bagwell had a chance to tie the major-league mark of four homers in a game with an at-bat in the ninth, but he grounded to third. "No question I was thinking about it," he said, "But I wasn't using the same mind-set. It was a strike, but it wasn't a pitch that you could hit out of the ballpark."

Bagwell went from one homer for the season to four by the time the game on April 22 was over. He would finish 1999 with 42 home runs.

Players with Most Raw Tools in Prime
César Cedeño
Jeff Bagwell
José Altuve*
Craig Biggio
Carlos Correa **

* Still Playing
** Still Playing, but not with the Astros

90

Astros Triple Play Beat Dodgers in 1978

**T**here is an old saying in baseball that the game is never over until the last man is out—no matter how bleak things might look.

The Astros on April 21, 1978 proved that. They beat the Dodgers in Los Angeles that day thanks to an extremely rare way to end a game. The Astros ended the victory by pulling off a triple play! What is almost as amazing, it was the third triple play executed by the Astros in the season's first month! They got their first on opening day against the Reds on April 6 and their second on April 11 against San Diego. Astro catcher, Joe Ferguson said after the game, "Before this season I'd never even seen a triple play." The former Dodger was a key for the Astros win. His three-run homer in the eighth put the Astros on top. Thanks to the triple play, that was the game-winning hit.

Consider that a triple play (getting three outs on one continuous play) is not terribly rare. There had been 717 of them in baseball between 1890 through 2018. Having one to close out a game is rare though. Fewer than 30 have been recorded.

Los Angeles had taken a 4 – 0 lead on J. R. Richard thanks to an RBI single by Ron Cey in the first and home runs by Rick Monday and Davey Lopes in the second.

The Astros rallied to tie the game with a four-run fifth inning off Dodger starter Rick Rhoden. A double by Bob Watson brought in the first run, and singles by Roger Metzger and Denny Walling plated two more. The fourth run scored on an error by Lopes.

The Astros took a 5 – 4 lead on an RBI single by Wilbur Howard in the seventh. But the Dodgers came right back and had a sacrifice fly by Cey and RBI single by Steve Garvey to retake the advantage.

Then came Ferguson's big three run homer to give them the lead to the last of the ninth.

After Bill Russell and Reggie Smith both singled off Ken Forsch, the hitter was Ron Cey. Moving the tying run into scoring position with a sacrifice bunt was not expected with the power hitting Cey at the plate.

Cey hit a ball right on the nose that got fans excited that an extra-base hit down the right-field line would tie the score. The runners were thinking that at well. Problem for Los Angeles was that Bob Watson at first base was able to glove the ball for the first out, then step on the bag to retire Smith, and pivot to make the throw to second where shortstop Metzger was waiting to hit the base before Russel could get back. Triple play! Game over. Astros win, 8 – 6.

91

Jim Bouton Book Goes Inside Astros

n June 1970, a book was published that made a lot of those in Major League Baseball nervous. Ball Four, by long time major-league pitcher Jim Bouton, was created from a collection of notes and anecdotes collected from the 1969 season when he pitched for two teams, but also included many memories from his best years with the New York Yankees.

For fans in Houston, it was a great book. Bouton had pitched for the Astros after starting the season with Seattle that year. For the first time, Houston had gone big time in the sports literary world. Fans all over baseball were reading about the Houston Astros.

At the time Bouton's book—like a couple of books written a few years before by another pitcher, Jim Brosnan, was shocking. In Brosnan's book, his fondness for martinis stood out as well as the use of "greenies" to pep up dragging players. The fondness for alcohol and amphetamines reappeared in the Bouton book. No steroids for PEDs yet, but more conventional (at the time) methods for handling the up and downs of the game.

In Bouton's book, fans learned of Astro manager Harry Walker's fining system and how Harry liked to talk and impart his "wisdom." Trainers and medical folks will cringe when they hear this, but in the book, Harry told Bouton the way to recover from a sore arm was to throw and throw some more. He said when he played in Pittsburgh and had a sore arm he would go stand on the third base foul line and throw the ball 400 feet over the right-field stands. Walker told Bouton he'd had a couple sore arms and cured them the same way. His belief was that people had to learn to reach a little bit further back and try harder.

The team song that was written called "Proud to be An Astro" gave fans further if not an off-color inside look.

Obviously, not all in baseball were happy to have Yankees, Pilots, and Astros exposed for some of their actions on the road—or the drinking and pill-popping—but what Bouton wrote was real. He did spare destroying marriages in print— at least until some of the spouses may have become more inquisitive about what went on in other cities. Fans never learned anything about the specifics, but what they did learn added a lot to watching some of their favorites just play the game.

92

George Springer Drafted by Astros in 2011

he MVP in the 2017 World Series George Springer was the eleventh player selected in the amateur free agent draft in 2011. He was the last choice from the Drayton McLane ownership regime and scouts. A very good choice, not just because what George did in 2017, but because what was available when the pick came up.

In a short phrase, the answer was "not much." That is why the selection of Springer was so good.

The 2011 draft was a good one in the first picks as it has turned out. In the first ten picks before the Springer selection, number 1 pitcher Gerrit Cole (who became as Astro teammate in 2018), number 6 Anthony Rendon, and number 8 Francisco Lindor have all made major contributions. Number three choice Trevor Bauer has been solid and the same could be said with number 9 Javier Baez.

No position player in the whole first round had hit more

home runs than Springer's 121 through 2018, nor have a higher OPS, let alone be a World Series MVP.

Pretty darn good choice by the outgoing Houston staff.

Springer had to spend two full seasons in the minors before coming to the Astros. He had holes (317 strikeouts in 263 games) but hit 61 homers with batting averages of .302 and .303, while driving in 87 and 108 runs and stealing 32 and 45 bases.

Photo Courtesy of Keith Allison

George Springer was a first-rounder and Series MVP.

The high volume of strikeouts had been a problem with Springer once he got to the Astros, but by 2018 he had cut them down by more than 50 from his 178 in 2017 and it showed.

The Astros didn't have a choice in the first round until number 11, but by selecting George Springer they did better than most teams above them and better than all of the following teams for sure. Twenty-two of the 60 players considered first-rounders in 2011, including those as supplemental picks in the first round for losing free agent players, had not even reached the major leagues through 2017. Meanwhile, George Springer had already starred for a World Series champion.

Sadly, for Astro fans Springer opted for free agency and joined the Toronto Blue Jays in 2021. For his seven years in Houston he hit .270 with 174 home runs, 458 RBIs and a World Series MVP honor.

93

Larry Dierker — Mr. Astro

o one has ever worn more significant hats in the Houston Major League Baseball franchise than Larry Dierker. Consider that he is one of the winningest pitchers in franchise history with a no-hit game to his credit. Then he was one of the most popular and skilled Astro radio and television commentators for twenty years. Add that his winning percentage is the second-best of all Houston managers. His teams winning four division championships in five years at the helm remains tops and it is easy to see why Larry is Mr. Astro.

As a player he made his debut on his 18th birthday on September 22, 1964 in the last week of the Houston Colt .45s. He appeared in three games that season, pitched nine innings, and allowed only seven hits and two earned runs.

Starting in 1965 he was a regular in the Houston rotation for the next 12 seasons. He won 137 games as an Astro with nine double-figure win seasons topped by 20 victories in 1969. His Houston career ERA was 3.28. Only Joe Niekro and Roy Oswalt had more wins in a Houston uniform. He has something neither Niekro nor Oswalt could accomplish on their own—a no-hitter—which he threw in his last Astro season. On July 9, 1976 Dierker beat Montreal, 6 – 0, and even drove in one of the runs with a sacrifice fly.

He finished his career in St. Louis in 1977 then worked for the Astros in ticket sales and broadcasting until 1997 when he was asked to take over as manager of the club.

In 1997, 1998, 1999, and 2001 he guided the Astros to National League Central Division titles. After leaving the job after the 2001 season, he left the club full time but picked up some freelance game work and wrote a couple of books on baseball. His most popular work, This Ain't Brain Surgery relived his managerial years including his comeback from a grand mal seizure that occurred during those years. In 2018, he started a website and podcast where fans can still hear his takes on the game.

Larry is a noted baseball historian and supplied anecdotes and vignettes on players and games from the past on a regular basis as part of his radio work for years.

In his honor as, unofficially at least, Mr. Astro, the Houston chapter of the Society for American Baseball Research (SABR) is the Larry Dierker chapter of the organization.

94

Tal, Gerry, Jeff & James — Houston's Building Winners GMs

Arguably the top three GMs in Houston Astro history had one significant thing in common. All three built teams that were postseason clubs, even if in two cases they were not around for the finish of the era and someone else was in their chair.

Tal Smith was first. He had been with the franchise from its Colt .45s start in the farm department then left for a few years but came back to run the show in the mid-1970s. Working around the financial limitations during the end of Judge Hofheinz's ownership and the credit company ownership, Tal was able to hire the right manager in Bill Virdon and build the Astros into a division winner and postseason team in both 1980 and 1981. After running the whole show until John McMullen bought the club in 1979, Smith and the new boss clashed at times, and after 1980 he was gone. Tal returned during the Drayton McLane Jr. years, serving as team president and working with GM Gerry Hunsicker to make the Astros champions of their division again.

Smith and Hunsicker had to manage the McLane budget, but built the Astros into a NL power. Gerry was GM from the end of 1995 through 2004. He was brought in from the Mets by Smith. During that period Houston won division titles in 1997, 1998, 1999, 2001, and was in the postseason again in 2004. He turned the reins over to assistant Tim Purpura prior to the Astros' first World Series in 2005. Hunsicker oversaw the drafting of Lance Berkman, Morgan Ensberg, Roy Oswalt, Brad Lidge, and the acquisitions of Moisés Alou, Carl Everett, Brad Ausmus, Bill Spiers, and more keys to the winning seasons.

It would be Jeff Luhnow, the GM for owner Jim Crane, who took over the franchise from McLane in 2012. Luhnow used an effective plan of keeping away from long term free agent contracts for veterans to expose top minor-league prospects to the major leagues if they looked like they might be able to play. At the same time the club invested in even more top draft choices—available thanks to the major- league club falling in the standings. To be fair his first years building the team were the greatest failures on the field in Houston baseball history. However, that was a sacrifice as part of the building plan.

Luhnow was a proponent of scout-aiding analytics to help determine which players were the strongest bets for success in professional ball. He used it heavily in building the major-league team and in helping his manager and coaches know what areas their players needed to most improve for maximum efficiency.

The result was a World Series-winning team in 2017 but was preceded by the worst three seasons in the franchises more than 50-year history. For a franchise that had never lost as many as 100 games in a season, having three in a row was hard for thousands of fans to accept. The first 100-loss season in 2011 actually was the last of the Drayton McLane ownership years as he cut costs and high-dollar free agent contracts to clear the deck for the Crane-Luhnow rebuild. Attendance and television ratings plummeted. However, it appeared the gamble had paid off when many from the Astro farm system, coupled with players acquired by the previous regime put together the best season in franchise history in 2017 by winning the World Series and then setting a new single-season victory total with 103 wins in 2018.

Luhnow had to supplement his scouting and development role to become a full-fledged GM by making some trades and free agent acquisitions to complete the Astro's winning roster. With the success of 2017 and the nucleus of the club in place for the next several seasons, Luhnow had pulled it off. Baseball had claimed the position as the top sports franchise in Houston. Enthusiasm was at a record high entering 2019.

Then came the sign stealing scandal. Owner Jim Crane was forced by MLB to suspend his manager, A.J. Hinch and General Manager, Jeff Luhnow. But he did more than that. He fired both of them.

The next men up were Dusty Baker as manager and James Click moving over from the Tampa Bay franchise as GM. Both were together for three seasons. In the Covid-shortened 60 game 2020 season the Astros were two games under .500 in the regular season, but still made the post season. They were able to advance to the American League Championship before losing to Tampa Bay four games to three, rallying from an 0-3 start to make it close.

The next season the Astros won another American League pennant, but dropped the World Series to Washington four games to three as neither team was able to win a home game. The Astros had the home field (dis) advantage.

Then in 2022 the Astros won both the AL and the Series. Yet, the working relationship between Click and owner Crane was not smooth. When the Astros offered only a one-year contract Click opted out. The new GM, Dana Brown, would have to see what he could do in 2023. As it turned out his work was not so easy.

Greatest Action-Filled Important Astros Games

Game 6 2022 World Series	Hou 4. Philly 1	Alvarez 3r HR
Game 5 2017 World Series	Hou 13, LA 12 (10 innings)	Bregman 1b Wins
Game 2 2017 World Series	Hou 2, LA 6 (11 innings)	Springer 2rHR Top 11
Game 4 2005 NL Division Series	18 innings	Burke Home Run Wins
Game 1 2022 ALDS		Alvarez HR Wins
Game 3 2022 ALDS	18 innings	Peña HR Top 18 Wins
Game 4 2004 NL Championship Series		Kent Home Run Wins It
Game 7 2017 World Series		Astros Win First World Series
Game 5 2023 ALCS		Altuve 3rHR in 9th Wins it

95

Jimmy Wynn Loses a Ball in the Astrodome Ceiling

When the Astrodome was new, it had a few kinks to work out. The grass was not growing well. And the translucent roof was a problem. Not enough light reaching the field for the grass, but too much light with girders intermixed for fielders to easily follow balls hit high in the air during daylight hours.

A famed video featuring outfielder Norm Miller has been played for years showing Miller looking up then around while the ball falls several feet away. That was from a team workout before the first season. Then, during the opening series of exhibitions with the Yankees and Orioles, problems showed up during play. Astro officials and players were very concerned. How could they ever play day games inside the building under those terrible conditions? They tried wearing special glasses. They tried different colored baseballs. They tried new ways to try to follow the ball. Nothing really worked. After the season's opening game against the Phillies, with the

Astros leaving on an eight-game road trip, it was decided to paint a section of the ceiling that served as the backdrop for balls hit in the air, which helped visibility but not the grass and still took some adjusting.

On May 22, 1965, when a game from the Astrodome between Houston and San Francisco was televised nationally on ABC-TV, finding the ball high in the air was still a problem for Jimmy Wynn.

In the top of the fifth inning, Giants catcher Tom Haller hit a ball off pitcher Bob Bruce very high into the Astrodome's "sky" toward center field. The problem was that even with the newly painted roof, Jimmy lost sight of it. He never could sight the ball against the glare and girders. Then he heard the sound of the ball hitting with a thud 50 feet from him. Turns out the ball had hit the ground and it was bouncing away. By the time anyone got to it Haller had gotten to third base. The Giants would eventually win the game 10 – 1.

The very next day things were worse. Jimmy lost a ball hit by Jim Ray Hart with two on and two out in the top of the first. His fellow outfielders unaware Jimmy was having trouble finding the ball figured it was only a routine out to end the inning and were in no position to help. The ball eventually bounded off the base of the fence with Wynn in pursuit and turned into a three-run inside-the-park homer against Ken Johnson in what would be his last start for the Astros. Mid-game, Johnson left the game as he was traded for outfielder Lee Maye. Johnson was the Astros most effective pitcher at the time.

After the game, Astro executive Tal Smith, general manager Paul Richards, and some players and coaches declared the roof needed some more paint. Coach Jim Busby hit fly balls to Wynn, Rusty Staub, and Nellie Fox. They caught them all, but not without some difficulty and declared the glare problem still needed to be reduced. As Smith said, "My recommendation is another coat of paint. This one will have to be darker than the off-white we used before—probably a green, blue, or black. You can section the dome into 12 pieces and we think it would be best to paint the two sections above home plate."

The extra paint was added, and from then on, losing the ball in the roof was not a common problem for the rest of the Astrodome's life as home of the Astros.

96

Longest Scheduled Road Trip in MLB History

On July 24, 1992, it was announced the Houston Astros had been sold by Dr. John McMullen to Drayton McLane Jr. Three days later the team started the longest scheduled road trip in modern Major League Baseball history. From July 27 through the next 28 days, the team would travel 9186 miles and hit eight cities. They would play 26 games.

The road trip was required because the Astrodome was going to host the Republican National Presidential Convention. Houston resident, President George H. W. Bush, was going to be nominated to run for a second term. He wanted the convention in his home town. Team owner John McMullen was going to get a substantial fee for subleasing the building. To counter complaints, he pointed out the Houston community figured to bring in $80-million in revenue from the convention. He was the good guy!

The player's union didn't agree, and to settle their

Barbara Bush and 1992 RNC sent the Astros on a long trip.

grievances, McMullen had to up the per diem amounts, arrange for a flight home mid-trip, and pay for wives to visit their husbands when the team was in Chicago. He also contributed $125,000 to two youth baseball programs on behalf of the union.

Prior to the trip, the Astros played an unimpressive 14-game homestand. They started with a 39 – 45 record and, when ready to leave on the trip, were only 44 – 54 and two and a half games further off the division lead than before the homestand started.

Things didn't look good to be gone for nearly a month. The Astro held their own. They were under .500 at 12 – 14, but a road trip that long would have figured to be much worse. The trip took the Astros from Atlanta to Cincinnati to Los Angeles, San Diego, San Francisco, Chicago, St. Louis, and finally Philadelphia. The club got one quick side trip home to Houston on an offday August 17, but were on the road the rest of the time.

The year before the Astros made their scheduled long trip, the Montreal Expos had one that lasted as long as the Astros

(26 games in 28 days), but it was totally unscheduled. A 55-ton chunk of ornamental concrete fell from the top of the Olympic Stadium one night. That happened in September and forced the Expos to play the rest of the season on the road.

Another stadium had a structural problem in 1994.The Seattle Mariners had a 21-day, 20-game road trip in 1994 when ceiling tiles at the Kingdome fell, making the building unusable. Had baseball not had a work stoppage on August 12, the trip would have continued, breaking the longest road trip record of the Astros. Of course, the Astros trip would remain the longest scheduled trip in modern major-league history. Montreal and Seattle are only footnotes.

While McMullen's move in many was just another sign his concern was money over winning and players, he had been trying to sell the club for two years before the McLane deal was finished. The trip did not help him in the eyes of his players or staff.

"It's like he [McMullen] is saying, 'We couldn't care less if you win," Jeff Bagwell told his hometown Hartford Courant. John McMullen had to sell the team. He would have never been forgiven for "The Trip."

97

2023 Got Off to a Rough Start

Coming off a second World Series title since 2017 the 2023 Astros started the year on the wrong foot for many reasons. Still they were able to stay at .500 or slightly above that for the first six weeks. And they did it both short-handed and with some players under performing. By the All Star break they were in second place in the AL West, but only two games behind the leading Texas Rangers. Rather amazing considering all that had transpired over the recent months and weeks.

In spring training expected starting pitcher Lance McCullers suffered some pain in his surgically repaired and 2022 tested elbow. He was shut down and began a build-up program that would likely not put him back on the Astros mound till June at the earliest. But during the season that return was sidetracked until 2024 when more surgery was needed to remove bone chips. He never pitched in 2023.

Then during the World Baseball Classic José Altuve was hit by a pitch that broke the thumb on his right hand. He would be sidelined till June. At the same time veteran Michael Brantley was still not ready to play after surgery on his right shoulder during the off seson. He had missed the end of the 2022 season and post season with the injury. His return was expected then scratched more than once as discomfort in his shoulder never went away. He was finally able to play during September.

Then there were the early in season injuries. The club lost two more starting pitchers when in successive games José Urquidy and Luis Garcia were felled. Urquidy's shoulder would not require surgery, but he went to the injured list. Garcia left his start after just eight pitches when an elbow ligament barked. The medics diagnosed a torn ligament. Tommy John surgery was prescribed. Garcia's 2023 and perhaps start of 2024 were no longer playable.

And then oblique muscle injuries to both Altuve and more seriously to Yordan Alvarez took them out of the lineup. Altuve had two short stints away. Alvarez missed six weeks. When he was injured he had been leading the team in both RBIs and HRs.

The Astros also had some hitting woes. Both new first baseman José Abreu and third baseman Alex Bregman began the season as sub-par hitters. Without the bats of Brantley and Altuve that was hard to take. The Astros were not scoring much, but help from Mauricio Dubon who started the year at second base and had a 20 game hitting streak and rookie outfielder Cory Julks were nice surprises.

Before he was hurt Yordan Alvarez' batting average was lower than usual, but his power and RBI game was top notch. Jeremy Peña struggled at times, but along with Alvarez and Kyle Tucker provided some punch. Alex Bregman was below normal. In fact he, Peña and off season acquisition José Abreu were hitting below .250. Hitting results was well below the norm. So was the pitching, but somehow the Astros stayed in the race.

The Astros were hanging in there with Hunter Brown, JP France and Brian Bielak picking up the innings lost with Urquidy and Garcia now out and McCullers ruled out for the year before he ever got back. Good enough to win again? That was the question for Astro fans.

Thanks to a strong finish they did win again...the AL West, at least in a tiebreaker with Texas. But the Rangers were too much for them in the ALCS ousting the Astros for a chance at more World Series glory.

98

Long Hitting Streak Took a Long Time for Eusebio

Outfielder Willy Taveras holds the Astros' longest hitting streak. In 2006 he hit safely in 30 straight games. He did it the usual way, by playing nearly every game over 32 days. He bested the mark established by Jeff Kent at 25 games over 29 days.

However, the record Kent broke had taken a long time to set. Tony Eusebio hit in 24 consecutive games during the 2000 season. Tony played his games over 51 days to squeeze past Art Howe's mark of 23 set in 1981.

It took Tony so long because he was only the backup catcher and pinch-hitter for the team in 2000. Rookie Mitch Meluskey was the starter behind the plate and had a good year as a hitter himself. Tony played only when needed.

To be able to get at least one hit in every game as a one-at-bat pinch-hitter for so many games was amazing. He hit .409 during the streak. His streak started on July 9 with a hit in four at-bats. The streak finally ended following a two-for-four game August 28. The next appearance had no hits.

99

Twenty-Five Hits in a 9-Inning Game 4 Times!

Before the late 1990s, and especially once the team moved into Minute Maid Park (Enron Field in 2000), the club was never known for being an offensive power. Yet, in two games way back in 1976, team records were set that remain.

The first record was set on May 30 in Atlanta during the second game of a doubleheader. After the Astros won the opener, 5 – 2, they exploded for a 16 – 5 win in the second game. That was when they set the team record by collecting 25 hits off Brave's pitchers. That is only one of the records. The other was that 23 of the hits were singles!

Cliff Johnson who had four of the hits also had one of the two extra-base hits, a double in the first off Roger Moret. Jerry DaVanon had a triple of Bruce Dal Canton for the other hit longer than a single. He had three hits and drove in a team-leading five runs. Twelve Houston players had official at-bats in the game. Eleven of them had at least one hit.

The hit total of 25 was duplicated at Cincinnati on July 2, but it took extra innings. Again, it was in one game of a doubleheader, but this time in Game One. The Astros beat the Reds, 10 – 8, in 14 innings. Greg Gross, César Cedeño, and Enos Cabell had four hits each. Cedeño's two-run homer in the 14th was the winning hit.

Having those two games with so many runs and hits was not common for the Astros in 1976. For the season, the team was only fifth in batting average at .256, 10th in home runs with only 66, and fifth in runs scored with 625. The record for the year was just 80 – 82.

The status of the team was far greater when they had 25 hits in a nine-inning game for the second, third and fourt times between 2019 and 2023.

In 2019 the Astros might have had their best team of all. They lost the World Series to the Washington Nationals in the strangest series of all time. Neither team won a single home game. The Astros had four so they lost.

But on the way to making that series they had a game in Baltimore that featured 23 runs and 25 hits. Houston hit six home runs including three by rookie Yordan Alvarez. Six players including Yordan had three or four hits with Yuli Gurriel getting four. José Altuve, Alex Bregman and Carlos Correa also hit round trippers.

The Astros would next have a 25 hit game in 2022. It was on August 18, 2022 against the Chicago White Sox. The Astros had been in the American League since 2013 and had established themselves has one of the top teams in baseball. Having won the AL pennant in 2017, 2019, 2021 and future winners in 2022 with a pair of World Series championships they could pitch AND hit.

In that game in Chicago they showed it. They racked up 21 runs on 25 hits. It started against Lucas Giolito, one of the Sox top starters. He lasted only three innings giving up eight of the hits and seven of the runs. Chicago used three more pitchers with none giving up less than four runs. The biggest sticks for the Astros were Alex Bregman, Christian Vazquez and Kyle Tucker. Each had four hits in six at bats and drove in eleven of the Houston runs. Bregman drove in four on two two-run homers. Trey Mancini and Chas McCormick also homered. McCormick had a three hit game as did Yuli Gurriel.

The Astros scored in seven of nine innings. Luis Garcia won his 10th game. He had entered the game 9-8 while Giolito was slightly better at 9-6. The better record did not result in better results that game by a long shot. Forty-six years after Houston had first registered 25 hits in a nine-inning game they had done it again on the way to a pennant and World Series victory.

They did it again in the midst of a tight pennant race in 2023. On August 27, 2023 in Detroit the Astros again had a 25 hit game featuring five home runs. Jeremy Peña had five of the hits as the Astros stayed within one game of the lead in the AL West behind the Seattle Mariners. Tucker, Dubon, Maldonado and Diaz all homered.

100

Scoring 12 Runs in an Inning is Astro Record

he 1975 Houston Astros finished the season, 64 – 97, which was the worst club record until the rebuilding years at the end of the McLane ownership years. In baseball, however, even the worst teams can have big days. Houston had one of those on May 31 when they whipped the Philadelphia Phillies, 15 – 3. What made the game unique was the Astros scoring a franchise-record 12 runs in the eighth inning. Up to then, Philly pitcher Wayne Twitchell had allowed Houston only two hits in the first seven frames.

Cliff Johnson had a game to remember. He entered the game as a pinch-hitter and doubled. As the Astros batted around, he came up again and belted a home run. However, it was not credited as a pinch- hit homer since he had already batted in that role.

The Astros sent 16 hitters to the plate in the eighth. They faced four different Philadelphia pitchers. They collected ten hits. All except Johnson's double and homer were singles in a nearly perfect inning with 12 runs scored and no one left on base.

Since 1975 the Astros have had many teams with more firepower than that club. So far, however, no team has ever had a bigger single inning.

101

First Test of Astroturf — April 18, 1966

O nce it was obvious grass would not grow or even be practical inside the Astrodome with the many uses other than baseball planned, the folks at Monsanto accelerated the development of an artificial grass replacement. The infield was in place early in 1966. On April 18, 1966, an artificial turf for baseball made its debut.

Astroturf changed the game; the Astrodome needed it.

Photo Courtesy of Matt Brown

It passed the test. The Dodgers won the game, 6 – 3, in a battle started by two future Hall of Fame pitchers—Robin Roberts for Houston and Don Sutton for Los Angeles. Only the infield was AstroTurf with the outfield being covered later that year. There were three errors in the game, but not caused by the new surface. The first was by Rusty Staub in the outfield who fumbled a single by Ron Fairly that let in the first run. The second error was on a wild throw to first by Dodger third baseman Jim Lefebvre. The third error was on a grounder by Bill Heath by Los Angeles second baseman Nate Oliver. The miscue came on the dirt surface behind the turf. The field had the standard dirt infield area. The artificial turf covered only the normally grass areas on the infield.

After the game, Lefebvre complimented the turf. "The ball still comes off quickly, but I've noticed a lot of improvement in the dirt area. They've done a lot of work on that."

Astrodome officials had put extra padding under the turf after complaints from the earlier exhibition that the surface was too fast and balls came off it with too much speed.

The Astrodome led the way in the introduction of artificial turf to baseball and ultimately other sports. The use of artificial turf peaked in the 1970s and 1980s before new strains of grass and methods of keeping it healthy allowed formerly artificial turfed fields to be converted back to grass.

102

Mets Announcer Lindsay Nelson Works from Ceiling

he Houston Astros have had several announcers who spent time with the club honored with the Ford Frick Award at Baseball's Hall of Fame. The two most remembered are Gene Elston, the first Astro voice, and Milo Hamilton, who spent more time behind a Houston microphone than anyone except for TV voice Bill Brown.

Lindsay Nelson, another Frick winner for his work with the New York Mets, did something on April 28, 1965 that no Astro announcer ever did or likely ever wanted to do. He broadcast from the gondola that used to hang beneath the roof of the Astrodome.

The idea of doing it was Joe Gallagher's. Gallagher was the Mets television producer who, later in life, moved to Houston and did some work with the old Home Sports Entertainment (HSE) on high school and college telecasts. In 1965 he, like most, was enthralled by the size and majesty of the Dome which had just opened.

While it was removed in later years, in those days an actual gondola hung from the roof right in the center of the dome 208 feet above the field. All during the first game of the series, Gallagher was asking questions of Houston officials like whether one could get into it and whether it was safe. The answer was a lukewarm, "I guess so." Other questions included how many it could hold and could a broadcast be done from there?

Gallagher went after the proper approvals and had to convince Nelson to make history. A couple of adjustments had to be made. Lindsay couldn't take any pencils or pens into the gondola to keep score. Dropping one could result in a lethal weapon if it hit a player or umpire on the field. But Nelson and assistant producer Joel Nixon agreed to ascend.

The gondola was lowered to about 12 feet from the ground and Nelson and Nixon got inside. The ride took about five minutes to go all the way up. Going up with the pair were a couple of locker stools, a pair of walkie-talkies, a microphone, binoculars, and a scorecard. Before going into the gondola Nelson asked an Astros engineer if he had ever been up there. The reply? "Up there? You think I'm nuts?"

Nelson kept very still in the gondola, which could sway with movement. Although he admitted when he first got up there that the players looked like ants and he couldn't really identify anyone. He was aided by his partners in the Mets booth.

Bob Hope was attending the game that day and insisted to wait before leaving the field to see if Nelson got back down okay. He did. The historic moment was never repeated.

Astro Announcers Honored with Ford Frick Award by Hall of Fame

Lindsay Nelson had a very illustrious career. In addition to his years with the Mets, he also worked San Francisco Giants games for a time and was a long-time network announcer primarily for NBC and CBS covering both college and professional football and Major League Baseball. For his baseball work he was honored with the Ford Frick Award for announcers by the Baseball Hall of Fame. Several former "voices" for Astros baseball have been honored as well. Gene Elston, Milo Hamilton, Harry Kalas, and Al Helfer have been elected. Elston and Helfer were on the original Colt .45s announcing team, and Gene was the longest tenured voice (25 years) until Milo Hamilton and Bill Brown surpassed him. Brown, DeWayne Staats, and the first Spanish-language radio voice for the club Rene Cardenas are strong former Astro announcers that have a good change to join Elston, Hamilton, Kalas, and Helfer in future years.

103

Best Promotions Ever! World Series Replica Rings

In 2018 the Astros staged the greatest promotions likely in baseball history when they had designed and made available to fans some well-executed replica World Series rings. All the fans had to do was attend one of what would turn out to be six games during the season. After an initial ring giveaway limited to just the first 10-thouand fans resulted in lines around the block and up to 30,000 upset fans who showed up too late, the club decided to go all out the rest of the year. They ultimately planned five more give-away dates in which every fan in attendance would receive a ring. When the season's last regular season game at home was played on September 23, the club had distributed about 250,000 rings. Every game where the rings were the prize was totally sold out. The Astros sold out 17 games at home in 2018. Six of them were "Ring Nights."

They continued the tradition every time they won the American League title or the World Series. Lots of rings were handed out for a good number of years.

There HAVE been some promotions from the past far less successful.

During the 1970s it was felt that baseball needed some new ideas to bring fans into the games Many felt the sport was stagnant and handling the boom that professional football was having. Even the National Basketball Association was on an upswing. Baseball was just baseball.

During the decade teams tried all sorts of things to attract new fans or at least ticket buyers. Post game concerts, in game fan contests, dress up nights and many other ideas were introduced. The promotions most popular with many fans involved getting reduced price, or even better, free beer. Obviously not totally thought out since drinking more beer often results in the lowering of inhibitions and less than ideal behavior by a number of those in the stadium.

For the Astros they learned their first lesson on August 6, 1971 during "Nickel Beer Night." The promotion didn't pack the Astrodome but it did bring in a high percentage of beer drinkers among the 21,915 on hand. There were a few minor incidents in the stands, but thankfully the Padres and Astros played a very speedy game. San Diego beat Houston 4-3 in just two hours, thirteen minutes.

The "fun" began after the final out. Drunken fans poured onto the field, pretending to hit by swinging imaginary bats at home plate while others pretended to throw the ball off the mound. Still others practiced their baserunning including sliding into bases. While disturbing those actions were harmless, but the more larcenous drunks invaded the Padre dugout trying to steal equipment.

In the future promotions involving beer would be much more under control. Foamer Night was one of those. It involved using a clock and rooting for their players to hit a home run at the right time.

The way it worked was an orange light would on every odd minute while the Astros were batting. If an Astro player hit a home run while the light was on the beer was free the rest of the night.

The odds were very much in favor of Astros management. The games in the cavernous and dead air Astrodome rarely saw home runs hit by anyone let alone the Astros. Furthermore beer could not be served after the seventh inning on any night.

But there was ONE time!! Trey Smith writing about in for Bleacher Report in 2009. Doug Rader became the beer drinkers friend when the light was on while he was hitting. He made contact and sent the ball deep to left field. The fans seemed to rise as one to get that ball in "Beer Land." Some fans were leaving their seats heading to the beer concessions as soon as the ball hit the bat. When it landed as a homer the stands almost emptied. It was chaos. Aisles jammed with the thirsty trying to climb their way to cups of the foaming liquid.

There were more Foamer Nights but no memories of another long ball hit at the right time. Promotions are far saner now with Dollar Hot Dog Night a current fan favorite.

104

Ricky Gutiérrez Took Bartolo Twenty Pitches Deep

he number of pitches thrown in games was not a statistic recorded for most of baseball's history. However, in modern baseball former Astro shortstop Ricky Gutiérrez held the record for most pitches seen in a single at-bat for two decades.

Facing Bartolo Colón in the eighth inning of a game played on June 26, 1998 in Cleveland, Ricky strung out his at-bat for 20 pitches. That was the modern record, and it lasted for twenty seasons until San Francisco Giant Brandon Belt took Los Angeles Angel hurler Jaimie Barria 21 pitches deep on April 22, 2018. For several reasons, Belt's feat against Barria was not as totally out of place as Gutiérrez long pitch at-bat against Colón.

Colón had not gone more than seven pitches to any Astro hitters before that at-bat. Only Gutiérrez in the third and Brad Ausmus in the fifth had gone seven deep. Fourteen Astro hitters were retired on three or fewer pitches.

So, when Gutiérrez led off the top of the eighth, what happened was totally unexpected. Colón was breezing with a 4 – 2 lead and had thrown only 84 pitches.

Colón jumped ahead on the count with two quick strikes. After a ball to make the count 1 – 2 came the first of seventeen more pitches. Two fouls and a pitch out of the zone made it 2-2 after six pitches.

It was 3 – 2 when Colón threw another ball on the 13th pitch. Six more fouls followed to get the count to 19. Finally, Colón fooled Ricky and got him to swing and miss on pitch number 20. The at-bat and its 20 pitches represented 18% of all the pitches Colón had thrown up to that point in the game. The whole thing was frustrating to Colón. Before he finally retired Gutiérrez, he was seen laughing on the mound while Ricky kept fouling off pitches. As for Gutiérrez, after the game he said, "It was no laughing matter. I wanted to get a hit, and he struck me out."

Colón would retire both Brad Ausmus and Craig Biggio on eight more pitches and be finished for the game, but he would be the winning pitcher, moving his record to 8 – 4.

While the Gutiérrez-Colón battle remained the most pitch-filled at-bat in official records for twenty years, stories from earlier days claim Luke Appling may have bettered it. There is an anecdote saying he had a 24 pitch at-bat. The problem is: no one is sure. The legend of this at-bat was that Appling fouled as many 16 (or 17) of the pitches on purpose to get even with an owner who would not give him a box of baseballs to give out to fans.

Another source says a hitter named Roy Thomas who was a slap hitting advocate of the bunt may have fouled off as many as 27 pitches in one at-bat during a game in 1899. His mark (even if verified, which it never was) must be discredited since he was playing under different rules at the turn of the nineteenth century when fouls were not strikes.

In 1901 the foul-strike rule (for the first two fouls while swinging) was adopted, and bunting foul with two strikes was an out. Some feel the rule was instituted just because of Thomas. Even if Thomas (or Appling) were contenders for the most pitches seen in an at-bat, no one knows for sure how many total pitches they may have seen. Gutiérrez's and Belk's totals were well-documented.

And finally, it must be noted that the third most pitch-filled documented at-bat was the 18 pitches Dodger infielder Alex Cora saw against Cubs pitcher Matt Clement in 2004. Cora had a much happier ending than Belt or Gutiérrez. Belt flied out. Ricky struck out. Cora hit a home run!

105

Tuffy Rhodes was Astro Footnote by Big Star in Japan

Based solely on his career as a Houston Astro, Karl "Tuffy" Rhodes is hardly a legend for what he did in a Houston uniform. He came up through the system, and in 1990, at 21 years old, got into 38 games for Houston. He hit one home run. For the next three seasons Rhodes played mostly in AAA with a few games with the Astros mixed in. He hit two more homers for Houston before moving on to the Royals and Cubs in 1993.

He had a dream minor-league season in 1993, hitting a career-high 30 home runs, driving in 89 runs, and batting .318. He made the Cubs' roster opening 1994, and after a big opening day, faded and showed perhaps his limit was AAA.

By 1996 at age 27, it was time to try Japan and perhaps make some real money before father time caught up with his body.

It was a great move. His first season with Kintetsu, he hit 27 home runs. He never quit hitting them. In his fourth season, he clubbed 40. In 2001 he was on a record tear and finished with 55 home runs, 131 RBIs, and a .327 average.

Notice that number of home runs: it equaled the all-time Japanese record set by Sadaharu Oh. Few traditional Japanese fans wanted a foreigner to challenge the mark—let alone break it.

Rhodes hit number 53 with ten games left. Six were against Daiei that was managed by Oh. His players would never let Rhodes see a pitch he could hit. Tuffy hit number 54 against Chiba and got his record tying number 55 against Seibu. There were four games left with three against Daiei.

He never saw a pitch close and was walked repeatedly. With one game left against Orix, Rhodes got some pitches to hit to break the record, but couldn't do anything with them.

A few years later, all the games were put aside. Alex Cabrera made it a three-way tie at the top in 2002, and finally Wladimir Balentien broke the record in 2013 when he hit 60 homers.

So, while Rhodes was not really an Astro legend, he started his career in the system, had some Astro at-bats, and became one of the biggest stars ever in Japan. And that is legendary by itself.

Photo Courtesy of Cake6

Tuffy Rhodes had a 55-home run season in Japan.

106

300-Home Run Milestones for Three Astros in 2009

he 2009 Houston Astros were not a very good team, but three of their members reached a major milestone. Lance Berkman, Carlos Lee, and Ivan "Pudge" Rodriguez all hit their 300th career homers that year.

Only Lance Berkman had hit all 300 of his homers in an Astro uniform. After his 1999 debut, he had averaged just over 27 home runs a season. Lee would wind up with 133 Houston homers, an average of just over 21 per season. Rodriguez played only 93 games with Houston and hit eight homers.

The first to reach the magic number was Rodriguez at Chicago's Wrigley Field on Sunday, May 17. In the fourth inning facing pitcher Rich Harden, Pudge drove a ball into the bleachers in left-center field for career number 300. Pudge would hit three more for Houston before returning to the Texas Rangers later in the season. Rodriguez hit 217 of his final career total 311 with Texas.

The second player to hit his 300th career homer in 2009

was Berkman. On Saturday, June 13, he hit the magic number off Diamondback starter Jon Garland. He connected in the top of the sixth with a runner on base and the Astros trailing, 1 – 0. His drive to deep right field was number 300 for him and put Houston on top, 3 – 2. They went on to win the game, 6 – 4.

As for Carlos Lee, his 300th came on August 8 at Minute Maid Park against his former team, the Milwaukee Brewers, with Claudio Vargas as the pitcher. During the last of the seventh, the Brewers comfortably led, 11 – 4. On a full count pitch, Lee became the third Astro to reach the 300 home run mark in the same season. In the history of baseball, it was the first time three teammates reached that level in the same year.

Lee's final career total of 358 home runs would wind up being the most hit by any of the three.

107

Astrodome Rain-In

It is not true that a game has not been affected by weather at Minute Maid Park. While no game has ever postponed by a rainout, games were moved and played in other locations due to Hurricanes Ike and Harvey in 2008 and 2017. However, one game at the Astrodome was postponed by a rainout, or more precisely, a rain-in.

The game between the Astros and visiting Pittsburgh Pirates was scheduled for June 15, 1976. On that day, however, Houston was hit with one of its famed sudden rain storms that have been known to drop ten inches of rain onto the below-sea level city. When this happens, areas hardest hit routinely have street flooding as over-taxed drainage and bayous that run through the city need time to handle it all.

The rain hit the Houston area shortly before noon, steady and hard. Still those who would play the game that night were not overly bothered. The Astros were all at the Astrodome by about three thirty p.m., and the Pirate busses were able to make it in from their hotel within the next hour, although the normally 20 minute trip took twice that time. Others had worse problems. Astros manager Bill Virdon, who planned on being in by about one p.m. spent over five hours stranded on a flooded street. By about seven p.m., more than 13 inches of rain was recorded at the Houston Ship Channel, and over ten inches was measured at the Texas Medical Center. Both areas are on the southern half of the city—where the Astrodome was also located.

Due to street flooding in the area, all major roads leading to the Dome were submerged. Even the Dome itself, built 45 feet under ground-level, had water coming down some of the ramps. The field was okay, minus a few drips leaking in, but who could or would make it to the game? Stadium workers were in short supply and the umpires couldn't navigate the streets. Only fans who could row boats in would likely show up.

Club President Tal Smith said, "We could have played since the players were there, but there would have been no fans and something would have had to be arranged with umpires." Actually, the umpires had tried to get to the game. They were staying in a hotel only about two miles away, but their car stalled in high water and they had to wade back to the hotel after scuttling their trip.

By 5 p.m., the game was cancelled. Tal Smith said it wasn't a tough decision. "Nobody could get there, and I thought the intelligent thing to do was cancel the game."

About 20 fans did make the game and were guests of the Astros at a stadium cafeteria. As for the players, both teams were fed on tables set up near second base.

Of course, getting home was a problem for some with cars that had flooded, but the rain had stopped or was very light by then and things were draining. Some didn't want to take a chance and get stranded and didn't leave the building until 10 p.m. or later. At least two players spent the night. Rob Andrews and Mike Cosgrove slept in an open luxury suite.

While Houston has had major storms since, never again was a game postponed.

108

Brian Bogusevic's Ultimate Walk-Off Grand Slam

Plus Johnson and Tucker Too!

He began his professional career in the Astros organization as a pitcher following his college career at Tulane. However, once Brian Bogusevic returned to his alternate college position in the outfield, he had his greatest moment in baseball.

It was on August 16, 2011 at Minute Maid Park when he came to the plate as a pinch-hitter in the ninth inning with the bases loaded and Houston trailing the Cubs by three runs, 5 – 2. The team's season-long losing streak was about to extend to eight straight it would seem. Carlos Marmol was the pitcher, and he was one of Chicago's top bullpen arms.

The ultimate grand slam was set up after J. B. Shuck singled after one out. He moved to second on a wild pitch. Then Clint Barmes singled Shuck to third. Matt Downs then walked to load the bases. That brought up the lefty hitting Bogusevic as a pinch-hitter. He had a strong at-bat even before the slam. He was able to foul off some good fastballs and laid off sliders in the dirt. Marmol, having a problem with control of his "out" pitch, finally came back with a fastball that caught too much of the plate and Bogusevic made him pay for it.

Hitting a game-winning walk-off homer was nothing new for Bogusevic. He had hit an opposite-field homer off the left fielder's glove while playing for the New Orleans Zephyrs against the Reno Aces in 2014. Of course, his Astro experience was special being in the major leagues and with his team down by three runs.

Hitting an ultimate grand slam has been accomplished only 32 times through the 2023 season. Hitting for the cycle and pitching no-hitters are far more common. Pitching perfect games are only slightly rarer.

Brian Bogusevic had been both an outfielder and pitcher in both high school and at Tulane University when he was drafted number 24 in the first round of the amateur free agent draft by Houston in 2005. For the first four years of his career he was a pitcher in the Astros system, but he never showed major- league stuff consistently and his records and ERAs were unimpressive. His best season on the mound was in 2007 splitting time between A and AA levels. He was 10 – 8 with a 4.61 ERA.

It was in 2008 that the Astros started thinking of him as a hitter when he batted .347 with four homers and 26 RBIs in 147 at-bats. He also stole nine bases in ten tries.

The next season, 2009, the full transition was made.

Once Bogusevic got a major-league shot with Houston, he had his moments, like his big hit in 2011, but could not win a regular or near regular spot in the lineup until 2012. Then he failed. He played in 146 games but hit only .203. After the season, the Astros and Bogusevic parted ways as he became a free agent. After one good year in the Chicago system with the major-league club, he was traded to Miami but never played on the major-league level. He moved to the Philadelphia system and, while mostly in AAA, he did get into 22 games with the Phillies in 2015. At 33 in 2017 with Boston's AAA team, he hit .278 with 12 homers and 40 RBIs in 76 games.

Whatever Bogusevic's future may hold out of baseball he retains one glorious memory when he hit a grand slam to move the Houston Astros from a 5 – 2 loss to a 6 – 5 win August 16, 2011.

While Bogusevic's feat is still unprecedented it is only one of three Astro Ultimate Grand Slams to win game. His is the only one of the Walk Off variety.

In 1975 Cliff Johnson hit one in St. Louis in the top of the ninth with the Astros trailing 7-4. They held on to win 8-7. And in 2023 in the heat of the pennant race Kyle Tucker also hit in the top of the ninth erasing a 6-3 Baltimore lead. His came off a 100+mph fastball from Felix Bautista, ranked as the top closer in the American League with an ERA (before the homer) of less than 1.00.

Others have hit game winning grand slams for the Astros, but only those three have ever hit ultimate slams leading to late inning victory.

Ultimate Grand Slam History

As a footnote to Bogusevic's ultimate grand slam is the story of the man who hit the first such home run. His name was Roger Conner and he won the final game of the season for Troy in the NL on September 10, 1881. His blast against Worcester in the last game of the season gave Troy an 8 – 7 victory and was described as a "terrific drive to right," by the Worcester Daily Spy newspaper.

Conner's home run will always be recorded as the first ultimate grand slam, but it was more; it was also the first grand slam ever in the NL!

109

Astros Records Most Unlikely to be Broken

he old line "records are made to be broken" may be true in many cases, but not all. Consider some of the feats recorded by Astros of the past that may be safe in large measure due to the way the game is played.

Will a pitcher ever record 20 complete games in a single season again? Larry Dierker did in 1969. Or how about throwing nine straight complete games? J. R. Richard set that record in 1979.

As for hitters, the Astros have two extremes. Craig Biggio went all season in 1997 never grounding into a double play. Someone can tie Craig, but never do better. On the other end, Miguel Tejada hit into 32 double lays in 2008. While that record could be beaten, it would be very hard to do. Not that anyone wants to break it!

Unless the rules change, no pitcher will ever drive in more than the 14 runs Shane Reynolds plated in 1999.

Unless the Astros get a larger home in the future, the attendance of 54,037 at the Astrodome on September 28, 1999 against the Reds won't ever be bettered. Minute Maid Park can hold fewer than 45,000 fans with a large number of standees, and even that number would require fans to suck in their stomachs and not breathe!

It may also be suggested there will never be a season at Minute Maid Park when the home team hits as few as 46 home runs as the woeful 2011 club did.

Likewise, the Astros will never hit as few as 82 homers in a full season as they did in 1981. Not that the '81 club needed homers. They made the postseason in that labor-shortened season.

Lance Berkman's record of 45 home runs by a switch-hitter will be hard to beat. Few switch hitters in all of baseball have hit more in a season.

Records ARE made to be broken. Some just require a whole lot of time and even changes in the way games are played to do it.

Houston Attendance Records

Season	Game (All at Larger Astrodome)
3,087,872 Minute Maid Park 2004	
3,052,347 Minute Maid Park 2023	54,037 vs Cincinnati 9/28/99
3,022,347 Minute Maid Park 2006	52,493 vs St. Louis 9/12/
3,020,581 Enron Field 2000	52,338 vs St. Louis 9/13/98
3,020,405 Minute Maid Park 2007	52,242 vs Cincinnati 9/29/99
2,980,549 Minute Maid Park 2018	52,199 vs Chicago Cubs 8/16/98
2,906,277 Enron Field 2001	52,186 vs St. Louis 9/11/98
2,706,017 Astrodome 1999	Postseason record: vs Atl NLDS 10/3/97

110

Astrodome Opened with Three Teams in 1965

I n 1965 when the Astrodome was opened to the world with the Yankees meeting the Astros, it was a very big deal. However, that Yankee-Astro game was only part of a much larger opening. Very few remember the Baltimore Orioles were also involved, and they played some games, too.

The Dome's first game was actually a day exhibition with their Oklahoma City AAA team. Houston won it 10 – 3 with Joe Morgan hitting the first "in-game" homer. But seeing the ball when hit in the air was a problem. Numerous balls were "lost" and fell untouched in the outfield. Almost immediately, Judge Roy Hofheinz admitted it was a problem that would have to be solved.

After the famed game with the Yankees, won by Houston 2 – 1 in 12 innings in front of a full house on April 9, which was played at night, the Baltimore Orioles joined the three-day party. On April 10 and 11, the Astros would play both the Orioles and Yankees in split doubleheaders. The total five games put almost 200,000 spectators in the seats of the "eighth Wonder of the World." The Astros would win three of those five games, but it wouldn't be easy.

The day games in those matchups continued to cause problems with visibility. More than a dozen fly balls fell untouched that might have been caught if they could have been seen against the background of glare and girders in the four day games. Some outfielders were even wearing batting helmets on defense—just in case.

Hofheinz felt the problems could be solved and, when the Astros played their first road trip, a wedge of panels were painted. They had to be painted a darker color a few weeks later, but it provided a much better background and far fewer balls were lost. Hofheinz was always suspicious that the grass would have problems, and it did from the beginning. After the roof panels were painted, it was obvious the already low level of sunlight getting in the building would be cut too much for grass to be a full-time option. The judge promised that an artificial surface not unlike what he called funeral grass would cover the field starting in 1966.

Thanks to the fame of the stadium, the first generation of artificial turf constructed by the Monsanto company was called AstroTurf and it soon was installed on outdoor fields that got heavy use as well as inside the Astrodome. The term became as generic as Kleenex or Coke even after other forms or artificial turf were invented to improve the coverage.

— 111 —

Enron Field Opening had One Similarity to Astrodome

**W**hen the Astros moved from the Astrodome to their new downtown retractable-roofed Enron Field for the 2000 season, they wanted to duplicate one thing from the Astrodome opening 35 years before. They wanted the New York Yankees to be the opponent in their first exhibition game.

There were no US Presidents or all the original astronauts or even the same fanfare, but it was a special night just the same. The ballpark was hoping to be the catalyst for the move to remake downtown Houston as not just a place to come to work in a high-rise office building and go home, but along with the already established theatre district a few blocks away, an entertainment hub.

Named after the once proud, but ultimately disgraced,

Minute Maid Park became the
Astros' home in 2000.

conglomerate Enron Corporation whose home was Houston, the ballpark featured natural grass, a roof that could be closed to beat the Houston summer heat and humidity, air conditioning and special unique features that included varied home run distances, walls of different heights, and even a sloped outfield in deep center field starting about 400 feet from home plate on to a 436 foot maximum distance. The flagpole was also distant, but inside the field of play. Perhaps even more distinctive was the short 21-foot wall in left field only 315 feet from home plate down the left-field line.

High atop left field was a working replica of a train engine reminiscent of the 1800s to represent the original use for the land—one of Houston's former train depots—Union Station.

The exhibition opener for the new ballpark was held on March 30, 2000. The starting pitching matchup was the key feature in 2000. The Yankees started Roger Clemens. The Astros started Doc Gooden. Clemens had a glorious seven-time Cy Young-winning career in Boston, New York, Toronto, and Houston while Gooden was near the end of his career and would only pitch a few exhibitions and only one regular-season game for the Astros that season. Gooden had been NL Rookie of the Year in 1984 and the league's Cy Young Award winner in 1985.

When he was with the Astros in 2000, he appeared in only one game, moved on to Tampa Bay, and finished as a teammate of Clemens with the Yankees before leaving the game.

In the exhibition game, the Astros saw Jeff Bagwell record the first hit in the building for the Astros, a single off Clemens. Once Clemens left the game, the scoring began. A four-run eighth by Houston decided the outcome. Daryle Ward's two-run home run was the first long-ball hit. Houston won, 6 – 5.

112

Billy Wagner Takes Line Drive Off His Head

During his 16-year playing career—the first nine with the Astros-- Wagner was one of the hardest throwing and effective closers in the major leagues. In Houston he had five seasons with 30 or more saves including two with 39 and a career high in his last season as an Astro in 2003 when he recorded 44.

His career total of 442 saves, including the first 225 as an Astro rank him in the top five all time.

And Billy did it throwing his whole career with the wrong arm!

You see, Wagner was born a righthander. He wrote that way and he threw a ball that way. Until he couldn't for a while in his youth. He wasn't even seven years old and he had broken his right arm twice. He was always athletically inclined with football and baseball his favorite sports. But he broke his right arm the first time while playing football. It healed but he broke it again climbing some monkey bars.

During the time he was sidelined he kept playing as best

he could by learning to throw a ball with his left arm. And he kept doing it.

According to neuroscientists it is much easier for a youngster to train other parts of the body and brain to transfer tasks to other parts with practice than teens or older adults.

And, Billy, being an athlete did just that. By his teen years he may have still written his name and eaten his food as a righty, but he was a lefty with a ball in his hand.

And what a lefty he was! By high school he was a pitcher who could throw in the low 80s. Even so, he wanted to attend college and play football. However coaches encouraged him to stick with baseball. His size at the time was a factor, he was only 5'5" tall and weighed 135 pounds, but his fast ball was what made him concentrate on baseball.

His first year at Ferrum College he gained 40 pounds and added three inches in height. He also found that by his first spring with the college team his fast ball could now reach 95 MPH.

During one year at Ferrum he averaged 19.1 strikeouts per game! After his junior year in 1993 when eligible to be drafted the Astros took him with their first pick. His fast ball was magical and while he began his pro career as a starter the Astro moved him to the pen to take advantage of the only pitch he really had at that point.

Hitters feared Billy Wagner. One time team-mate and future Hall of Famer, Randy Johnson, said Wagner threw the ball harder than he did.

During the 2003 season Billy reportedly threw 159 pitches at greater than 100 miles per hour. The rest of the National League recorded only 14. And the entire American League had only 26. Was Wagner aided by the radar gun at home games? That was a debate, but his margin over the field indicated that he was still head and shoulders ahead of the field with velocity.

Billy did have one scare with the Astros. It was his head and not his arm. In July of 1998 Arizona D-Back Kelly Stinnett got a hold of one of Wagner's fastballs and shot it right back at Billy.

With no time to react, the ball crashed into the side of Wagner's head. Billy went down on his back with his legs flopping wildly. There was fear in the air in Phoenix.

But miraculously, while Wanger suffered a concussion and was sidelined for more than three weeks he recovered. As he later remembered, "You don't practice this, because you can't practice this. There is one chance in a million it comes back at you. You just don't expect it."

Wagner was lucky. He had turned his head just enough to make it a glancing blow tearing off some skin near his left ear before bounding away.

Surviving that close call and after seeing time with the Phillies, Mets, Red Sox and Braves, the Astros all time leading closer should be memorialized as one of the greats in the Baseball Hall of Fame in Cooperstown, New York.

Astros Relief Saves Leaders	
Billy Wagner	225 over 9 years
Dave Smith	119 over 11 years
Brad Lidge	123 over 6 years
Fred Gladding	76 over 6 years
Joe Sambito	72 over 8 years
José Valverde	69 over 2 years
Doug Jones	62 over 2 years

113

Retired Number 32 — Cancer Took Jim Umbricht Early

**A**s time passes, some of the retired numbers from Astros of the past become more historical footnotes in books such as this than truly remembered players. Perhaps none more than the owner of number 32, Jim Umbricht.

Fans who look him up on-line don't see anything special. In fact, his career was very short. In a career that lasted only two full major-league seasons and parts of three others, the left-handed pitcher won nine, lost five with a 3.06 ERA. He never started a game but worked 88 games in relief with three saves. If one peruses his bio, something stands out. He was only 33 years old when he died.

Umbricht's move to the top as one of the NL's top relievers had been long. He started pitching in the minors with the Pittsburgh system on the lowest level in 1953. In 1954 and 1955 he was out of baseball while in the US Army, but played on the team at Fort Carson, Colorado. He returned to professional baseball in 1956 and made his major-league debut with Pittsburgh in 1959—for one game. He made his second appearance in 1961—again for only one game.

The Houston Colt .45s selected him in the expansion draft after that season, and by 1962 he had made it. He was 31. He was 4 – 0 with a 2.01 ERA in 34 games.

Umbricht had another strong season in 1963 when he pitched in 35 games while recording a 4 – 3 record and 2.61 ERA. How he was able to accomplish it was amazing. Prior to the season, a malignant melanoma was discovered in his right leg. He had been golfing with GM Paul Richards and mentioned a lump that had developed in his groin area. He thought it was beginning to affect his pitching motion. When Richards saw it, he got Jim on an immediate flight back to Houston. Umbricht was in surgery the next day that took eight hours as malignant growths from his groin, thigh, and shin were excised. He was also infused with cancer drugs in the hope that amputation could be avoided. Initially the treatment seemed to work, and Umbricht was able to return to the mound in May, 1963. He was often in great pain, but he toughed it out. His teammates knew what he was going through and held him in great respect.

However, cancer was not beaten. After the season, Umbricht complained of shortness of breath and a cough. Chest X-rays showed the cancer had metastasized massively. The prognosis by December was grave.

Jim was honored at baseball dinners all over the country for "beating cancer" to pitch in 1963, but he and those close to him knew the truth. He had only taken the disease to extra innings. He entered M. D. Anderson Hospital in early March 1964. He only had a short time left. His last request was to be kept alive until opening day. He couldn't quite make it.

He died on April 8, 1964. The season opened at Cincinnati April 13. Umbricht's former roommate, Ken Johnson, beat the Reds that day, 6 – 3. Following the game Johnson said, "There was a little extra reason for this one. I thought about him right before the game. All the players did." Nellie Fox, who had been added to the Houston roster when Umbricht was released in December, had a two-run single and Jimmy Wynn a two-run homer to lead the Colt .45s' offense. All the players wore black arm bands in memory of their fallen teammate.

Jim's body was cremated and ashes were spread over the construction site for the Harris County Domed Stadium. His brother, Ed who dropped the ashes said, "The Astrodome is Jim's headstone." In his honor, the team retired his number. He was the first player in franchise history to die while an active player. Don Wilson would be the second. His number 40 is also memorialized.

114

Sad Story of Ken Caminiti

When Ken Caminiti was playing third base for the Houston Astros he was one of the more popular players on the team. He might have been the best defensive third basemen in the National League, although he wouldn't be recognized for it till he moved on. He wasn't the greatest hitter, but he played the game hard.

Ken played ten seasons with Houston. After his first eight he moved to the San Diego Padres as a free agent. He did not win a Gold Glove and was named to only one Allstar game as an Astro. He was solid and Gold Glove quality as a third baseman and decent but not great with the bat. In four of his eight seasons he hit has high as .294 in 1992 but had four seasons in the .250s or less. His best home run season saw him hit 18 and was in double figures all seasons except 1994 after he became a regular player. When he moved to San Diego he won two Gold Gloves and an NL MVP. There was a big reason why.

The move to San Diego brought about a new Ken Caminiti. His bat was among one of the best in baseball. He hit no less than .290 in three of his four Padre season. He hit 26, 40, 26 and 20 homers. He had to battle through some injuries.

But he found steroids, too. Those supplements raised Caminiti from the ranks to the NL MVP in 1996 after he hit 40 home runs, drove in 130 runs and batted .326. Those were San Diego native Ted Williams numbers and not Ken Caminiti!

Dan Good's book, "Playing Through the Pain", is an outstanding chronicle of Ken's life, career and sadly death. It was in San Diego when Caminiti first used steroids for two reasons. To help his body recover from a number of injuries and ultimately help his offense vastly improve.

PED's were not at the root of Ken's downfall. Rather they were just the highlight of his playing career. Even before he broke in with the Astros in 1987 Ken was not averse to taking a drink...or ten!

Cammy had been introduced to drinking alcohol before he was a teen. Drinking became a regular thing from then on. Eventually, he was not reluctant to using drugs, too. Marijuana, cocaine, pep pills and finally cocaine and heroin years later.

During his time with the Astros team mates and training staff recognized he had an alcohol addiction and tried to help him. He was enrolled in off season programs. Teammates Craig Biggio and later Jeff Bagwell tried to keep him away from the wrong influences. The trio were great friends. His wife was trying, too.

Nothing fully worked. Cammy loved his wife and family but strayed at times on the road and during the offseason. Usually due to the lure of drugs.

But he was such a good guy. After his run in San Diego ended after the 1998 season the Astros brought him back. In oft-injured limited play he was good. Thirteen homers, 56 RBIs and a .286 avwerage in just 78 games for 1999. In 2000 the first year of what is now Minute Maid Park he hit .303 with 15 homers and 45 RBIs. He only appeared in 59 games. The injuries and additional problems were evident to those close by. He was let go after the season had concluded.

Caminiti tried to hang around. The Texas Rangers gave

him a shot in 2001, but he ended the year— and career with the Braves. He had fallen in trouble with the law over his addictions and was sentenced to prison. His actual time behind bars was very short.

He had earned a lot of money in his 15 years in the major leagues. But when it was over his marriage had ended, too. With fewer watching over him his demons took over. He died in a near slum New York apartment of a drug overdose. It was in early October 10, 2004.

He was buried on the Cambo Ranch in South Texas, which he and friend Craig Biggio had purchased together years before as a hunting destination. As years go by fewer remember Ken. Dan Good's book tells the story that fans of him as a player never knew, but his close teammates and friends knew all too well.

115

Joe Espada Becomes Astros' 20th Full-Time Manager

**T**he Houston Astros appeared in their 7th straight American League Championship Series (ALCS) in 2023. That is an American League record. (The Atlanta Braves hold the Major League record with eight straight in the National League.

But even with that continued level of success the Astros were in search of a new manager following the resignation of 74 year old Dusty Baker at the team's post season end.

The team did not look far for a suitable replacement. Bench coach Joe Espada was elevated to the job on November 13. According to General Manager Dana Brown, "We got looking and came up with the right man. Joe is a good fit for the club.

Why true? The Puerto Rican native had been the manager's right-hand man as bench coach under two winning managers. He joined the team and took the job under A.J. Hinch and continued when Baker took over after the punishment for the 2017 electronic sign stealing affair cost Hinch his job.

And the Astros kept winning. Of the seven straight ALCS appearances Espada was bench coach for six.

Espada began his professional baseball career as a minor league player after being a second round draft pick of the Oakland A's in 1996. He was the 96th player selected overall. In college at the University of Mobile he set a school record by hitting .442 in his final season.

While he reached the AAA level as a player during a nine year career he never had a major league at bat. His best season was at Midland in the Texas League in 1999 where he hit .338 with a superb .420 on base percentage. He was a good contact minor league hitter with a career .275 batting average and .367 on base percentage. He walked 314 time and only struck out 315. Alas, he had no power which kept him from prospect status. Defensively as a middle infielder he was above average.

When it appeared his dream of staying in baseball would have to take a non-playing route he became a minor league coach and instructor for the Marlins and finally made the major leagues as a coach with Miami in 2010. He served three years there before jumping to the Yankees to serve as a special assistant to General Manager Brian Cashman. Eventually he got back into uniform as the Yankees third base coach. After two seasons in that role he jumped to the Astros to be manager A.J. Hinch's right hand man on the bench.

As far back as 2019 Espada was rumored to be a candidate to replace Hinch as manager when A.J. was fired. But the veteran Baker got the job to use his experience to take over a still very talented, but shaken team.

Espada while a candidate for other jobs with Texas and both Chicago teams stayed on after no offers were forthcoming. That turned out to be fortunate for both Espada and the Astros.

"This is a dream come true. I had a front row seat with two incredible managers. It is an honor working being hired to replace Dusty Baker, a future Hall of Fame manager," said Espada at his introduction. "This is a very special place."

116

José Lima Only Latest of "Unique" Players

osé Lima's time as an Astro was relatively short. His time as a star with the team as a player was even shorter, as was his life, but when the right-handed pitcher was around it was always, "Lima Time." Few, if any, personalities have ever shined brighter. As former teammate Lance Berkman put it, "He was one of the characters of the game."

For two Astro seasons, he was also one of the best pitchers in the NL. He was a key part of two Houston division title teams in 1998 and 1999. After coming to the Astros in a trade from Detroit for the 1997 season and working unimpressively out of the bullpen, he got a chance to be a starter in 1998 and came through.

Lima was 16 – 10 with a 3.70 ERA. He started 33 games, had three complete games, and one shutout. In 1999, he was even better with a 21 – 10 record and 3.58 ERA. Lima was never dominating, but he was a workhorse who gave his manager Larry Dierker a lot of innings and kept his team in games.

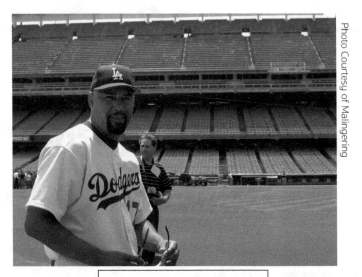

Photo Courtesy of Malingering

Before becoming a Dodger, José Lima was a star in Houston.

However, it was Lima's outgoing personality that caught the real attention. He would do an interview with anyone. He would sign autographs, pose for photos and talk with all fans. He fancied himself a singer and would appear at any chance to sing Latino favorites. And he did all these things with great exuberance.

Lima took charge of the music in the clubhouse after games—whether his teammates were into high volume Latino music or not. They half-heartedly might have complained privately, but publicly, he was just being Lima. He was the outgoing personality many would have liked to be, but just weren't built for it.

I manned a field-level position at the end of the Astros dugout at Minute Maid Park. Most players would ignore the TV happenings. Not José. On days he was not pitching, he would keep up running conversations. Sometimes he would volunteer "inside information" that he probably shouldn't have. Once when an Astro pitcher took a line drive off his forehead and had to leave the game, Lima was asked if he would go into the clubhouse and come back with a report.

When he returned his eyes were wide and he excitedly said, "He's okay, but he has big marks on his forehead from the stitches on the ball!"

Alas, for all his popularity in 1998 and 1999, things faded in 2000. He had a mental and physical problem with pitching at the new cozy Enron Field. Except for deep center field, all the dimensions had less distance to the wall than at the Astrodome. In addition, the noted "dead air" in the Dome was gone. Baseballs flew greater distances and with greater speed, especially when the roof was open.

Lima who had always surrendered a significant number of long fly balls that were caught for outs in the Astrodome no longer had that to help him out. Always victimized by more home run hitters than the average 16 – 20 game-winners, moving to Enron Field hurt him badly.

It got into his head before a game had been played when he saw pitchers taking batting practice loft ball after ball into the seats above the scoreboard in left field. At the line, the fence was only 315 feet away and it was only 340 feet at the start of the power alley on that side.

Lima was never the same in Houston after he saw that hitting display. He would start 33 games in 2000 but finish with a 6 – 12 record and a horrendous 6.65 ERA. He would surrender 55 more hits than innings pitched and give up a NL-high 48 home runs. His worst outing was early against the Chicago Cubs. On April 27, he gave up 13 hits and 12 runs in only five innings. Five of the 13 hits were home runs, including back to back homers by Eric Young and Ricky Gutiérrez leading off the game. Then he gave up home runs to Henry Rodriguez and Damon Buford also in the first inning! Four home runs and five runs before the opening frame was closed.

Lima never had another game that bad, but it set the tone for his season. Early in 2001 Lima was traded back to Detroit for Dave Mlicki. He moved on to Kansas City where he was 8 – 3 in 14 games in 2003. Then the next season with the Dodgers, he put together his third best career season after his big two in Houston back in '98 and '99. Lima was 13 – 5 with a 4.07 ERA. Lima Time hit the west coast. He left the Dodgers as a free agent back to Kansas City and on to the Mets in 2006, but his skills and the magic were gone.

He tried the minor leagues and wound up his pitching career in independent ball in 2009. He was 36 years old.

Then on May 23, 2010, his body was found in his apartment in Pasadena, California. He had died of a heart attack at 37 years old. Lima suffered from a cardiac arrhythmia brought on by cardiac hypertrophy and fibrosis of his heart.

Fans of the Astros from the late 1990s will never forget José Lima. And his teammates from the time won't forget "Lima Time" either.

117

More Astro Legends for Reasons Beyond the Game

By the 1990s when José Lima was around, the term "flake" was rarely heard in baseball, meant to describe someone who was a bit different than the norm. Perhaps because it could be attached to players for politically incorrect reasons, it has pretty much disappeared in usage. Lima would have qualified without any P. C. concerns, but Dick Farrell certainly did, too. And he has the distinction among Houston legends as being the first.

Farrell, most known by his nickname as "Turk", which he picked up as a kid since his father was "Big Turk", was obtained by the original Colt .45s in the expansion draft from the Los Angeles Dodgers. As a youth Farrell contracted polio which caused his left leg to shrivel a bit. Neighborhood kids called him "Peg Leg" for a few years until he recovered and proved his worth as a multisport high school athlete.

Farrell had pitched for the Phillies regularly from 1957 through the start of 1961 when he was traded to the Los Angeles Dodgers. After some good seasons with the Phillies, he didn't perform well for either the Phillies or the Dodgers in 1961, so he was left off the Dodgers protected list prior to the expansion draft. The Colt .45s took him with their fourth choice. He had been a reliever up to this point. The Colt .45s saw him as a starting pitcher. They may have heard of his prank-filled years, but looked more at his skills.

Pranks? He nailed Satchel Paige's shoes to the floor. He stuffed limburger cheese in the catcher's glove, then bet a teammate that the catcher, Clint Courtney, who was not known for personal hygiene, wouldn't even notice it for at least an inning. Apparently he didn't, but the home-plate umpire did and ordered Courtney to change gloves.

At the initial Colt .45 spring training at Apache Junction, Arizona in 1962, he often carried a revolver or two with him to shoot rattlesnakes as he walked across some open land to get to the ballpark. He had developed a reputation for being "different" earlier in his career with a number of bar room activities and a somewhat rowdy off-the-field reputation with Philly teammates Jim Owens and Jack Meyer. Reporters dubbed then "the Dalton Gang" for their exploits.

In addition to shooting snakes, old bottles, rabbits, and almost any suitable targets on his walks to the ballpark, he took at least one solo road trip. As Bob Aspromonte remembered, Farrell asked to borrow his car one day. Reluctantly Aspromonte allowed it. When Farrell returned it later, the car was filthy on the outside and filled with dead snakes. Well most of them were dead. A couple were still moving.

Farrell has also tried to sneak a live rattlesnake into outfielder Walt Bond's pants. Bond wanted Farrell's head for that stunt.

During the first season, owner Roy Hofheinz had supplied

the club with western style suits complete with hats to wear on the road. Most of the players hated them but had to comply for fear of being fined. Farrell wasn't wearing his outfit one time in Los Angeles and claimed he had dropped off the gear at the cleaners and they mistakenly sent if off to Disneyland instead of his hotel. As Farrell was quoted in Robert Reed's Colt .45s: A Six Gun Salute, "I'll wear it, but only if it's presentable. I wouldn't want to bring shame to Buffalo Bill."

In addition to toting his six gun in Arizona, he was a major-league prankster in Houston. He once marked up a game ball with an X that told opposing hurler Lew Burdette to "Spit Here." Burdette was not averse to slipping some illegal spitballs during games.

Farrell had been a reliever before joining the Colt .45s. As a starter, he was the team's best in the first season. He even represented the team as a National All-Star in 1962, even though he would eventually become the only pitcher in Houston history to lose twenty games in a season.

Turk became a solid member of the Houston community and worked hard in the offseason trying to sell both tickets and Houston Colt .45 baseball in general. But sometimes things just happened. OK, finding a baby alligator and keeping it in the trainer's room whirlpool was not exactly in the category of "just happened" but was typical Turk Farrell. That occurred one spring after the club had moved training camp to Cocoa Beach, Florida.

Taking a line drive off Hank Aaron's bat that caromed to Joe Morgan for the out was hardly normal, but Farrell was unhurt. With maturity, Farrell was good for stories about the old days, but he developed as a pitcher. Noted originally for his blazing fastball Farrell had to learn how to pitch. He was a starter only during his Houston six-season stint, but was a major leaguer for 14 seasons and retired at age 35. Sadly, like José Lima, he did not live long past that. He was killed in a traffic accident in Great Yarmouth, England. He was there supervising safety for offshore oil drilling rigs. He was only

43 years old. His body was brought back to Houston where he had his greatest playing memories and his family lived.

Another "unique" Astro played third base for the early Astros.

Doug Rader was one of the Astros most popular and successful players from the late 1960s to mid- 1970s. He had big shoes to fill, replacing the club's first third-sacker Bob Aspromonte, who had held down the job from the franchise's founding as the Colt .45s in 1962.

Rader was a different player than Aspromonte. He had more power, but a lower average. No one in Houston history won more Gold Gloves for defensive excellence at his position. He won five straight from 1970 through 1974. He also hit 25 home runs, which stood as the Houston best for a third baseman from 1970 until Morgan Ensberg hit 25 in 2003 and set a new mark with 36 in 2005.

Rader went on to manage the Chicago White Sox, Texas Rangers, and California Angels, but to this day he is remembered more for his antics while playing for the Astros.

Rader, when introduced as manager of the Angels, came right out and said, "I am not a flake. Never was." Eyes around the room dropped and smiles had to be hidden.

Rader may have matured by his managerial days, but he was at least "different" at times while he was a player. Consider the time Astro teammate Norm Miller and his wife paid an unexpected visit to Rader's house and Rader greeted them at the front door totally without clothing. Or how about how he would torment Jesús Alou, who had a weak stomach. Sitting on a birthday cake or "decorating" the cake with something from a toilet was a ploy he used.

It was well-documented that Rader had, on at least one occasion, teed up a golf ball in the Astro clubhouse and given the ball his best swing. As Larry Dierker remembered in Jim Bouton's update to Ball Four, "He'd hit the ball—real hard too—and it would ricochet around the room while the players dived for cover and hoped it wouldn't hit them." Rader later claimed that he only did it when no one was in the room. Others do not concur.

Dierker says all the Rader stories are true and some just can't be printed, but that wasn't even close to what he was. Norm Miller thought he might have been the smartest man on the team. Dierker says, "He was hard on anyone he thought was full of themselves. Best example of that was Joe Pepitone. He gave Pepitone a hard time about being a pretty boy." As Dierker continues, "When we went to spring training and we had two or three young inexperienced guys who might have felt out of place, he would take them under his wing. He would take down the high and the haughty and protect the young and the vulnerable. That showed me a side to him that didn't jive with him being the big strong tough wild man."

Yet Rader was still different.

Rader would give great advice to the very young. Once, when retired pitcher Jim Bouton and a former teammate were conducting an interview with Rader and asked his advice for young players, his response was, "They should chew the gum that comes with baseball cards then eat the cards."

"Just any baseball cards?" Bouton questioned.

"No, they should only eat the cards of the good players. Say you got a kid who is small. Let him eat a Willie McCovey card. Willie's six four. The kid may grow. You can never tell."

Another example cited by Steve Bisheff of the Orange County Register in 1988 told of the advice Rader gave to nervous-flyer Mike Ivie on a flight to Montreal. Rader knew Ivie was scared of flying so he sat down next to him and said, "The airlines don't like to talk about it, but I'm sure you'd want to know about the Laurentian Condition."

"It forces the snow in Eastern Canada to fall up instead of down over the Laurentian Mountains. The pilots see it coming and they have to turn the plane upside down. It's tough on takeoffs and landings." Up to this point, Ivie was getting even more nervous. Then Rader finished, "Look there's snow over the Laurentians. Let us pray."

No wonder Ivie never stuck in the major leagues. He already had developed a problem throwing the ball back to the pitcher while he was catching. Now he had to worry about upside down snow in the Laurentians!

The Astros opened the 1974 season in San Diego. Ray Kroc, owner of McDonalds, had recently purchased the team. The Padres had a rough night, and at one point Kroc commandeered the public address mic and apologized to the fans. "Ladies and gentlemen, I suffer with you. I've never seen such stupid ball playing in my life."

After that, not only did Kroc hear from the Commissioner of baseball, but also from Rader. "What does he think we are, a bunch of short-order cooks or something?" Rader's words were duly noted and the next time the Astros were in town, the Padres held a Short-Order Cook Night.

Doug was ready. He was given the lineup card to present at home plate, and when he strolled out, he was wearing a chef's hat and apron and carried the card to the plate in a frying pan, flipping it with a spatula.

Norm Miller, a character himself, was Rader's roomie for a time. He tells a story in To All My Fans from Norm Who? about a time Rader ordered room service then made the delivery man stay in the closet until he finished eating it. Rader also made his own luau tent in the corner of a spring training locker room that featured tiki torches. Rader thought the island life was natural since in an earlier life he had been a pirate.

Doug Rader kept himself and those around him on their toes. They never knew what might be next. And that did partially cover the fact he was a very good player. If nothing else, the five Gold Gloves should show that. He played eleven years and hit 155 home runs, carrying a lifetime .251 batting average. Nothing great, but good enough to hold down a starting job for nine of those eleven seasons.

After his playing career ended, Rader stayed in baseball and was manager of the Texas Rangers for two full and one partial season between 1983 and 1985. He coached with the

White Sox and managed again with the California Angels from 1989 through most of 1991. His 1989 Angel team won 91 games and finished third in the American League West.

Doug Rader was an Astro legend for more than just what he did on the field. But he was way off when he was contemplating writing a book. "I'm going to write a book. This won't be one of those tell-all deals like Jim Bouton's Ball Four. It's going to be a family book. I'm writing down a lot of things that go through my head, so there probably will be a lot of blank pages."

Family book? Blank pages? No chance with Doug Rader. Doug's one-time roommate during his Astro years did write a book. Norm Miller was a major-league outfielder from 1965 through 1974. In 2009 he published, *To All My Fans from Norm Who?*

He was unique not always for what he did, but for the situations he found himself. A native of the Los Angeles area, he made his debut with Houston after originally being signed as an amateur free agent out of high school then moving to the Houston Colt .45s system in the first-year draft.

His first major-league experience was during the weekend that the Astrodome was about to open for the first exhibitions in 1965. Norm is the clueless outfielder in right field trying to find fly balls in the daytime glare from the roof. The video of his struggle appears on many historic films.

His actual debut in the majors at the end of the 1965 season, when he was called up to join the team in Los Angeles, was memorable as well. In the ninth inning, manager Lum Harris called down to the end of the visitor's dugout where Miller had been hanging out watching his first major-league game from a major-league bench.

"Get a bat," was the call. The Astros and Dodgers were involved in a close game. Pitching for the Dodgers was lefty Claude Osteen. As Norm told the story in To All My Fans, from Norm Who? "I grabbed the first bat I got my hands on and I noticed they were waiting for me at home plate. I didn't even stop to loosen up or get pine tar on the bat. As I got closer to home plate, the umpire glanced at me and said, 'Welcome to the big leagues.' That was nice, I thought. As I was ready to step into the batter's box, the umpire tapped me on the shoulder. I turned and he gazed through his mask. 'Son, it's a lot easier to hit up here without a jacket on.'

"My teammates were on the dugout floor, laughing. No wonder my name had not been announced by the public-address announcer yet. He didn't know my number. How do you walk up to home plate your first time in the bigs and then take your jacket off without losing your cool? You don't"

Luckily for Norm, the first at-bat had a very happy ending. He got a single off Osteen. He then met Dodger first baseman Wes Parker, but, distracted, he was not sure if he had gotten a steal sign or not and took off. He stole the base and got to meet idol Maury Wills, too.

A lot of things happened to Norm. In the minor leagues, he passed out on home plate. He had been hanging out between games of a doubleheader in a super air-conditioned clubhouse in Phoenix before the second game. Outside it was more than 100, and Miller was already tired from playing the first game in that heat. Norm was the leadoff man and he went directly from the clubhouse to home plate. Bad move. He passed out from exhaustion. When he went down, the home-plate umpire trying to add some humor to the scene immediately called, "He's out!"

Norm was out, really. Diagnosed as suffering from heat exhaustion brought on by dehydration, Miller was sidelined for a few days.

Miller also got himself in a little trouble on his team's first trip to Hawaii when Honolulu was in the Pacific Coast League. This was the one stop all the players loved. Norm unfortunately spent some of his first afternoon drinking Mai Tais with teammate Howie Goss, who was not in the lineup that night. Norm was. Still loopy from the alcohol, he was exposed in the bottom of the first inning by the leadoff man for the Hawaii Islanders. Playing right field, Norm had to deal with a slicing liner. He saw it but too late. He took a couple of steps in and threw up his glove, but not until the ball had hit him square in the forehead. Miller went down like a rock. He was done for the night, but only one of several players who heard the wrath from manager Mel McGaha after the loss for surfing, swimming, tanning, or excessive drinking prior to the game in minor-league paradise.

During his major-league career, he was never a star, but had milestone moments like being hit by a pitch from Don Drysdale in his first game against the future Hall of Famer as teammate Joe Morgan had predicted. Drysdale, it was widely known at the time, liked to hit rookies the first time they faced him.

He was warned that, if he got a hit to right field against the Pirates, he shouldn't make a big turn. Miller forgot and was thrown out by Roberto Clemente. Some things a player just has to learn the hard way through experience.

Norm was a player that had good fundamental skills but none that said "future super star," so was vulnerable to coaching suggestions to be able to keep his job. He and many other Astros had problems with manager Harry Walker.

Walker was a manager who ran the whole show. He wanted his pitchers to work one way. He wanted his hitters to do things his way. The problem was, he wanted all his hitters to do it the same way. He even had a bat model he wanted them all to use. Many of the bats suspiciously got broken. As for the hitting style, he claimed he had convinced Matty Alou to use it and it had made Alou a NL batting champion. It was called "pop and glide." It essentially required the hitter to wait as long as possible at the plate, which was not a new concept, but then stride and hit off the front foot, often taking the pitch to the opposite field. While it sounded like it might work for some—like the slap hitting Alou who had virtually no power—it did not fit for all any more than using the same bat model.

Miller was trying to follow the pop-and-glide formula to stay in the lineup, but got frustrated when he kept grounding out to shortstop. So, as Norm mentioned in his book, he came into the dugout after yet another 6 – 3 scorebook notation and said, "I'm through 'popping and gliding'. I'm going back to my 'leap and sweep.'" Norm pointed out he was then back to the bench for a few games.

Then there was his broken ankle which happened at the Astrodome when Norm was playing right field. A ball was hit over his head and he ran as hard as he could chasing it. Unfortunately, he got to the wall before he got to the ball—which hit the barrier and bounded away. Norm had slammed into the fence so hard he was down and in real agony. When the trainer asked him what hurt—after the hitter had circled the bases for an inside-the-park home run—Norm told him his head hurt, his knee was killing him, and his left ankle? Well, as Norm described it, the ankle was pointing north, south, east and west.

The broken ankle ended Norm's season, but not all was bad. After his wedding two weeks later (which he endured with a cast and crutches), he was able to spend more time at home.

Early in the 1973 season, Miller's Astro time ended as he moved to the Braves and even had a last shot with the Dodgers. He retired in 1975 at 28 years old and moved into a successful sales and real estate career the rest of his life.

As a major leaguer, Norm was never a regular for a full season. His best year with in 1969 when he played in 119 games and got 409 official at-bats. He hit .264 that year with 4 homers and 50 RBIs. Norm Miller was a player in which there were more stories about him than achievements on the field. That's why he is legendary.

And finally the man with the final word. The very unique "One Tough Dominican" as he billed himself, Joaquin Andujar.

If there any one word to describe the game of baseball, the one coined by former Astro, Cardinal, and A's pitcher Joaquin

Andujar fits. When he was asked about the sport, he replied, "There is one word for it, youneverknow!" Such is the essence of America's longest successful team sport. A team even with a better lineup than another can still be beaten on a given night. A future Hall of Fame pitcher can be touched up for a home run by the rawest rookie who may never play more than a handful of games in the majors. As the "One Tough Dominican" so aptly put it, baseball can be a humbling game.

Andujar may have had some tough days during his 12-year major-league career, but one thing you DID know when he started a game was that his team would have a good chance to win. Joaquin won 127 and lost 118 with a solid 3.58 ERA during his career. He was an Astro from 1976 until midway through 1981 when he was traded to the Cardinals for outfielder Tony Scott prior to his free agency after the season.

In seven seasons with the Astros, he had a sub .500, 44 – 53 record, but a solid 3.67 ERA. He was a starter in 113 or his 202 Astro appearances with his best seasons in 1977 when he was 11 – 8 and 1979 when he was 12 – 12. Overall his best years were in St. Louis, where he won 20 games twice and lowered his ERA to 3.33.

One time during his career, he told Montreal's Bill Lee not to throw him a fastball. Lee took up the challenge, and Andujar hit a homer for the game's only run in a 1 – 0 Astro victory.

While Andujar was caught up in the suspensions handed down for players caught using or dealing cocaine prior to the 1986 season, he bounced back to finish out his career in 1988 back in Houston where he had started it all and the word "youneverknow" earned a spot in all-time baseball lexicon as the best way to describe the great game.

BIBLIOGRAPHY

Bouton, Jim. 1970. Ball Four. Champaign, Illinois: Sports Publishing, Inc.

Brown, Bill. 2016. Breathing Orange Fire: José Altuve. Houston, Texas: Bill Brown.

—. 2017. Houston's Team, Houston's Title. Houston, Texas: Bill Brown.

Brown, Bill, and Mike Acosta. 2013. Houston Astros: Deep in the Heart. Houston, Texas: Bright Sky Press. Dierker, Larry. 2003. This Ain't Brain Surger. New York, New York: Simon and Schuster.

Footer, Alyson, and Terry Lawrence. 2006. Inside the Magical Seasons. Houston, Texas: Tate Publishing Co.

Good, Dan. 2022. Playing Through the Pain. New York, NY, Abrams Press

Izenberg, Jerry. 1987. The Greatest Game Ever Played. New York, New York: Henry Holt and Co. Jr., José Ortiz. 2006. Armed and Dangerous. Champaign, Illinois: Sports Publishing, Inc.

Lucas, Greg. 2017. Houston to Cooperstown. Indianapolis, Indiana: Blue River Press.

McTaggert, Brian. 2016. 100 Things Astro Fans Should Know and Do Before They Die. Chicago, Illinois: Triumph Publishing.

Miller, Norm. 2009. To All My Fans, from Norm Who? Houston, Texas: Double Play Productions. Morgan, Joe, and D. Falkner. 1993. Joe Morgan: A Life in Baseball. New York, New York: Norton and Company.

Ray, Edgar. 1980. The Grand Huckster. Memphis, Tennessee: Memphis State University Press. Reed, Robert. 1999. Colt .45s: A Six Gun Salute. Houston, Texas: Gulf Publishing.

Titchener, Campbell. 1989. The George Kirksey Story. Austin, Texas: Eakin Press.

Watson, Bob, and Russ Pate. 1997. Survive to Win. Nashville, Tennessee: Nelson Publishing. Wynn, Jim, and Bill McCurdy. 2010. Toy Cannon. Jefferson, North Carolina: McFarland Publishing.

Public Broadcasting System (PBS) 2023 The Astros Edge: Triumph and Scandal in Major League Baseball